The Resistible Rise
of Benjamin Netanyahu

The Resistible Rise
of Benjamin Netanyahu

NEILL LOCHERY

BLOOMSBURY

NEW YORK · LONDON · OXFORD · NEW DELHI · SYDNEY

Bloomsbury USA
An imprint of Bloomsbury Publishing Plc

1385 Broadway   50 Bedford Square
New York   London
NY 10018   WC1B 3DP
USA   UK

www.bloomsbury.com

BLOOMSBURY and the Diana logo are trademarks of Bloomsbury Publishing Plc

First published in Great Britain 2016
First U.S. edition 2016

© Neill Lochery, 2016

ISBN: HB: 978-1-63286-471-0
           EPUB: 978-1-63286-473-4

Library of Congress Cataloging-in-Publication Data is available.

2 4 6 8 10 9 7 5 3 1

Typeset by Integra Software Services Pvt. Ltd.
Printed and bound in the U.S.A. by Berryville Graphics Inc., Berryville, Virginia

To find out more about our authors and books visit www.bloomsbury.com.
Here you will find extracts, author interviews, details of forthcoming events,
and the option to sign up for our newsletters.

Bloomsbury books may be purchased for business or promotional use.
For information on bulk purchases please contact Macmillan Corporate and
Premium Sales Department at specialmarkets@macmillan.com.

For my family, with much love

Contents

Preface

When the polls closed in Israel on 17 May 1977, the anchor of the Israeli television election coverage excitedly announced an 'upheaval'. After 29 years in government in various guises, the Israeli Labour Party had been thrown out of power to be replaced by the Likud and Israel's first non-leftist Prime Minister, Menachem Begin.

It was a crucial moment in Israel's history, and since 1977 the Likud has become the natural party of government in the country. Its leaders all became prime ministers: Begin, Yitzhak Shamir, Ariel Sharon and the subject of this book, Benjamin Netanyahu.

In 1977, Benjamin Nitai (as Netanyahu was then called) did not reside in Israel and was working in the United States as a consultant for the Boston Consulting Group. He had previously completed four years of study, gaining a B.Sc. in Architecture and an M.Sc. in Business Management at MIT. To all intents and purposes he looked like a man who was heading for a successful corporate career in the United States.

Just under two decades later, he was elected Israel's youngest Prime Minister – and today the name of Benjamin Netanyahu is one of the most recognized on the planet. The story of his rise to power is one that has intrigued me since I first heard his name mentioned in the mid-1980s.

Since then, I have spent the best part of a quarter of a century researching and writing about Netanyahu's career, and its impact on Israel and the rest of the world. While preparing to write this book, I went back and read my earlier writings and was surprised how different my assessment of him is today from when I started out all those years ago.

I think what has changed the most has been my perception of the sizeable disconnect between Netanyahu and of the country he has led for a greater length of time than any other Prime Minister, apart from. David Ben-Gurion. Over the years, Netanyahu became more American and less Israeli, and not the other way around.

In many ways, Netanyahu's story is that of an outsider: a man who didn't fit into the notoriously closed political and business elites in Israel. For all its successes on the battlefield, Israel has always possessed many of the characteristics of a small country – with well-established elites protecting their positions against newcomers and outsiders.

Economically inefficient with high levels of political and business corruption, it has been a largely closed society even to new Jewish immigrants. Take away the military and Israel could easily resemble small European democracies such as Ireland and Portugal, with all the problems of nepotism and corruption that are associated with those countries.

The concept of the outsider remains very strong in Israel. Despite his prolonged period in office, Netanyahu remains an outsider to a vast number of Israelis: viewed as an American imposter who has taken over the country and tried to reshape it into a small political, economic and cultural outpost of the United States.

As a historian, I found this paradox of a man considered to be an outsider or foreigner emerging as the most important leader of the country in modern times truly fascinating. Furthermore, no matter how long Netanyahu remained in office, the notion of his being a stranger did not go away.

While I was writing this book I witnessed two examples of the perception that he does not belong to the tribe. The first was when he publicly started lecturing President Barack Obama in the Oval Office over the Iranian nuclear programme, and an Israeli politician said to me, 'Netanyahu is so not Israeli in his conduct with the President.'

The second occasion occurred after Netanyahu won a largely unexpected victory in the Knesset elections in March 2015. The next day some Israeli members of my faculty at University College London were in tears, arguing that he, along with his wife, had somehow stolen the Israel that my colleagues belonged to and remained committed to preserving.

The debates, divisions and repercussions over the question of the ownership of Israel remain one of the most intriguing and unresolved issues of the Jewish state. To further complicate the issue, many of the same people who regard Netanyahu as an outsider – or even an impostor – at the same time look towards him as the 'goalkeeper' of the state who offers protection against those who would willingly wish to damage or destroy it.

In short, many Israelis remain uneasy about Netanyahu, but see him as the best possible protection for the country that exists in an increasingly dangerous neighbourhood. One of the most interesting parts of the writing of this book has been to see how Netanyahu has cleverly and systematically played on the fears of Israelis in order to advance his own political career.

The fear factor has never been far away throughout the political career of Netanyahu, and for different groups of Israelis is best given in listed form:

1. Fear for personal security.
2. Fear for the security of the state.
3. Fear of making peace with the Arabs.
4. Fear of not making peace with the Arabs.
5. Fear of international isolation.
6. Fear of globalization.
7. Fear of increased religious extremism.
8. Fear of increased secular influences.
9. Fear of economic reforms.
10. Fear of economic decline.

Netanyahu has been able to invoke all ten of these fear factors, even when many of them were seemingly paradoxical. The basis for his rise has been his success in understanding what makes many political constituencies in Israel tick, tuning in to its fears and concerns about the present day and the future.

Before I started writing the book I made a list of the successes of Netanyahu's career and his two periods in office, and tried comparing it with similar lists for other political leaders who had been in power for an extended time in the same era. The list for Netanyahu was very short.

The book is therefore not a study of success, but nor is it a study of failure. For many Israelis the litmus test is survival. By and large, Israelis remain pessimistic about their future prospects. Netanyahu's older brother Yonatan, who died in the mission to rescue hostages held in Entebbe in 1976, summed this sentiment up in a letter to Benjamin in November 1975:

> I feel profoundly apprehensive about the future of the Jewish state. Shedding illusions, I see that the process aimed at annihilating us is gathering momentum and the noose is tightening. It won't be a rapid process, though our strength will diminish from one war to the next. There's a chance (just a chance) that we may come out of it whole, if we can manage to drag it out for a few additional decades.[1]

For Benjamin Netanyahu the story of Israel, as well as his own career, has been all about survival. So success for him personally is not measured in the chorus of approval of the outside world, or in the signing of peace agreements. It is important to remember this point and how it is different from definitions of success or failure for American and European leaders.

As I researched and developed the book, I became intrigued how Netanyahu fitted into the history of Israel, and how his character and temperament were different from those of the previous leaders of the country. The book, as a result, provides a perspective on the history of Israel and the wider world during the Netanyahu era as well an insight into the man.

The process of writing this book has been one of the most interesting and thought-provoking for me to date. The book challenges many of the myths about Netanyahu (good and bad). It illustrates the complexity of his character, as well as the difficulties of leading a country as politically, socially, economically and religiously divided as Israel.

In organizational terms, the book is divided into what I define as the nine most decisive moments in Netanyahu's career. These decisive moments are arranged chronologically and are used as springboards to tell the story of Benjamin Netanyahu from the start of his political career right up until the present day. The narrative within each section focuses on the route to the decisive moment, and why it was so important to the rise of Netanyahu.

I chose to write the book in this way in order to avoid the dryness of some modern political biographies that adopt a more conventional chronological birth-to-death format. For me, both as a writer and a reader, what intrigues me more is how leaders deal with and react to the most decisive moments in their careers.

Finally, the test of a history book as I see it is that it makes the past relevant to the present day and to the future. In writing the book I kept a close eye on trying to achieve this aim. Though it is foolish to predict the future development of events in the Middle East, it is relatively safe to say that Netanyahu will be remembered as an Israeli leader of historic importance.

Introduction

For much of the world, Benjamin Netanyahu is a right-wing nationalist zealot, but for many Israelis he is too centrist, too soft on the Arabs, and backs down too easily in a fight. One thing is clear; Netanyahu has become a hugely polarizing figure in Israel, the Middle East, the United States and the wider world.

The story of Netanyahu's meteoric rise to power, his ability to survive scandals and political crisis that would have finished off most leaders, as well as his famed capacity for making political comebacks, all makes for a fascinating narrative. His story is also the story of our times, and Netanyahu himself is a product of these times.

Benjamin Netanyahu has been at the centre of Israeli and Arab–Israeli politics since 1990, when he became the Israeli voice for CNN and its coverage of the Persian Gulf War and the preceding political crisis. His night-time interviews (prime time in the United States), sometimes given when Saddam Hussein's Scud missiles were falling on Israel, coincided with the television news revolution that made 24/7 broadcasting the norm.

With his soft American accent, sound bite answers and telegenic face, Netanyahu became an overnight international star. He even had a memorable nickname, 'Bibi', that made him all the more engaging to presenters and audiences in the United States.

For decades, Israel had been crying out for a spokesman who could articulate its point of view in a manner that would be easily digestible for an international audience. In 1990, Netanyahu's boss, Yitzhak Shamir, a veteran from the pre-state Jewish militias, spoke heavily accented English (and heavily accented Hebrew for that matter) – with a slow, quiet, flat voice which was only occasionally punctuated by rises in intonation (more often than not in the wrong places).

Although not in the government at the time, the former Prime Minister Yitzhak Rabin was always keen to put himself forward to deal with the foreign media. While more articulate than Shamir (in both English and Hebrew), Rabin spoke as slowly and quietly as a grandfather trying to coax a grandchild to sleep. The list could go on, but suffice it to say that the arrival on the international media stage of Netanyahu was a hugely important moment not only for him, but for Israel and its efforts to get its message across to an often sceptical international press corps.

Netanyahu's appearance on the centre stage represented part of a wider cultural revolution in Israel that ushered in an Americanization of its politics, media and business. In many ways, Netanyahu was the catalyst for these changes and for the shift away from the East European-influenced culture of the founding fathers (and mothers) of the State of Israel, towards a more modern style of politics.

Television studios soon replaced smoke-filled rooms. American spin doctors were hired to guide their candidates through the maze of new media, and direct on style and manner when communicating with the electorate.

Later came American-style primary elections that were meant to reconnect Israeli politicians with the voters, but instead highlighted the new centrality of money, and the ability to raise it in staggering proportions. With money came corruption, and with corruption came prosecutions, and eventual loss in belief of the political system. As for Netanyahu, it is worth remembering that he helped usher in this political revolution even before he had held a cabinet post or any local leadership position.

Netanyahu was given television time that was well beyond his rank of a deputy Foreign Minister (Shamir had appointed him to the role so that he could keep a close eye on the Foreign Minister who the PM didn't trust). He never seemed to be far from a television studio. His aids recount that he carried up to six shirts each day (all the same colour) and was always carefully groomed as if he were living on the small screen.

On Israeli television, his Hebrew language sound bites were just as tight and well delivered as his English ones, and called for a new domestic political agenda. The centre of this was a proposal to change Israel's election system to allow separate votes for Prime Minister and for the

Knesset (parliament). Early on in his political career, and perhaps a tad vainly, Netanyahu thought of himself as being more popular with the Israeli public than the Likud party of which he was a member.

For a time, the story turned sour. Events ganged up on Israel's young rising star as he started to make basic political mistakes. 'All talk and no substance' said a veteran member of Netanyahu's own Likud party. And the charge was repeated across the country as Netanyahu struggled to come to grips with new political realities in Israel, the Middle East and beyond.

The Likud party lost to Yitzhak Rabin's Labour Party in the 1992 Israeli elections and found itself out of power for the first time since 1977. The old guard of the Likud was ushered away, either willingly or with a firm push. Many Likud party members saw Netanyahu as the man of the hour, the youthful, charismatic politician who could lead the party out of the political desert of opposition and back to its rightful place at the centre of power in Israel.

For the first time in its history, the party allowed all of its members to select its leader – and Netanyahu won a comfortable victory. Two important veterans of the party leadership, Ariel Sharon (who didn't run, rightly believing that Netanyahu would win) and David Levy, refused to accept Netanyahu's legitimacy to lead the Likud. They promised to challenge his leadership at a later date, and both were true to their word.

To make matters worse, Netanyahu became a victim of the political revolution for a while. Soon after he arrived at Likud party headquarters in Tel Aviv to start the revitalization of the party, he discovered that the Likud was effectively broke. The party had blown large amounts of cash it didn't have, but had borrowed from banks on the failed 1992 election campaign. Fundraising, as a result, in both Israel and abroad became a key part of his job and this impacted upon his own political strategy for positioning the Likud at the political centre-right of Israeli politics.

The most well-funded of the major political groups were the settlers – with groups such as Gush Emunim (Block of the Faithful) able and willing to help Netanyahu. Naturally, there was a political price involved in this, and the Likud leader moved closer towards the settlers, and further away from the political centre-right he knew he needed to dominate if the Likud were to return to power.

The disconnect between the financial needs of the party and its political needs was exposed by the signing of the Oslo Accords by the Rabin government and Yasser Arafat's PLO in September 1993. To the outside world, the Oslo Accords were the Middle Eastern equivalent of the Berlin Wall coming down – in that it was widely welcomed, but nobody was particularly sure what lay at the end of the yellow brick road.

From the majority of Israelis who watched the White House signing ceremony transfixed to their television screens, there was at least tepid support for the peace deal. For Netanyahu, however, the sight of Yasser Arafat hugging an Israeli Prime Minister was almost too much to bear. And here, his personal narrative of his childhood, upbringing and family history comes to the fore – as an expression of the moral as well as political disgust and distress that Israel could have let Arafat into the peace process.

This profile uses the juncture of the Oslo Accords to take the reader back to Netanyahu's formative early years. Among ordinary Israelis there is a disjuncture between Netanyahu the leader and, when the lights go off and the camera is not running, Netanyahu the man.

You can ask most Israelis to name three aspects of the personal life and history of their second longest serving PM and they will probably respond with information about his wife, his fondness for Cuban cigars and that his brother was Yoni Netanyahu.

Put simply, Israelis know very little about their PM's personal history and what makes him tick. In addressing this disconnect the book looks at the two key Netanyahu family members to help explain his strong ideological and personal incomprehension towards the Accords: his father, Benzion, a scholar of Jewish history and the Zionist political movement, and his elder brother, Yonatan (Yoni), one of Israel's most decorated soldiers.

Both family members had a profound influence on the character of Bibi the politician, and, a point that is most often overlooked, his sense of detachment and loneliness at being a perennial outsider even in his own party. Benzion Netanyahu helped shape his son's hawkish views towards the Arabs.

Central to Benzion's scholarly work was the traditional Revisionist Zionist ideology as articulated by the Zionist leader, Ze'ev Jabotinsky. In essence, the Jews faced racial discrimination and any attempts to try to reach compromise with the Arabs were futile. In other words, the Arabs would never come to accept the existence of the State of Israel.

From his father's thinking his son developed a sense of self-sufficiency and need to plan for a permanent existence, as Israelis are fond of saying, 'in the dangerous neighbourhood of the Middle East'. He also inherited from his father a strong belief that Israel could only achieve successful relations with stable democratic states where regimes were changed by the ballot box and not by the gun. Much to the disappointment of his son, Benzion never achieved mainstream acceptance for his work on Jewish history, and remained on the fringes of international academia.

Yoni Netanyahu was charismatic and a brilliant soldier and officer, who served in and commanded one of the most elite units in the Israeli Defence Forces (IDF), known in Hebrew as *Sayeret Matkal* (Israeli special forces). Like many older/younger brother relationships, Yoni was a hero to Bibi – and the man he most wanted to emulate. Bibi followed in his brother's footsteps joining *Sayeret Matkal*, but was not considered to be senior officer material.

He did, however, take part in one of the most famous *Sayeret Matkal* operations, the storming of a Sabena passenger airliner at Lod Airport that had been hijacked by members of Yasser Arafat's Black September group on route to Tel Aviv in 1972. His *Sayeret Matkal* commander that day was Ehud Barak, who later succeeded Netanyahu as Prime Minister in 1999, and subsequently served as Netanyahu's Minister of Defence in his second government.

In 1976, Yoni's death during another daring Israeli mission to rescue over a hundred hostages held at Entebbe in Uganda left a deep void in his younger brother's life. Yoni was the only Israeli casualty of the operation, which was later retold in two Hollywood films. His younger brother placed the blame for his brother's death squarely on the shoulders of the PLO, and its leader, Yasser Arafat. Following Yoni's death, his younger brother became the guardian of his memory and the protector of his name.

It also helped motivate him to become a self-taught expert on international terrorism, publishing books and articles that called for Israel and the Western Powers to take a tough line against terrorists. This expertise proved to be the catalyst for Netanyahu's initial political ambitions and decision to devote himself to politics rather than business.

When Netanyahu witnessed Rabin shake Arafat's hand in 1993, his response was a mixture of political disgust and personal anguish. Moreover, Netanyahu vowed, at the time, that he would never be put in a position of having to deal with or meet Arafat, who he saw as the unrepentant and unreformed godfather of international terrorism.

The toxic mixture of abhorrence and distress at the signing of the Oslo Accords can partly explain why the Netanyahu bandwagon derailed in the period from September 1993 up until the assassination of Yitzhak Rabin in November 1995. This book recounts in detail the events of 1995, Netanyahu's *annus horribilis*. During the course of that year Netanyahu's political immaturity, inexperience and apparent superficiality were all ruthlessly exposed, as suicide attacks from Hamas and Islamic Jihad killed Israeli citizens.

As is traditional in Israel, when the country is under attack Israelis shift to the right politically speaking. This quickly translated into a large lead for Netanyahu's Likud over Rabin's Labour Party in opinion polls. Unless Rabin was willing to abandon or freeze the implementation of the Oslo Accords (and there is evidence that he was considering such moves), Netanyahu looked likely to achieve his aim of becoming Prime Minister.

The book recounts, in chapter four, the events surrounding the assassination of Yitzhak Rabin in November 1995 and the reasons why many Israelis felt that Netanyahu was partly to blame for creating the conditions that allowed an extremist right-wing Jew to kill the Prime Minister. The rise in political violence prior to the assassination was put down to Netanyahu's fiery oratory and harsh anti-Rabin remarks at anti-Oslo political rallies.

The assassination of Rabin proved to be Netanyahu's darkest moment, both as a man and a political leader. He survived calls to resign as head of the Likud for largely two reasons: the alternative leader, Dan Meridor, dithered at this key juncture, and both Sharon and Levy felt the timing was wrong.

Both Netanyahu and the Likud took a hammering in the polls throughout December 1995 and January 1996. When the radical Islamic groups Hamas and Islamic Jihad carried out a new wave of suicide attacks in February and March 1996, however, the polls in Israel showed the parties once more neck and neck.

This book shows how Netanyahu came to power in the 1996 elections and how his government lurched from crisis to crisis before collapsing in 1999. It then focuses on his years in the wilderness and his return to power. Its key aim is to fill the void, by presenting a clear picture on this complex man, who is viewed as being both strong and weak at the same time.

PART ONE

Rise

I

Interview

Successful or not, all careers have decisive moments along the way, the importance of which is only understood in retrospect. On a cold, clear January night in Israel in 1991, Benjamin Netanyahu experienced his first decisive moment which would catapult his career into a new orbit, and make him an international television star at the dawn of the era of 24/7 global news networks.

On 17 January 1991, the Persian Gulf War began when the United States-led coalition launched massive air strikes against Iraqi forces. The following night Netanyahu was in a CNN studio in Israel giving a routine interview to the network when the warning sirens sounded to signify an incoming missile attack.

It was a time of high tension in Israel, with Saddam Hussein promising to attack the Jewish state with Scud missiles containing chemical warheads. In the weeks leading up to the war, gas masks had been distributed to all Israelis, who were told to prepare a sealed room in their homes to try to help reduce the effects of a chemical attack.

In the television studio, Netanyahu, the CNN correspondent Linda Scherzer and the rest of the CNN team donned their gas masks and continued with the interview. Scherzer addressed Netanyahu by his nickname 'Bibi' and asked him a routine question about his reaction to comments made earlier in the night as to how Israel would respond to any attack from Iraq.

His response, slightly muffled by the gas mask, came over as strong and resolute: 'What it does demonstrate in a dramatic way is the threat that we are facing – and we would like to see that threat removed.'

Next came one of those perfect sound bites that would characterize his television persona: 'I cannot tell you when: I cannot tell you where and I cannot tell you how, but we will make sure that Israel is safe.'

The reality of the interview was quite shocking. Here was a deputy minister of the Jewish state donning a gas mask against a possible chemical attack half a century after the Holocaust. The appalling significance of this point was largely lost on the television audience as 'Sheriff Netanyahu' tried to lay down the law to Saddam Hussein.

From a television perspective, the interview was brilliant political drama, and herein lay the crux of the debate about 'Bibi'. He was theatrical, compelling and convincing, but his words lacked any real attachment to political reality. As we now know, Netanyahu was no better informed about Israel's 'when, where and how' response to an Iraqi attack than the journalist who asked him the question.

He was a deputy minister who did not sit on the Israeli Security Cabinet; he was not a trusted confidant of his boss, the Israeli Prime Minister, and he was not privy to any substantive discussions about Israel's response. He was essentially a spokesman winging it, but doing it with some style. In retrospect, the performance was of greater importance than the quality of the script.

Straight after the interview, Netanyahu became hot property. All the news networks wanted him on their shows and he soon assumed the role of the main Israeli spokesman during the war. In Israel, much of the Hebrew press mocked Netanyahu's style. All drama and no substance was the general consensus among Israeli journalists. They weren't alone. Several leading members of the Likud argued that Netanyahu was a political lightweight who, sooner or later, would fade into the background.

Most Israelis simply didn't get him, or like him. Amidst a political culture that was characterized by its insular nature and with a small, centralized elite that was largely detached from the changes that were taking place as a result of the media, Netanyahu didn't fit in. Within the international media, it was a completely different story. After Netanyahu's gas mask interview, news networks across the globe couldn't get enough of him. At the time of the Persian Gulf War and beyond, Netanyahu found himself being taken more seriously by foreigners than by his fellow Israelis.

This under-estimation of Netanyahu's ability by Israelis helped explain why his political rivals did not attempt to block his career at this early stage. It would be folly to suggest that the interview for CNN and the subsequent ones he gave to the international press during the war were only important for the advancement of the career of this ambitious politician. They were not. The timing, style and tone of the message could not have been better for Israel, which found itself diplomatically isolated, and whose public relations efforts to present its side of the story had hitherto been mediocre.

The political career of Netanyahu began before 1991, but it was during this transitional year for Middle Eastern and world politics that he came to prominence as the spokesman for a small nation that once again found itself at the centre of dramatic international events. Prior to 1991, the energetic and ambitious would-be politician had been based at the centre of the diplomatic world in the United States: from 1982 as deputy head of the Israeli mission to the United States, and from 1984 to 1988 as Israel's Ambassador to the United Nations.

Both postings provided a whirlwind of opportunity to build a profile and for networking, which Netanyahu grasped with both hands. Later in 1988, largely on the back of his success in the United States, and his father's long-standing connection with the revisionist Zionist movement, he had been elected to the Israeli Knesset on the list of the Likud. Soon after, he had been appointed as deputy Minister of Foreign Affairs – and this was the position he still held in 1991. It was a relatively junior role within the Israeli government, but it provided him with open access to diplomats based in the country and to the foreign media.

It is important to remember that Netanyahu did not appear out of nowhere. Previously, he had been identified in Israel as one of the 'Likud Princes', a small group of young *Likudniks* whose speedy elevation to national leadership was based on the centrality of their fathers in the movement. In a small country where the elites are centralized and tightly bound, this initial help up the diplomatic and political ladder remained an important factor in kick-starting the careers of the privileged.

At the start of the 1990s, Netanyahu would have to be characterized as something of a late bloomer within this group, with several of the other so-called Likud Princes occupying loftier positions than the deputy Minister of Foreign Affairs. The time Netanyahu had spent in the United States proved to be very useful in the long run, but in the short term it gave several of his political rivals in the Likud the opportunity to steal a march on him.

Where Netanyahu stood head and shoulders above his peers, however, was in his oratory. Arguably, this was to become the single most important factor in Netanyahu's rise to the top, and in his ability to hold on to power, sometimes against all the odds. It was a skill he had cultivated during his university days, and had perfected in the corridors of power in Washington and at the United Nations.

Many people can still recall the first time they saw Netanyahu interviewed on international television channels and the lasting impression it made on them. There had been reports circulating among the foreign diplomatic corps, and intelligence officers based in Tel Aviv, about this articulate, young, telegenic Israeli politician who spoke beautiful English with a clipped American accent.

All of this was in contrast to most of the other members of the higher echelons of the Israeli political elite who generally either mumbled, or barked, their way through speeches and television interviews. More often than not they spoke in grammatically confused, unfinished sentences with heavy accents that revealed their East European origins. In Hebrew, their articulation was usually equally poor with several leaders using the lowest forms of the language.

There had been historic exceptions to this rule on both the English and Hebrew language fronts, but by 1991 these leaders had long exited the political arena. So in retrospect, although nobody gave it much thought back in 1991, the timing of Netanyahu's arrival on the international stage could not have been better for the man, and, from a public relations perspective, for Israel.

The timing was perfect for Israel for a number of reasons. It is important to go back, for a moment, to the long hot summer of 1990. Israel was heading towards one of its decisive moments when a clash between the newly installed ultra-nationalist governing coalition and the outside world appeared inevitable.

The government, which was led by the veteran Yitzhak Shamir, was arguably the most hawkish in Israeli history and included parties from the far-right as well as the religious parties. Naturally, its composition and policies did not go down well in Washington, where there was a growing sense of polarization of opinion about Israel. While support was still relatively strong on Capitol Hill, at the White House there was a deep sense of frustration that the Israelis were seemingly not inter-ested in moving the peace process forward.

Specifically, President George H. W. Bush and his Secretary of State, James Baker, were alarmed at the pace of Israeli settlement in what was described by the State Department as the Occupied Territories. The fear was that it was the intention of the Israeli government to settle widely in the West Bank (and to a lesser extent the Gaza Strip).

Bush and Baker had adopted a more critical line towards Israel from the outset of their administration, in January of the previous year, than the previous administration of President Ronald Reagan. For its part, the Israeli government made no secret of its desire to settle widely in the West Bank and the Gaza Strip, with the intention of changing the facts on the ground: specifically altering the demographic balance between Jews and Arabs in the area. The end of the Cold War was drawing near and with the Soviet Union allowing its large Jewish population to emigrate to Israel, there appeared a plentiful supply of immigrants for Israel to settle in the West Bank.

On top of this there was an ongoing Palestinian *Intifada* (upris-ing), which had started in December 1987. While the intensity of the campaign, characterized by stone-throwing Palestinian youths, was diminishing, the political and public relations damage it inflicted upon Israel was not over.

For more than two years, American news networks had regularly broadcast scenes from the West Bank and the Gaza Strip of Israeli soldiers using live rounds and forceful non-lethal measures against the stone-throwers. The resulting heavy casualties among the Palestinians led to calls for greater American pressure to be brought to bear on Israel to show greater restraint.

Through the first part of the summer of 1990, the world waited for the catalyst that would spark what was expected to be one of the biggest diplomatic crises in US–Israeli relations. Then, as so often happens in the Middle East, while people are eagerly watching one area something quite unexpected happens elsewhere, which changes nearly everything.

On 2 August 1990, the world awoke to the news that Saddam Hussein's Iraqi armed forces had invaded Kuwait. Few, if any, European, American or Arab diplomats or intelligence services had foreseen the invasion. Within 48 hours Iraqi forces were in complete control of

Kuwait, and the world speculated as to whether Iraq would push on into Saudi Arabia.

Many Middle Eastern experts at the time of the invasion were left dazed and confused by the invasion. One thing was clear from the outset, however: the old bipolar lines of the Arab–Israeli conflict, which had dominated the region's recent history, were about to become very blurred.

The diplomatic crisis and eventual war that resulted from the Iraqi invasion did lead to major developments and changes. One of the most significant was the arrival on the international political and media stage of Benjamin Netanyahu. In short, it made a star of this previously little known junior Israeli politician.

Without the Iraqi invasion, Netanyahu might very well have reached the highest circles of political power in Israel, but it is less likely that his rise to the apex of power in Israel would have been so meteoric.

The crisis and eventual war led to a number of firsts, new alliances and developments on the political side as well as on the battlefield. One area that is sometimes overlooked in today's world of instant online news is that the Persian Gulf War of 1991 was the first 24/7 cable news conflict. The war as a result helped make not only Netanyahu, the interviewee, but also the news presenters of Ted Turner's CNN.

The brief that Netanyahu was left with – to act as the spokesman for Israel's defence in the international media – was a difficult one. Soon after Iraq's invasion the Bush administration set out with the aim of building as big a coalition as possible for a potential military campaign against Saddam Hussein.

At the centre of this coalition were the Arab states. President Bush made it clear that he wanted as many of them to commit forces to the Allied coalition as possible. Sensitivities in Washington centred upon allowing any military action against Iraq by the United States to be perceived as a modern take on the Crusades.

As a result, not for the first time in its short history Israel found itself as something of a strategic liability to United States policy aims in the Middle East. The conventional wisdom in Washington was that the Arab states would not join any coalition that contained Israeli military forces, either directly or indirectly.

One Arab who was acutely aware of this point was Saddam Hussein. The Iraqi leader announced that if Iraq were to be attacked by the

US-led coalition, he would respond by launching missile strikes against Tel Aviv, with the intention of bringing Israel into the war and thus splintering the coalition.

During the intensive diplomatic talks to find a peaceful resolution to the crisis, Saddam Hussein attempted to link a potential Iraqi withdrawal from Kuwait to an Israeli one from the West Bank and the Gaza Strip. Once again, the subtext to this Iraqi manoeuvre was to try to sow the seeds of division within the US-led coalition. In Israel, Saddam's attempts at the linkage were viewed with considerable concern.

The former Prime Minister and veteran Labour Party politician Yitzhak Rabin briefed the international press corps, pointing out that he feared the world would pay Saddam Hussein with Israeli currency. Rabin's slightly cryptic comments revealed the concerns of many Israelis, that the United States might be willing to eventually cut a deal with Iraq, which would see it apply additional pressures on the Israelis to make far-reaching concessions to the Palestinians.

The final parts of the complex jigsaw puzzle that Netanyahu faced as he entered the international stage centred upon the Palestinian Liberation Organization, and its leader, Yasser Arafat. At the key juncture of the Iraqi invasion of Kuwait the PLO found itself knocking on the doors of the White House in Washington and 10 Downing Street in London.

Arafat and the PLO had seemingly renounced violence on 13 December 1988, and accepted a two-state solution for the Israeli–Palestinian conflict. In essence, this meant that the PLO had effectively recognized Israel's right to exist within its 1967 borders, with the PLO-proposed Palestinian state being limited to the West Bank and the Gaza Strip.

Naturally, the United States and European leaders welcomed this shift in policy as well as Arafat's public declaration of it at the United Nations. The PLO leadership believed that it had met the criteria that Washington had set it as pre-conditions for being allowed to enter the Washington-led diplomatic talks on the Israeli–Palestinian track of the Middle East peace process.

Netanyahu's boss, Yitzhak Shamir, viewed Arafat's statements and the changes in PLO policy as a trick.[1] Whatever Arafat's and the PLO's motives, this shift, by the summer of 1990, was starting to have the desired effect from a Palestinian perspective. The period of quarantine during which the Americans wished to test the sincerity of Arafat and the PLO's commitment to non-violence and acceptance of the two-state solution was drawing to a close.

The Bush administration appeared increasingly willing to involve Arafat and the PLO in the process, as did several European leaders. This was not good news for the Israeli government trying to deal with its increasingly prickly relationship with Washington.

In Europe, while opposition to Iraq's invasion of Kuwait remained strong, there was a feeling that Israel had made an already bad situation worse with its seeming intractability towards the Palestinians. Saddam Hussein's attempts to link resolution of the Palestinian issue to that of the Iraqi–Kuwaiti issue had resonated in some European capitals that were already more receptive to Arafat's message than the United States had been.

The charge made by Saddam Hussein of the West's double standards in dealing with the Israeli occupation of the West Bank and Gaza Strip and the Iraqi one of Kuwait, while clearly aimed at sowing the seeds of division, appeared to make sense to some Europeans who were determined to avoid an armed confrontation with Iraq. Among the Palestinians, Saddam Hussein's linkage was hugely welcomed, as was his call for the destruction of Israel.

There were political ramifications for all of this, with Yasser Arafat voicing his support for Iraq and thus distancing himself from the American-led coalition. At the end of the war, this was to prove one of the costliest mistakes of Arafat's career. At the onset of the war, however, the pressure was firmly on Israel.

When all these international factors were taken together it meant that, when Netanyahu appeared on international television essentially spinning Israel's position, he was operating from an apparent position of weakness. To a certain extent this made his performances in the media during the crisis and resulting war all the more compelling and impressive.

When the war started, Netanyahu was on television screens across the globe. 'We know how wars start, but we don't know how they end' was the message he put out when asked how he envisaged the war developing. Dressed in dark suits, crisp white shirts and club striped ties, he acted as the Israeli point man for the foreign media. All wars have been important for Israel, but the Persian Gulf was different in many respects from previous ones, and Netanyahu's performance crucially had to reflect these changes.

When, on the second night of the war, Saddam Hussein attacked Israel with the first of the 39 Scud missiles launched during the course of the conflict from western Iraq aimed at Tel Aviv, and the rest of Israel's coastal areas, it was the first time that Israel's major population centres had come under direct missile attack. While today this has become more commonplace in subsequent Israeli wars, with both Hamas and Hezbollah being characterized by missile strikes targeted against Israeli cities, in 1991, it was something new for Israelis to have to contend with.

In maximizing his threat to Israel, Saddam Hussein declared that the missiles would carry chemical warheads that would cause massive casualties. In the weeks prior to the war, Israelis became accustomed to carrying gas masks everywhere they went and preparing a shelter in their homes. In order to try to lighten the fears a little, Israeli children and young women decorated their gas mask cases, thus making them into something approaching a fashion accessory.

With the threat of being killed by an explosion from a Scud or from the potentially deadly chemical fallout, thousands of Israelis simply packed their bags, left Tel Aviv and headed for Eilat, in the south of the country, or Jerusalem, where they believed (correctly) that Iraq would not dare bomb.

In the end, the Scud missile threat was partially neutralized by the inaccuracy of the missiles – they were operating very close to or even beyond their maximum range – and by Allied bombing and sabotage efforts against the mobile Scud launchers in western Iraq.[2] At the outset of the war, the United States, desperately trying to keep Israel from retaliating to the Scud attacks, rushed Patriot defensive missiles to Tel Aviv that aimed to shoot down the incoming Scuds.

The supply of the Patriot missile batteries was a major public relations triumph in reassuring Israelis, but actually had little impact on the war. A leading member of the Israeli government said after the war that the missiles had only intercepted a couple of Scuds and that the collateral damage from the Patriots was as significant, if not greater, than the damage caused to Israel by the Scuds.

Perhaps the biggest lesson Netanyahu took from the attacks on Israel related to the response of the Israeli Prime Minister to the Scud attacks. Twelve days before the first Scud missile was launched against Israel, while Netanyahu was reminding the world of Israel's right to self-defence and its history of retaliation along the lines of an eye for an eye, Israel's Prime Minister slipped quietly out of the country with two of his advisors and a senior Israeli Defence Forces commander, General Ehud Barak.

Their mission was a private meeting with King Hussein of Jordan in his country house near London in order to finalize a secret agreement between Israel and Jordan.[3] Shamir and his team spent the weekend at the King's residence, coming to an important understanding with the King.

In essence, Israel and Jordan agreed that Israel would not violate Jordanian air sovereignty: this made it very difficult for Israel to mount bombing raids on Iraq. In return the King promised to prevent Iraqi planes flying over Jordan, which made it difficult for Iraq to bomb Israel.[4] The King also banned Iraqi troops from entering Jordan. This move, in turn, removed the threat of an Iraqi land-based attack on Israel.

Netanyahu was not privy to these discussions or the outcome of the meeting. As ever, Shamir played his cards close to his chest, not officially informing the United States of the talks or their outcome, as well as keeping most of his political colleagues in the dark. The agreement worked and Israel did not respond to the Scud attacks. The Israeli Air Force was readied for attacks over Iraq, which avoided violating Jordanian airspace by flying first south rather than east.[5] The missions, however, were cancelled, many at the last minute, due to Shamir's intervention or poor weather.

Shamir's restraint was widely welcomed by both the United States and by the majority of the Israeli public. On a strategic level, his actions helped keep Jordan out of the war and prevented a potential Iraqi invasion or internal coup. It was a sign of the relatively lowly political position of Netanyahu that he was kept largely uninformed by Shamir about the strategic agreement with Jordan. Opinion polls conducted at the end of the war in Israel gave Shamir a significant bump in support for both his leadership and for the Likud.

Support for Netanyahu deepened during the war, where he was seen as having effectively won the public relations battle against the Arabs and other anti-Israel groups. His impressive performance meant that he had arrived on the political scene and the political agenda appeared to be moving in his direction. As the internal political fallout from the war developed in Israel, it soon became clear that Netanyahu's star was burning brighter, but there were several other Likud Princes who appeared better placed to succeed the high-flying Shamir when he chose to step down as leader.

There were also two other senior members of the Likud, Ariel Sharon and David Levy, both older than the Likud Princes, who believed themselves to be strong candidates to succeed Shamir. Not all *Likudniks* were taken with Netanyahu's style. Many felt him to be something of a theatrical performer who lacked depth: a classic case of style over substance. More problematic for the relative newcomer to politics was his lack of a real power base within the party organs, the majority of whose members were tied to Sharon, Levy or one of the more senior Likud Princes.

Netanyahu, however, was making big plans to deal with this problem, and also to effectively bypass some of the party institutions. In the meantime, there was much public relations work to do for Israel's unofficial spokesman in the arena of the Arab–Israeli conflict.

2

Madrid

On 30 October 1991, Benjamin Netanyahu found himself where, arguably, he felt most comfortable: at the centre of the world stage amid the sea of flashbulbs and television cameras of the world press that had gathered to cover the opening of the historic Madrid Peace Conference.

This was the first time that Israel and the Arab states had sat in the same room and attempted to negotiate an end to the conflict. The Palestinians were also present in the room as part of a joint delegation with the Jordanians.

Netanyahu's presence at the conference was confirmation of his heightened importance to Yitzhak Shamir following the Persian Gulf War and of the deeply problematic relationship between Shamir and Israel's Minister of Foreign of Affairs, David Levy. Put simply, Shamir did not trust Levy and vice versa.

As a result, Shamir decided to attend the Peace Conference himself, leaving the disgruntled Levy at home to play Cinderella. On the surface it was a strange decision, given that the conference had been arranged by the United States for the participating countries to be represented at foreign minister level.

Netanyahu for one wasn't complaining about Shamir's decision. Relations had soured between him and his superior at the foreign ministry in Jerusalem, and the two men were not on speaking terms. There were tales of petty jealousies over Netanyahu having played such a prominent role in the PR campaign during the Persian Gulf War. Levy did not speak English and was largely absent from the international news coverage during the war.

In retrospect, both men were hugely ambitious and were looking towards future battles. For Netanyahu, the Madrid Peace Conference was a win-win situation. While Levy sulked back in Israel, Netanyahu was able to put together his own team to offer PR support to Shamir rather than have the ministry draw up the list of experts for him. It was clear from the outset that for Shamir, whose political style was to try to say as little as possible, and who wasn't afraid of long silences, Netanyahu represented the perfect foil.

The conference was the result of months of exhaustive American diplomacy led by the Secretary of State, James Baker, and supported by the frequent personal interventions of President Bush. In Washington, the successful military outcome to the war with Iraq was viewed as providing an opportunity to advance negotiations between the Israelis and the Arabs.

The preparation for the conference proved as difficult as the Bush administration feared it would be. Two issues were particularly hard to resolve. The first was securing the agreement of the Syrians to attend the conference. President Hafez al-Assad was widely regarded as the leader of the Israel rejectionist camp in the Arab world, and had turned down previous overtures to enter into negotiations with it. The second was securing the participation of the Israelis at the conference. Eventually, as the British Ambassador in Tel Aviv, Mark Elliot, wrote, Shamir was convinced by:

> Prolonged persuasive efforts by the US administration, dwelling on the unprecedented opportunity for peace with moderate Arab regimes and spiced with occasional reminders that the US remained Israel's paymaster.[1]

The Ambassador further added:

> Seen from the outside world, he [Shamir] drove a pretty hard bargain, achieving the great goal of direct talks with Israel's Arab neighbours without having to pay any price in terms of the status of East Jerusalem or explicit acknowledgement of the PLO.[2]

All in all Shamir was left feeling extremely satisfied that he had been able to achieve the difficult balancing act between managing his right-wing coalition and the Americans. Some members of the Israeli coalition government remained dissatisfied with Shamir's decision for Israel to attend. They argued that he hadn't secured 'explicit prior assurances' from the Americans in defining the direction and the limits of the process, and had also been forced to accept the presence of the PLO behind the scenes.[3]

In preparing for the conference, Shamir correctly predicted that it would be a theatrical event during which all parties would initially play to their domestic audiences by outlining their most hawkish positions towards the peace process.[4] Political spin came to play an important part at the conference, as both the Syrians and the Israelis traded speeches that were laced with recriminations from the past conflicts rather than offering any new path forward.

It was for purposes of spin that Shamir took Netanyahu to Madrid rather than for any substantive advice on policy. The opportunity to excel at what he was good at – for both the domestic and international audiences – further raised the profile of Netanyahu, much to the displeasure of his formal boss in the ministry of foreign affairs. The message that Netanyahu was tasked with putting out was that the Prime Minister and the Likud clearly enjoyed strong support in Israel for their handling of the threats to Israel during the Persian Gulf War.

In terms of the peace process, Israel would consider some limited, and unspecific, concessions towards the Arabs in exchange for peace and the United States needed to be careful not to push the Israeli government too hard. In Israel, there was widespread resentment at American attempts to pressure Israel into handing over lands in exchange for peace.[5]

For Netanyahu, the Madrid Peace Conference was an overwhelming personal success, coming on the back of his strong performance during the Persian Gulf War. Although not wholly party to Shamir's tactics and strategy for the conference, and the subsequent bi-lateral and multi-lateral negotiations, Netanyahu's television skills made him an effective spokesman for the Israeli government. In political terms, however, he was still some way from the top tier of the Likud with Shamir, Levy and the Minister of Defence, Moshe Arens, at the apex of the elite.

Arens was the closest of the leading figures to Netanyahu at this point. In some respects he acted as a mentor to the younger man. Writing much later, Arens told the *Washington Post*, 'I have been friendly with Netanyahu for many years . . . and it is true my relations with him, because of the age gap, were in many ways like those of father to son.'[6] It was Arens who had given Netanyahu his first job as political council at the Israeli Embassy in Washington in 1982, and it was Arens who helped get Netanyahu appointed as Israeli Ambassador to the United Nations in 1984.[7]

In 1988 Arens was appointed as Israel's Minister of Foreign Affairs, and he helped appoint Netanyahu into the government as his deputy with a remit to deal with relations with the United States Congress. Both Arens and Netanyahu were educated at MIT and both men spent extended periods living and working in the United States.

Arens was arguably the most articulate senior member of the Israeli government when dealing with the English-speaking international press. His tone, however, could be likened to a teacher speaking to a not very bright student. He was often over-defensive, and this made him a much less attractive prospect for television interviewers than the more suave Netanyahu.

The patron/client-style relationship that characterized Arens and Netanyahu's friendship was commonplace in Israeli politics, particularly in the two major parties, Likud and Labour, that had run the country in various coalitions since 1948. Indeed, at the time Netanyahu was launching his political career there were few other ways to get a foothold on the greasy ladder. Israel's party list electoral system, in which the political parties presented a ranked list of candidates to the electorate, encouraged patron/client ties.

In order to obtain a realistic slot on the party list, candidates needed the support of one or more of the major figures in the party. In Netanyahu's case that patron was Arens, and, to some extent initially, Shamir as well. The system encouraged strong elite control over the parties – as well as political deals – as members of the elite used the party list as a means of increasing their position within the party.

It was no coincidence that the rise of Benjamin Netanyahu corresponded with the process of democratization of Israeli politics. At party level, American-style primary elections were introduced first by the Labour Party, followed by the Likud and the others. It proved a popular move with the electorate. In political terms, it loosened the control of the party leaders over the electoral list, and as a result over the party itself. Initially only the party's central committee were given the vote, but this was soon widened to give a vote to party members.

The side effect of the changes was that the focus for political advancement shifted from supporting the elite to attracting as much popular support as possible among party members. The easiest way to achieve this was through the media, specifically television, in order to talk directly to the party members. Naturally, Netanyahu used this format effectively to start to develop a strong camp in the party for himself. Primary elections eventually caused problems of their own, but at the start of the 1990s they were very much in vogue.

The veteran leaderships of both the Likud and the Labour Party were not inclined to support a shift towards primaries. Why would they when potentially it would reduce their patronage powers to their supporters in their respective parties? Both sets of leaderships, however, found it difficult to resist primaries given the popular support for their introduction.

The 1992 election was to be the first in which Likud and Labour would have a ranked party list of candidates for the Knesset determined by a primary vote. As it turned out, this came to help Netanyahu's rise in the party by allowing Netanyahu and several other Likud Princes to essentially leapfrog the generation above them in the party and those who had been viewed as the natural successors to Shamir. There was a similar development in the Labour Party, whereby the young guard did well in occupying spots near the top of the list.

The other major area of reform that came to impact on Netanyahu's rise to power was the electoral system itself. The party list system had produced coalition governments in Israel since 1948. Indeed, no one party had ever achieved an overall majority in the Knesset. From 1948 until 1977 the Labour Party (in various guises) had ruled Israel in coalition governments comprising it and several other parties (usually including the National Religious Party).

From 1977 to 1984, the Likud had become the main party of government again with various coalition partners (specifically the various religious parties in Israel). From 1984 until 1990, Israel witnessed what were known as the years of the national unity – when Labour and Likud had ruled together.

In 1990, the government had broken up amid much rancour when the Labour Party leader, Shimon Peres, attempted to form a narrow-based centre-left government. This, known rather unflatteringly in Israel as the 'dirty or smelly' exercise, created strong momentum for reforming the electoral system, to strengthen Israeli democracy and the ability of elected governments to govern.

The aim of the reforms were twofold: to weaken the power of the smaller parties and to strengthen the influence of the Prime Minister. There was deep dissatisfaction among Israel's secular parties that the power of the religious parties had become too great. This led to various electoral reform proposals aimed at raising the number of votes that each party needed to win in order to secure its first seat in the Knesset.

This made perfect sense to Labour and Likud, both of whom thought that they would benefit from any increase, as it would – in all likelihood – lead to one or more smaller parties failing to get a single seat in the Knesset. In such circumstances, the votes of these parties would then be redistributed to the party with which it made an arrangement before the election. The debate here centred on how far the threshold should be raised with various proposals put forward.

Netanyahu was much more interested in the second debate about electoral reform: the potential introduction of direct elections for Prime Minister. As ever, he viewed the implications of this reform from a self-serving perspective. In 1991, Netanyahu believed one important thing about his future prospects: his best chance of becoming Prime Minister was through a direct election for the post.

The concentration on the self over the collective was something that has characterized much of Netanyahu's career. As it turned out, his judgement was probably correct on this, but he failed to understand the damaging consequences of giving Israelis a separate ballot for Prime Minister and for the Knesset.

On this issue, Netanyahu was out of sync with the Likud and its leadership. Yitzhak Shamir made it clear he opposed the idea and felt that Netanyahu's position on the direct election was self-serving. Shamir did not want to take part in any 'beauty contest', as he called it, in order to secure the premiership. This was one of several reasons why Shamir's support for Netanyahu started to cool in the period prior to the 1992 elections in Israel.

The impetus for political reform in Israel quickened over the second part of 1991, when it became clear that the narrow-based Likud-led government was crumbling and it looked increasingly likely that Shamir would have to call for early elections. The attention of Shamir, however, in the weeks and months that followed the Madrid Peace Conference was largely taken up with dealing with increasing pressure from the United States on Israel to make concessions in the negotiations with the Arabs.[8]

At the same time, thousands of Soviet Jews were arriving in Israel, and, with the collapse of the Soviet Union, Israel hoped that at least two million immigrants would arrive in the following decade. The newly arriving immigrants placed strains on the Israeli economy. Jobs needed to be found for them as well as housing and social services.

The result was that Israel needed $10 billion in loan guarantees from the United States to successfully absorb this potentially massive wave of immigration. The Bush administration saw this request as an opportunity to try to leverage Israel on the political front, and made a counter-demand for an Israeli freeze on settlement building. The loan guarantees, as a result, became the dominant issue in the final months of the Shamir government.[9]

The Shamir government refused to accept the terms of the offer from the Americans and the loan guarantee issue developed into a fully fuelled US–Israeli crisis. Shamir saw it as a one-off in an otherwise good state of relations between Jerusalem and Washington.[10] He was deluding himself.

Netanyahu, with his experience in dealing with Congress, was drafted into action, to see if Congress was willing to lean on President Bush to release the loan guarantees. There was some surprise in the Israeli government that a US President would take such a course of action, coming as it did so close to the US presidential election in November 1992. Bush risked alienating the powerful American Jewish lobby group, AIPAC, and losing large chunks of the Jewish vote in the election.

The Bush administration, however, had become exasperated by the lack of progress in the negotiations in Washington that followed the Madrid Peace Conference. They increasingly felt that the Israelis were doing no more than treading water and keeping the talks going without offering any concessions. At the same time, the apparent pace of settlement building in the West Bank was quickening with the government constructing settlements rather than expanding the large existing blocks near the Green Line (the border between Israel and the West Bank).

The Americans feared, with some justification as it turned out, that the Israelis would continue to stall the talks in Washington indefinitely, while they put facts (i.e. new settlements) on the ground in the West Bank that would prevent the creation of any potential Palestinian state. In retirement, Shamir admitted that his stalling tactics were designed exactly for this purpose.

Netanyahu watched the deepening crisis in US–Israeli ties with great concern. Both President Bush and Secretary of State James Baker were sending the Likud and Israel a clear signal: the Israeli government had to choose between getting the money to absorb the newly arriving immigrants and its settlement programme in the West Bank. It wouldn't be allowed to have both.

The Americans were essentially making the Israelis prioritize the two major ingredients of Zionism: immigrants and land. By continuing with the settlement construction in the West Bank, Shamir chose to prioritize the development of new lands over the immigrants. The message was not lost on the Soviet immigrants in Israel who, without the loan guarantees, faced a bleak and protracted process of absorption after their arrival in Israel.

It was a major challenge to the authority of the Likud, and Netanyahu, along with several other *Likudniks*, argued that the Bush administration was trying to directly intervene in Israeli politics. They were correct, and the meddling became deeper at the start of 1992.

The British Ambassador, writing at that time, predicted that the Likud would be 'the governing party of the next decade'.[11] Much of the reasoning for this prediction was based on the poor performance of the opposition Labour Party. As the British suggested:

> There is no immediate threat from the left wing, whose thunder Shamir has in large measure stolen. The Labour Party has agonised through the year [1991] over its position and its leadership, ending up with the mixture as before – Peres and Rabin in charge.[12]

On 29 January 1992, Likud and Labour agreed to an election date of 23 June, thus starting nearly five months of political campaigning that took place first inside the parties, followed by the election campaign. On 19 February, Yitzhak Rabin narrowly defeated Shimon Peres to become the leader of the Labour Party for the second time. Rabin's victory came to have a major impact on Israeli politics.

Known as Israel's 'Mr Security', Rabin had been identified as the man they most wanted to lead Israel. By this stage, the more dovish Shimon Peres had been labelled as unelectable by Washington, after failing to win a decisive victory in the four most recent elections in Israel since 1977.

Bush and Baker saw Rabin as not only more electable than Peres, but also potentially more flexible than Shamir and the Likud in negotiations with the Palestinians and the wider Arab world. Rabin soon confirmed the American assessment by announcing that he would be willing to accept the conditions laid down by the Bush administration for the granting of the $10 billion of loan guarantees to Israel.

The Americans, in short, achieved their goal of creating the conditions whereby, after years of policy fudging, the Israeli electorate would be offered a real choice of priorities by the two major parties in the country. Put simply, the Likud giving greater importance to the settlements, and the Labour Party prioritizing getting the funds to successfully absorb the Soviet immigrants.

Netanyahu was among several members of the Likud who felt that Shamir had been cornered by the Bush administration, and that Rabin was receiving more favourable treatment from Washington. Netanyahu's mentor, Moshe Arens – whose positions on the negotiations were closest to those of Netanyahu – had for some time been trying to persuade Shamir to give the Americans some concessions.[13]

One of Netanyahu's rivals, the Likud Prince Roni Milo, tried to convince Shamir to give up the Gaza Strip to the Palestinians. His argument was based on the fact that nobody in Israel really wanted Gaza – with all the chaos and darkness that its occupation of this narrow strip along the Mediterranean Sea had brought for both sides in the conflict. Shamir refused. He would fight the forthcoming election without promising the United States, the Palestinians and the wider Arab world any meaningful concessions.

Within the Likud there were increasing murmurs that Shamir's strategy placed Israel on a collision course with the United States. Shamir looked out of touch and tired. He had served as Prime Minister since

1983 (except for a two-year period between 1984 and 1986 when Shimon Peres had occupied the position as part of a rotation agreement with Labour, during which time Shamir had served as Minister of Foreign Affairs). The British Ambassador summed up the mood towards the Likud in Israel:

> The Likud which for so long appeared to have replaced Labour as the natural party of government began to look vulnerable – increasingly divided internally and tainted with corruption. Shamir's preference for inaction began to look like a habit of indecision. The pressure for clean government and constitutional reform was growing too, as was a public antipathy to the cramping compromises on daily politics imposed by the religious parties.[14]

The tensions within the Likud were reflected in the leadership contest that took place on 20 February 1992, among the 3,300 members of the Likud's Central Committee. Netanyahu was part of the Arens camp that supported the 77-year-old Shamir who defeated his two bitter Likud rivals, David Levy and Ariel Sharon. Shamir secured 46 per cent of the vote to Levy's 31 per cent and Sharon's 23 per cent.

The result illustrated the increasing concern over Shamir's leadership, as well as the strong support that Levy enjoyed in the party from its members of Sephardic origin.[15] The belief was that Shamir would not serve a full term if he was re-elected in June 1992, but would stand down after a couple of years. The battle to succeed Shamir was already well underway.[16] Shamir argued that all the intense internal fighting in the Likud at the time took place when everybody in the party was convinced that it was going to win the general election.[17]

For Netanyahu, the key race of his career to that point was about to take place. He sought a high position in the Likud primary, to rank in its party list for the election. This was a basic requirement in order to stand a chance of becoming a minister in the government, if the Likud emerged victorious in the general election in June.

Voting took place with the 3,300 Central Committee members of the party casting their ballots in a carnival atmosphere at a Tel Aviv fairground. Voting was in rounds, with seven places selected in each round. Shamir had already secured top spot as leader of the party. To a large extent, the political story of the vote was an agreement between the

Shamir–Arens camp and the Sharon camp to effectively try to divide the list of realistic spots for their supporters at the expense of David Levy and his faction.

The result was as expected, with only a couple of Levy supporters making the list. The key result of the night was that Netanyahu was placed in the first group of seven. This was largely based on the alliance of the Shamir–Arens and Shamir camps, but it was nonetheless very impressive and had far-reaching consequences. In generational terms, Netanyahu effectively moved himself to the top of the Likud Princes by achieving a higher place on the list than people such as Benni Begin (the son of Menachem Begin).

The primary election marked Netanyahu's arrival as a major player in the Likud. The result was no accident. Netanyahu had spent a great deal of time and effort since the Madrid Peace Conference developing his political machine. A small but dedicated team of advisors lobbied members of the Central Committee well before the official campaign started. While the leadership of the party appeared to be embroiled in a series of public quarrels, Netanyahu worked energetically to achieve the top spot among the younger generation of Likud leaders.

In retrospect, the model he used for the Likud internal elections in 1992 came to serve him well as he continued to climb the political ladder. Despite all his hard work, it almost ended disastrously when he clashed with the leadership of the party over the issue of the introduction of the direct election for Prime Minister.

Both Shamir and Arens were opposed to direct elections for Prime Minister. Shamir argued that it did not fit with the political culture for the electorate to choose between individuals rather than an ideological platform.[18] On his part, Arens agreed that the direct contest risked becoming a beauty contest between the leaders of the two major parties in Israel.[19]

Netanyahu understood that both men were responsible for the advancement of his political career to date, and in all likelihood, would be so for the immediate future. For Netanyahu, however, this was an issue on which he didn't want to compromise, even if it meant damaging his internal position within the Likud.

Both Shamir and Arens gave Netanyahu something of a working over in a private meeting, in which Shamir warned him that his career prospects would suffer if he went ahead and voted in favour of the reform. Shamir issued the whip to Likud MKs to vote against, but with the Labour Party under Rabin supporting the bill the outcome was considered too close to call. The pressure on Netanyahu from the Likud further increased when it became known that his vote could turn out to be the casting one.

It was significant that two of the biggest advocates of the direct system were Netanyahu and Rabin, who both believed that they were personally more popular than the party they led. Rabin was already leader of the Labour Party, but at the time Netanyahu was not close to becoming leader of the Likud. So for Netanyahu, his support of the direct election was aimed at enhancing his chances of the premiership much further down the line. Self-interest was a strong motive for both Netanyahu and Rabin, but to some extent both men were in similar positions within their respective parties.

Rabin had been elected in an open primary against Peres who largely still controlled the party organs such as the Central Committee. Rabin was more popular among the party supporters than Peres, hence his victory. Within the Likud, Netanyahu was still reliant on the patronage of Arens and Shamir. Among the 'old guard' of veteran Likud Central Committee members he was widely distrusted and seen as an intellectual and political lightweight. By 1992, he was, however, the favourite of party supporters who adored his media performances.

Whatever his motives, Netanyahu stood his ground on the vote for direct elections. In private, his small team of advisors warned him of the dire consequences of his actions. Shamir was not a man known to forgive people easily, especially those who he believed had betrayed him from within his own camp. Regardless of this, Netanyahu cast his vote in favour, and to his horror was the only member of the Likud to do so, and his vote did turn out to be the decisive one in the Knesset. On 18 March 1992, the Knesset passed the legislation for direct election for Prime Minister to come into effect after the June 1992 election.

The forwarded date at least meant that Shamir, given his advanced age, would not be faced with the prospect of ever having to win the premiership. It was a small mercy for Netanyahu as he made his way back to his tiny office in the Knesset. The silence in the corridors of the Knesset among the Likud MKs was deafening.

Though he probably didn't know it at the time, Netanyahu had just taken the first major decision of his political career. It was one that left him isolated and vulnerable within the Likud. True to form, Shamir never forgave him. As the election campaign got underway, however, Shamir was too busy with his Machiavellian internal Likud political games to worry much about the man who had gone off message.

Meanwhile, the electorate was registering its discontent with the political games in the Likud with opinion polls indicating that Labour under Rabin (as the Labour Party electoral list was marketed) was making inroads into voting constituencies that had hitherto been considered Likud strongholds. Shamir was not a man to panic, but things were soon to get worse for the Likud and a victory that appeared all but assured during the previous year looked to be at risk.

Only unity would bring victory, suggested a Likud member of the party's electoral committee. The cold reality was that the wheels were coming off the wagon, and due to petty jealousies the party's biggest electoral star found himself benched for the campaign. The Likud would fight the 1992 election with Netanyahu as a peripheral figure. The party that had spent two years turning in on itself needed to find a way of derailing the Rabin electoral bandwagon.

3

Earthquake

Soon after the polls closed on 23 June 1992, Israeli television announced dramatically that there had been a (second) political upheaval. Labour under Rabin had replaced Likud as the single biggest party in the Knesset. The electorate had punished the Likud. Its number of seats fell to 32, some 12 fewer than the 44 seats the Labour Party secured.

Almost immediately, senior figures in the Likud attempted to blame one another for the poor showing in the polls. Amid all the recriminations in the party, there were clear reasons for the defeat. Netanyahu, who by virtue of being benched for large parts of the campaign emerged relatively unscathed from the defeat, carefully noted the reasons why the electorate had turned against the Likud in the election.

Most of the voters who deserted the Likud on 23 June had voted for other parties from within the Likud block. The election did not, as a result, reflect a major political realignment in Israel. Indeed, when the official results were published, it became apparent that the Likud block comprising of the Likud, along with the parties of the far-right and the religious parties, had won more votes than the Labour block.

Instead, the victory of the Labour Party was largely a technical one, caused by the divisions within the Likud and the right, along with the failure of one rightist party to win enough votes to cross the electoral threshold. The party also failed to set the correct arrangement for the transfer of its votes. The British Ambassador concurred and wrote, 'Rabin won a narrow victory in June'.[1] Netanyahu understood it was disunity and division that handed Labour its victory, and this understanding became a major influence on his political development in the years following this electoral defeat.

Netanyahu, along with all the pollsters and commentators, noted one key electoral constituency that was voting for the first time in 1992 and that turned against the Likud in their thousands. The ex-Soviet immigrants to Israel punished the Likud for the failure to devote enough resources towards their absorption into Israel. By failing to agree to the terms outlined by the Bush administration in order for the Americans to agree to $10 billion of loan guarantees, the Likud alienated one of the most significant voting groups.

Netanyahu understood two important points about the new immigrants: their vote for the Labour Party was essentially a protest vote, and the majority of the ex-Soviet Jews still held hawkish views about the conflict with the Arabs. This made them potential allies for a future leader of the Likud. For his part, Netanyahu devoted a great deal of time to developing relationships with the group, foreseeing their continued importance to the outcome of future general elections.

In Washington, President Bush and Secretary of State Baker greeted the outcome of the 1992 election in Israel as a vindication of their policy of refusing to grant the loan guarantees to Shamir. In reality, the reasons for Rabin's victory were much more complex. Rabin and his small, dedicated team managed to run the campaign as if direct elections for Prime Minister had already been introduced. Wherever possible, the Labour Party was hidden as it was deemed to be a vote loser.

Rabin managed to blur his policy towards the settlements, arguing that there needed to be a distinction between security settlements and political ones. Cleverly, he never clearly articulated how he defined each category and the differences between them. He did talk about the need to redistribute funding away from the settlements to developing infrastructure projects within the Green Line in Israel.

In doing this, Rabin managed to retain American support without agreeing to a settlement freeze. The Persian Gulf War also played a role in Rabin's victory, with its challenge to the notion that Israel would only be safe from attack by retaining large buffer areas of land. The range of Saddam Hussein's Scud missiles made any buffer zones redundant.

On a superficial level, Israel appeared a changed country following Rabin's victory, one that was not only welcomed in Washington, but in Europe as well. The British Ambassador recorded his impressions:

There was a palpable air of fresh optimism and expectancy. Rabin caught the mood when he told the Knesset 'This is a time of great opportunities . . . it is no longer that all the world is against us . . . we must overcome the sense of isolation that has held us in its thrall for almost half a century'.[2]

The outside world's wish for a Rabin victory to end 15 consecutive years of Likud presence in the government was granted. Political leaders, diplomats and large parts of the international media rushed to congratulate Rabin and celebrate the apparent demise of the Likud.

In the days that followed the election, the Likud was in a state of shock. The outcome of the election had been widely predicted in opinion polls conducted by both parties and the media, but there had been a hope of a late swing to the Likud – as had happened in several previous elections. Israelis are notorious fibbers to pollsters. In previous elections, opinion poll responses had been slightly distorted by voters indicating that they were not going to vote for the Likud when they fully intended to do so.

In 1992 it was different. There was no late comeback, and no surprise outcome. The Likud awoke on 24 June 1992 to the cold reality that the party, which only 18 months earlier had appeared to be the natural party of government, now found itself in opposition.

Like most electoral defeats for political parties that have been in government for a long time, the development of a deep understanding for the reasons for the defeat did not emerge quickly.[3] Instead, the party entered a period of internal bloodletting, followed by a search for quick-fix solutions to reconnect the party with the electorate.

Yitzhak Shamir's announcement of his resignation from the leadership of the Likud came as little surprise, given his advanced age and the scale of the Likud loss. What came as a much greater surprise to the Likud, and to Israel, was the announcement by Moshe Arens – two days after the election – of his retirement from political life.

Arens was Shamir's anointed successor, and would probably have stood an excellent chance of succeeding his old boss as head of the party. Arens' reasons for leaving public life were complex. Publicly, he cited his own relatively advanced age – he was 67 in 1992 and if Rabin and Labour had served a full term would have been 71 at the time of the next general election. After serving in government for nearly a decade he also didn't fancy four years on the opposition benches.[4]

On a political level, he argued during the press conference announcing his resignation that 'Likud's failure at the polls was largely because the public did not see the Greater Eretz Israel slogan [integration of the West Bank into Israel] as a sufficient response to the problems of the Occupied Territories'.[5] Put simply, the Likud needed to come up with new messages in order to reconnect with key sectors of the electorate.

In Arens' memoirs of his time in government he makes light of his decision; a brief passage dedicated to the event concludes with the words: '... I believed in service, I do not believe in servitude. The time had come to close this chapter of my life.'[6] Whatever the motives, in the blink of an eye the two veteran leaders of the Likud most responsible for its policies towards the conflict had departed front-bench politics.

For Netanyahu, the resignation of Arens left him with an opportunity he had not foreseen coming so soon. If Arens had decided to run for the leadership of the Likud, Netanyahu would have backed his old mentor and political patron. With him out of the field, there was now nothing to stop Netanyahu from throwing his own hat into the ring for the leadership election. If he were to stand a realistic chance of victory, it was clear that he would only do so if primaries were confirmed as the method for electing the new leader.

With Netanyahu's strong support and lobbying, this prerequisite fell into place on 28 June 1992, as the Likud agreed on a system of primaries to elect all future party office holders and candidates.[7] The following day, 29 June 1992, Benjamin Netanyahu announced his intention to run for the leadership of the Likud party.

He had already moved to recruit a small team of key advisors who were drawn from both the public and private sectors. More importantly, he had received promises of financial support from several American Jewish business leaders with whom he had cultivated relationships over the previous decade.

All but two of the other Likud Princes whom Shamir hoped would succeed him kept their powder dry and did not enter the race.[8] The exceptions were Benni Begin and the ex-Minister of Transport, Moshe Katsav. Earlier in the year, on 9 March, Begin's father, Menachem, had passed away. Menachem Begin was the giant of the Revisionist Zionist movement and his death, at the start of the election campaign, cast a long shadow over the Likud's campaign.

Benni was little like his father: he largely lacked the political skills and personal charm of Menachem. Benni Begin saw the Likud's defeat in 1992 as a reflection of internal difficulties and not a rejection of its policies towards the West Bank. He was viewed as arguably the least attractive of the Likud Princes to the wider electorate, and the major charge against him was that it was difficult to foresee him leading the Likud to victory at the next general election.

The other Likud Princes, with the exception of Katsav, held back largely to assess their chances of success. The Netanyahu candidacy dominated the print and television headlines, and it wasn't clear if there was much room for another candidate. Once it became apparent that Netanyahu was doing well in opinion polls, the potential for a challenge from a Likud Prince further receded.

Netanyahu rapidly found himself the best organized and the highest funded of the candidates from his generation. Two big beasts from the older generation, however, waited in the wings to trip up the man they regarded as a political upstart. Ariel Sharon believed that the leadership of the Likud would be his one day. He was smart politically, and clever enough to sense that the wind appeared to be blowing in the direction of Netanyahu's candidature. He decided to wait.

Sharon announced he would not run in this election, while making it clear that he would not be bound by the result. In other words, he would mount a leadership challenge at the time of his choosing. For Sharon, this was a near-fatal mistake. With Sharon out of the picture, albeit on a temporary basis, Netanyahu's biggest challenger was David Levy.

Levy, the ex-Minister of Foreign Affairs, was a populist candidate in contrast to the ideologue Benni Begin. He described himself as an 'opinion poll on two legs'. The two men had continued their feud from Netanyahu's time in the ministry of foreign affairs into the internal politics of the Likud. Not surprisingly, the contest for the Likud leadership brought their personal animosity back into the public arena in a way that shocked even hardened veterans of the Likud and political commentators.

On 14 January 1993, Netanyahu appeared on television, admitted to an extra-marital affair and accused a rival in the Likud of blackmail. Extra-marital affairs were nothing new in Israeli politics, but owning up to one on television was a first – along with accusing a member of his own party of blackmailing him in order to force him to withdraw his candidature for the leadership of the party.

During the interview, Netanyahu labelled the attempted blackmail 'the worst political crime in Israeli history, perhaps in the history of democracy'. He went on to add that 'criminals who use the methods of the Mafia' were behind the blackmail.[9] American-style politics had just landed in Israel, with all the sickening falseness and insanity of a television soap opera.

The scandal, dubbed 'Bibi-gate', allegedly started when an anonymous caller telephoned his wife and threatened that an intimate tape of her husband with another woman would be made public unless he withdrew from the race. During his interview, Netanyahu admitted to the affair, said that his marriage to Sara (his third wife) was in crisis and without naming him accused David Levy of being behind the blackmail attempt.[10]

The interview took place in time for the Israeli press to investigate the issue and to splash the whole story over their front pages. The press soon discovered that the woman in question was a certain Ruth Bar, a media consultant who had been hired to help him with the 1992 Likud primaries. Her photograph was displayed over the front pages of local newspapers.[11]

Bar's husband, who had suspected for some time that his wife was having an affair with Netanyahu, filed for divorce. While Israelis immersed themselves in the alleged details of the extra-marital sex life of the front runner in the Likud leadership race, Netanyahu's handling of the affair raised important questions about his leadership credentials.

Netanyahu's admission on television of the affair was widely ridiculed by his political enemies, and by large sections of the Israeli media. It was seen as a knee-jerk reaction to the alleged attempt to blackmail him. Even his advisors thought that his strategy could be seen as a panic reaction.[12] The case against Netanyahu was strengthened when, despite the best efforts of the Israeli media to locate the tape, and despite Netanyahu's admission, it was never found. Indeed, the very existence of the tape was increasingly brought into question.

The Levy camp threatened to sue Netanyahu for the damage they alleged had been done to their candidate by accusations of a blackmail attempt. 'Bibi-gate' did little to halt the Netanyahu bandwagon in the campaign. Opinion polls taken in the aftermath of the affair indicated that it had little impact on the intentions of Likud voters in the forthcoming leadership election. While Likud voters appeared little swayed by the scandal, there was concern over the attitude of religious voters in a national election if the self-confessed adulterer Netanyahu was the candidate of the Likud in the direct election for Prime Minister.[13]

Whatever was said, or agreed, in private between Benjamin and Sara Netanyahu at this point in their marriage, the result was that this was the moment when the Netanyahus became a team. Sara become a central figure in the Netanyahu camp, appearing beside her husband at political events.

Sara's conversion from a wife who stayed in the background to her more prominent role worried many of Netanyahu's key aides, who feared that she was not up to dealing with the kind of scrutiny that the local and international press would subject her to if Netanyahu were to win the leadership contest.[14]

Aides, however, soon learned to bite their tongues and keep quiet about the 'Sara factor', as one of them put it. At this stage, Netanyahu's team heavily managed any contact she had with the press.[15] Two things became clear: the Netanyahus were not about to separate, and Sara's influence over her husband was substantial, including an alleged veto over who was to be admitted into his inner entourage.

For a man of such apparent charisma and charm, as well as rugged good looks, Netanyahu was not good at forging meaningful relationships with women. During his early years he attracted a number of suitors from both Israel and outside it. Some relationships broke down over his alleged infidelity, others simply through natural causes and changes in career or country of residence.

It is difficult to explain this emotional and sexual drifting. There is little evidence that points to a specific woman breaking his heart or being the love of his life. No woman appeared to have damaged him or scarred him emotionally. One of his key aides suggested that Netanyahu was so focused on political power and so much wanted to become Prime Minister that there wasn't much room for anything more in his life.[16]

He enjoyed the company of women, but remained suspicious of their motives – just as he did with male friends and colleagues – and never really connected with them on a deep emotional level. He also liked his private life to remain private and this makes his public admission of guilt over the affair with Bar all the more difficult to comprehend.

The story of Netanyahu's first meeting with Sara, and the development of their relationship, remains one of the oddities of the Netanyahu narrative that has developed and been modified over the years. Critics of Sara (and there are plenty in Israel) tell the story of the girl from a humble background meeting the jet-setting politician on a flight from Israel to the United States, on which she was an air stewardess. David Margolick, who wrote an extended character piece on Netanyahu for *Vanity Fair* in 1996, summed this up:

> Contemporaries describe his current wife, Sara Netanyahu, who was born in a small town near Haifa to a religious family, as quite ordinary. One of Bibi's American friends called her an 'A-I-R-E-S-S,' his way of telling me not just that Sara had been a stewardess when she met her husband but that she was not nearly the intellectual equal of Bibi or either of his first two wives.[17]

Quite soon after their first meeting, Sara became pregnant and a few months later, in March 1991, they married. It was not long after their wedding that Netanyahu began the affair with Ruth Bar, who had been brought in by Netanyahu to work on his image. Clearly, with the Likud elections so near and with political power beckoning, Netanyahu understood that the stakes were getting higher, and he simply could not behave in a manner that would allow his enemies to make political gains.

As the Likud race entered the final stages, Netanyahu tried to shift the political agenda back on to politics. The Levy camp, however, sensed that 'Bibi-gate' provided it with ammunition to attack Netanyahu's lack of judgement and to illustrate that he cracked under fire. 'This man is not fit to lead the Likud or the country' was the spin that the Levy camp tried to put on Netanyahu's character. It wasn't completely successful, but Netanyahu's actions in January 1993 raised question marks about his temperament, which to this day have not been put to rest.

At the time, Netanyahu was quick to put the attacks on his character down to either Levy or to the left-wing bias in the Israeli press. The questions about his judgement outlived the career of David Levy, and in recent years have also originated from members of the Israeli press more closely associated with the right in Israel.

After the bitter campaign between Netanyahu, the two candidates, along with Benni Begin and Moshe Katsav, awaited the results of the election on 24 March 1993 with some trepidation to see how the 145,000 Likud members had cast their ballots. In the end, Netanyahu won handsomely, taking 52.1 per cent of the votes. The margin of victory over Levy, who was second with 26.3 per cent, was gratifying for Netanyahu. Benni Begin, who polled 15.1 per cent, followed David Levy, and former Transportation Minister Moshe Katsav was last with only 6.5 per cent.

Netanyahu had easily passed the 40 per cent threshold to avoid a second round of voting. In reality, despite last-minute rumours of a decline in his support, Netanyahu proved his critics in the Likud wrong. Those who had not taken him seriously most certainly had to following this result.

His victory took place amid a worsening security situation in Israel, with a spate of attacks against Israeli citizens. Netanyahu devoted much attention during the campaign to what he saw as the failure of the Rabin-led government to deal with this threat. Netanyahu's stump speech rhetoric was crisp and seemingly seductive:

> This government says that it is impossible to fight the knifings, that
> it is impossible to fight terrorism. How do they put it? Terrorism
> has only one solution: a political solution. In other words, there is
> no solution to terrorism except retreat.[18]

He went on to attack the government's policy towards negotiations with the Arabs: 'In the peace negotiations, the government only offers concessions,' he said, and the consequences for Israel would be 'to bring the Syrian army on the Golan Heights closer to us, to shrink and reduce the size of this country, to bring the border to the outskirts of Petah Tikvah [a town just outside Tel Aviv]'.[19]

In his fiery victory speech he chided the government's record, as he put it:

> We can fight terror. We know how to, and we will do it! If
> [members of the government] don't know how, they should step
> aside . . . We will, through parliamentary and other means, organize
> to topple this government as soon as possible.[20]

Brave promises from what was still an essentially inexperienced politician who, by Israeli standards, was still a member of the young guard. In retrospect, his eagerness to please the party faithful and his promise to attack the Rabin government on all issues was merely macho chest puffing, but it set the tone for his leadership of the Likud for the subsequent two years.

On internal Likud issues, Netanyahu used part of his victory speech to try to rebuild bridges with his rivals, including Levy. He failed. Levy neglected to congratulate him, and told aides that he planned to try to take over the party internal committees to make sure that his influence continued.[21] Ariel Sharon continued to circle Netanyahu from the political shadows, promising the new leader that, just because he had been elected the leader of the Likud, it did not mean that he would eventually be the candidate of the Likud in the direct elections for Prime Minister.

Sharon told his supporters, the local media and anybody else who would listen that he felt he was the legitimate leader of the Likud and that Netanyahu, and his hardline rhetoric, would not bring success. It remains rare in politics for a comprehensive victory such as Netanyahu's to be so quickly undermined by his rivals – who steadfastly refused to accept his authority.

The most striking part of the victory, noted by local journalists, was Netanyahu's gushing tribute to his wife, whom he kissed and thanked for standing by him.[22] Israelis were not used to this American-style political culture. Some journalists at the event described Netanyahu's conduct during it as 'stomach churning'.[23] Netanyahu's point of reference might well have been a young, pre-presidential Bill Clinton during the 1992 campaign amidst the Gennifer Flowers scandal.

The link between Clinton and Netanyahu did not stop with their extra-marital controversies. Netanyahu carefully studied and learned from the Clinton political machine. Both men were highly articulate and came across well in the media. Both had also built formidable campaign machines that were backed with big money from American donors.

At the outset of their national campaigns, both men were relative outsiders, neither of them particularly liked nor rated highly by the majority of the grandees of their respective parties. In the end, both became the political stars of their generation and came to reflect the changed political culture in the era of the telegenic politician.

Despite the remaining internal challenges to his leadership, Netanyahu's victory was quite remarkable within a movement, which, in its entire history to this point, had only been led by two leaders. The basic *Likudnik* rationale for voting for Netanyahu was the belief that a Likud led by him would soon return the party to what it saw as its rightful position in government.[24]

One thing that party members forgot, however, was that even with Netanyahu at the helm it would, in all likelihood, be another three and a half years before Netanyahu and the party were given the opportunity to win a general election.[25] Before that point, Netanyahu would have to develop his credentials from leader of the opposition to become more statesmanlike. Coming as it did, in one of the most turbulent periods in Israeli history, this challenge would prove to be one of the greatest of Netanyahu's political career.

PART TWO

Opposition

4

Rebuilding

An Israeli Prime Minister lay, bleeding heavily, in the back of his limousine as it tried to navigate its way through crowds of supporters. An early winter night rally in Tel Aviv that was meant to break the cycle of internal political violence in Israel had led to the ultimate Jewish taboo being broken. The world watched in horror as scribbled statements were read out by barely believing officials, amid screams from bystanders who had gathered after hearing early reports of the shooting.

Soon Rabin was pronounced dead, killed by a fellow Jew. Israel had had its Kennedy moment. People would remember for the rest of their lives where they were, and who they were with, when they heard the news. A Jewish gunman opposed to the peace agreements with the Palestinians and the subsequent withdrawal from parts of the West Bank and Gaza Strip assassinated the Israeli Prime Minister on 4 November 1995.

Most Israelis were shocked by the assassination of Yitzhak Rabin, and what it said about Israel's flawed democracy and divided society. For Netanyahu, the murder of Rabin was a political disaster. In the days that followed his death, the Israeli media and leftist politicians singled out Netanyahu as being, to some extent, culpable for the tragic events of 4 November.

In retrospect, this was decidedly Netanyahu's most decisive and his darkest moment. It was what his political enemies, including those in the Likud, had been waiting for. It seemed to confirm that the tactics and strategy he had employed since assuming the leadership of the Likud in 1993 to oppose the Rabin government and its policies was wrong. Tags that were linked to Netanyahu at the time included rabble-rouser and extremist. Rabin's murder led to a character assassination of the Likud leader, whose political future looked close to being over.

In the immediate aftermath of Rabin's death, opinion polls indicated a steep drop in support for Netanyahu personally, and for the parties of the right in general. Prior to Rabin's death, however, all looked to be going well for Netanyahu and the Likud, who had held a healthy lead in the polls for over a year, and had looked well positioned to win the 1996 elections.

The previous two and a half years since Netanyahu's leadership victory had been one of the most turbulent periods in Israeli history. For Netanyahu, the challenges had started from his very first day as leader of the Likud. What followed included aspects of tragedy, comedy and farce that would have been more at home in a Shakespeare play than in a weak, relatively immature political democracy.

Back in March 1993, safely installed in his new office at Likud headquarters and in his new 'mini suite' at the Knesset, Netanyahu soon discovered one particular home truth. The Likud was effectively broke as a result of the 1992 election campaign.[1] The election defeat in 1992 robbed the party of a large chunk of its state funds. Netanyahu's predecessor, Yitzhak Shamir, had never been a great fundraiser, even in the United States, where there were rich seams of Jewish donors to be tapped. There were also laws that, to some extent, governed the financing of election campaigns in Israel.

Through the spring and summer months of 1993, Netanyahu tried to repair the black hole in the Likud's finances. He was as likely to be spotted heading into a bank, as appearing at a political rally. He opened his black book of contacts in the United States and badgered wealthy American Jews to help clear the debt of the Likud.

It wasn't simply a case of clearing the overdraft. There was a need to raise funds for the 1996 election campaign, which would have seen Netanyahu run against Rabin in Israel's first direct election for Prime Minister. Netanyahu's advisors worked to try to balance the demands of fundraising, which often meant extended trips to the United States, with his management of the reconstruction of the Likud party machine under his control.[2]

With David Levy and Ariel Sharon, along with their very vocal supporters, continuing to pose an internal threat to Netanyahu's leadership, he responded by moving the political goalposts in the Likud. In amending the party constitution to make it extremely difficult to challenge the incumbent leader before the 1996 election, he caught both Levy and Sharon off guard and illustrated to both men that his political skills were not to be underestimated. The rank and file of the Likud largely fell in behind him, as they believed that he was the most electable of the senior figures in the party.[3]

Netanyahu was therefore largely able to reconstruct the Likud party organs and machine under his control, and with donors loyal to him rather than the Likud bankrolling the exercise. Developing tighter control over the Likud did not lead to the end of internal dissent against his leadership, but it created the impression that, at the very least, Netanyahu was a competent party manager. This compared favourably to Rabin who, distracted by affairs of state and a genuine indifference, largely ignored the Labour Party that he was supposed to be leading.

Rabin and his government were busy with managing a peace process with the Palestinians. Initial hopes for progress were soon thwarted. At the start of 1993, while Netanyahu was running for the leadership of the Likud, the situation on the ground was depressing. The British Embassy summarized the sentiment:

> The year began badly with a row over the deportation of some 400 Hamas activists to a barren Lebanese hillside. The euphoria of Labour's election victory and the high hopes for progress at the Washington peace talks had faltered. Hostile Palestinians and a sceptical West could not quite believe that the new policies of territorial compromise and reordered priorities meant a real change of Israeli heart.[4]

Less than a week after Netanyahu was elected as Likud's leader, on 30 March 1993, Rabin closed the Occupied Territories. This followed a rise in attacks against Israelis in the month, which led to 15 deaths. As a result of Rabin's measures, there was an immediate and drastic drop in violence within the Green Line. Naturally, this proved extremely popular with the Israeli public.

It was something of an embarrassment to Netanyahu and the Likud, who argued that the territories were an integral part of Israel and should not be sealed off from it.[5] Netanyahu's campaign message that the

Rabin government was soft on terrorism no longer seemed relevant, given Rabin's robust response to the attacks. While the Israeli public got used to the idea of the Occupied Territories being cut off from the rest of Israel, Netanyahu switched his focus to Israel's northern borders.

Within the Likud, there was an understanding that Rabin would prefer to strike a peace deal with the Syrians rather than advance the Palestinian track of the peace process. With plans for Palestinian autonomy seemingly put on the back burner, Rabin, and the Chief of Staff of the IDF, Ehud Barak, were keen to explore the potential of reaching a deal with the Syrians with the help of American mediation from the new administration of President Bill Clinton.

During the 1992 campaign, Rabin had pledged that Israel would never come down from the Golan Heights, but few believed this would be the case. It was widely understood in Israel, and internationally, that Syria would demand the return of all of the Golan Heights, which Israel had captured during the 1967 Six Day War, in exchange for peace.

The Heights, with its views into Syria, were seen as strategically important to the security of northern Israel. A withdrawal from the Golan Heights was not unthinkable for most Israelis, but polling at the time indicated that most opposed the idea of giving up the territory.

Netanyahu saw a political opportunity to remind Israelis about what he saw as the dangers of the Rabin-led government agreeing to a full withdrawal from the Golan Heights. The Israeli–Syrian relationship was complex with the countries involved in what amounted to a proxy war with one another in Lebanon. A stark reminder of this came on 21 April 1993 when scores of rockets, fired by Hezbollah, fell on Galilee in northern Israel.

In order to help highlight the Golan issue, Netanyahu decided to hold the Likud Convention in the Golan on 17–18 May. Despite this high-profile event and the usual round of interviews with the local television and print media, Netanyahu was struggling to gain any traction with voters. Quickly dismissed by Rabin as something of a loose cannon, and, at the other end of the political spectrum, distrusted by the Settlers movement – whose political patron remained Ariel Sharon – Netanyahu struggled for political take-off.

His political troubles aside, arguably Netanyahu's biggest problem during his first year at the helm of the Likud was his lack of access to Israel's agenda towards the peace process. Rabin played his cards very close to his chest, often not telling his cabinet and Labour Party colleagues details of his diplomatic manoeuvrings. Netanyahu's instinct that Rabin was planning to offer the Golan Heights to Syria in exchange for peace turned out to be spot on.

Rabin made the offer to the US Secretary of State, Warren Christopher, who passed it on to the Syrians. Details of this diplomatic process that eventually failed are now well documented, but, at the time, the meetings took place under a veil of secrecy. This made it difficult for Netanyahu to attack the government's policies, as he simply did not have enough information as to what was really taking place away from the public gaze.

In interviews with Israeli media, Rabin continued to make it clear that he favoured a Syria-first option, and that any deal with the Palestinians would not be forthcoming. Netanyahu knew too little, too late, to mount an effective opposition to the government's policies.[6]

He wasn't the only one in this position. Rabin's Minister of Foreign Affairs, Shimon Peres, was equally in the dark as to Rabin and Christopher's diplomatic efforts with Syria. Rabin trusted few people, and certainly not his long-standing political rival in the Labour Party. Peres only learned of Rabin's offer of the Golan Heights to the Syrians following the Prime Minister's death, when Rabin's aides and the Americans briefed him on the Syrian negotiations.

On the Palestinian front, however, Peres proved to be much more the lead man than Rabin, who continued to divide his time between the Syrian track, domestic issues and trying to keep his quarrelsome coalition government from collapsing. Peres was to help bring about what was hailed as an historic breakthrough in the conflict with the Palestinians, one that was to have far-reaching consequences for Israel, and for the political career of Benjamin Netanyahu.

Unbeknown to Netanyahu (and at this stage Rabin as well) on 20 January 1993 an Israeli academic named Yair Hirschfeld met with a senior Palestinian figure, Abu Ala, in Oslo to start the secret negotiations that would produce the Oslo Accords.[7] The first of the resulting agreements were signed before the end of the year. As the British Ambassador optimistically summarized:

> 1993 will be remembered in Israel as the year of Rabin's handshake
> with Arafat on the White House lawn; and the possibility at last

of peace to the long standing struggle between Jew and Palestinian Arab for control of the Holy Land.

Before a startled, delighted and nonetheless somewhat doubting world, Prime Minister Rabin and Chairman Yasser Arafat announced that Israel and the PLO had decided to recognise each other's existence and commit themselves through a firm timetable to negotiate a permanent settlement to a dispute that has led to four wars . . .[8]

That this should have been done not by representatives of the younger generation who forged the deal but by two grizzled survivors of so many recent years of terrorism and violence was inexpressibly moving to those who watched the television coverage. In Israel, as Rabin said, 'the mood was of great expectation albeit mixed with deep apprehension'.[9]

The British Foreign Secretary, Douglas Hurd, described the signing as the Middle Eastern equivalent of the fall of the Berlin Wall in Europe. Nothing, he promised, would be the same again. With the benefit of hindsight it is clear that much of this optimism was misplaced. The key point, however, was that at the time of the Rabin–Arafat handshake on the White House lawn the Israel–PLO deal was backed by the majority of Israelis.

This level of support was to decline as home truths were established during the subsequent months that saw an increase – and not a decline, as had been anticipated – in the levels of violence in the conflict. For Netanyahu, the Rabin government's agreement with the PLO presented a curious mixture of difficult challenges in political positioning terms, and an opportunity to try to unify the right in Israel under his leadership.

At the time of the signing ceremony, Netanyahu was in Europe fundraising for the Likud. He immediately cut his trip short and returned to Israel. There was much speculation and rumour about Netanyahu's reaction when he returned to Israel. Journalists from local newspapers reported that Netanyahu and his key aide, Eyal Arad, had held an impromptu 'panic stricken conversation at a gas station' near Ben-Gurion Airport.[10]

Prior to the Israel–PLO agreement, Netanyahu had a clear strategy to win power, which he hoped he would be able to achieve before the date of the next scheduled national elections. The first part was to raise substantial campaign funds that he would use to bankroll Likud candidates in the forthcoming elections. Here, he very much endorsed the American election model, which suggested the larger the campaign funds the greater the chance of victory.

Other political leaders in Israel remained light years behind Netanyahu on this score. The aim here was that the funds would help buy loyalty from those *Likudniks* who were part of Netanyahu's expanding political faction. Campaign funding was becoming an increasingly grey area in Israeli politics, with loopholes making it easier for people such as Netanyahu to raise money directly from wealthy donors.

The second part of Netanyahu's strategy concerned the likelihood that the Rabin-led governing coalition would collapse before 1996 and that elections would have to be moved forward to a date much earlier than scheduled. All of this centred upon the instability of the coalition and a criminal investigation that involved Aryeh Deri, the leader of the ultra-orthodox party Shas, which was part of the coalition. Netanyahu calculated that there was a good chance that Shas would leave the coalition either as a result of a police investigation into Deri, or due to tensions between Shas and the fiercely secular left-wing party Meretz.

In truth, Shas and Meretz were odd bedfellows in the coalition given their opposing views on secular–religious issues. All the issues relating to Deri and Shas' participation in the coalition were coming to a head just prior to the announcement of the agreement between Israel and the PLO. On 9 August 1993, the Israeli Attorney General had demanded the suspension of Deri from his position as the Minister of the Interior.

Netanyahu's hope was that he could tempt Deri to leave the governing coalition and rejoin the Likud-led camp. Prior to 1992, Shas had been an important member of the Likud-led governing coalition. Looking ahead to the direct elections for Prime Minister, Netanyahu understood the importance of the ultra-orthodox voters for his chances of success in beating Rabin.

It was widely presumed that these highly disciplined voting constituencies would vote for parties such as Shas in the Knesset (parliamentary elections) and then vote in the direct election for Prime Minister following the advice of their religious and political leaders. On his part, Netanyahu had been extremely proactive in building bridges and deepening his ties to Shas and its leadership.

In doing this, he skirted over his two divorces and admission of adultery in his third marriage, focusing instead on the religious conservatism of the Likud versus the allegedly more secular nature of the Labour Party. Naturally, to sweeten the deal, he made sure that Shas understood just how grateful he would be to them, and that he would ensure they were rewarded politically in any government he led.

Unlike Rabin, who continued largely to ignore the impact of the electoral changes on the politics of Israel, Netanyahu understood that the fundamental impact of the new system was that it shifted coalition bargaining from after an election to before it. Put simply, candidates running for Prime Minister needed to effectively strike endorsement deals from the political leaders of key voting groups.

Of course there was no guarantee that voters would follow the directives of their respective constituent leaders, but in the case of the ultra-orthodox it was thought highly probable that this group of voters would follow the directive of its religious and political leaders.

On 25 August 1993, as the Israeli press, for the first time, started to publish articles about the possibility of an imminent agreement between Israel and the PLO, Netanyahu believed that both Deri and the religious leaders of Shas were well disposed towards him and would support him in the direct election for Prime Minister.

All in all, in the weeks prior to the announcement and signing of the Israel–PLO deal, Netanyahu's prospects looked very rosy. Ahead in the polls against Rabin, and with the Likud looking set to improve on its disastrous 1992 election result, and with the ultra-orthodox leadership turning a blind eye to his adultery, Netanyahu had good grounds for optimism. What he needed most was to capitalize on his healthy political stock by forcing early elections.

In order to try to help force this issue Netanyahu was set to launch a major public relations campaign across the country calling for early elections. Posters and bumper stickers were produced and billboard space booked up by the Netanyahu team. The aim was to create momentum for the two key municipal elections to be held at the start of November 1993 in Jerusalem and Tel Aviv, and to use this as a launch pad for the national elections. Netanyahu and his Likud colleagues believed that the veteran Mayor of Jerusalem, the 82-year-old Teddy Kollek, was vulnerable to a major challenge from a youthful leading figure in the party.

Kollek had first been elected in 1965, but by 1993 the demographic make-up of the city had changed with many young secular Jews abandoning Jerusalem, as the ultra-orthodox population in the city increased. The latter was seen as more likely to vote for a Likud candidate than the secular incumbent mayor. Tel Aviv was a completely different case, but there was a feeling that a moderate Likud candidate could take the city.

In the end, the Likud did take both cities with Ehud Olmert winning in Jerusalem, and Roni Milo in Tel Aviv. Their victories on 2 November 1993 did not have the immediate impact on the Likud at a national level. To some extent, however, they stopped the perception of the decline of Netanyahu and the Likud that had occurred since the Israel–PLO deal had been signed on the White House lawn on 13 September.

While Netanyahu was quick to try to take his share of the credit for the two key successes, it's important to remember that municipal elections in Israel, as in many other countries, are largely fought on local and not national issues. The success of the Likud in Jerusalem and Tel Aviv was not an endorsement of its national platform towards the peace process or the popularity of Benjamin Netanyahu.

The success of the Likud in the November local elections served as a brief break from the storm, rather than a solution to the problems that had engulfed the party since the signing of the Israel–PLO agreement. Netanyahu's early election strategy was effectively dead in the water. His advisors reminded him that, in the immediate euphoric period that followed the deal, it would be Rabin and Labour who would benefit from early elections and not Netanyahu and the Likud. The agreement, as well as damaging Netanyahu and the Likud nationally, also opened up a can of worms over the party's response to the agreement.

Here, Netanyahu appeared to adopt a rigid, ideological approach to the agreement, stating that he opposed and furthermore, if elected, would not implement it. He cited the PLO and Arafat as being unreformed and unrepentant terrorists who continued to wish to destroy Israel. His opposition to the agreement was not only based on his opinion of Arafat and the PLO, but also on his deep-rooted commitment to 'Greater Israel', that had been one of the central planks of the Revisionist Zionist movement since the creation of Israel in 1948.

In essence, 'Greater Israel' meant the inclusion of the West Bank into Israel. Within the Likud, there were those who cited the legitimacy

for this inclusion on religious grounds – the lands had been promised to the Jews – and those who maintained that the lands were vital
for security reasons. Naturally, there were those who used a mixture of
both rationales to justify their support for retaining control over the
Occupied Territories.

The feeling in the party was that the deal with the PLO removed
any realistic possibility of achieving the dream of 'Greater Israel'. For
his part, Netanyahu, while well versed in the use of religious imagery
and symbolism in his speeches, belonged to the group that emphasized
the value of the West Bank to maintaining and strengthening Israel's
national security. For Netanyahu, there was no greater threat to Israel's
security than a PLO-led Palestinian state in the West Bank and Gaza
Strip.

His opposition to the deal with the PLO was therefore based primarily
on the grounds of security and not ideology. The opposition, however,
was steadfast and inflexible, a point that irked several of Netanyahu's
senior colleagues in the Likud.

The question of the Likud's response to the agreement was on the
surface very clear: non-acceptance of the agreement, no recognition
of the PLO and no negotiations with it. Netanyahu imposed a strong
whip on the Likud members of the Knesset when Rabin had brought
the deal before the Knesset for the ratification vote on 23 September
1993.

In his speech, on the first day of the two-day debate, Netanyahu
warned that the deal with the PLO resembled British attempts to
appease Hitler during the 1930s. In press articles published in the same
month, Netanyahu pushed the comparison. In a *New York Times* op-ed
entitled 'Peace in Our Time', he wrote:

> Earlier in this century, Neville Chamberlain thought he could
> buy 'peace in our time' by handing over the mountain defenses of
> Czechoslovakia to Hitler, who promised to accept a deal of 'land for
> peace.' On his deathbed, Chamberlain said, 'Everything would have
> been all right if Hitler hadn't lied to me.'
>
> The Rabin Government is now betting the security of Israel on
> Yasser Arafat's promises. But his promises are worthless. He has
> violated every political commitment he has ever made. Since his
> 'breakthrough' promise in 1988 to stop PLO terror, his own Fatah

faction has launched more terrorist attacks against Israel than any other Palestinian group. Similarly, he repeatedly 'recognizes' Israel for some political gain – only to take it back later.

An armed PLO state looming over Israel's cities and overflowing with returning 'refugees' (a million to start with, says the PLO) is a far cry from a responsible compromise that would give Israel security and Arabs autonomy. Instead of giving peace a chance, it is a guarantee of increased tension, future terrorism and, ultimately, war.[11]

From the outset, Netanyahu's rhetoric was strong and intended to indicate his belief that the deal with the PLO posed an imminent threat to Israel's security. He portrayed Israel as a small country that would be in mortal danger if it handed over lands that were vital for its security.

His efforts in the Knesset debate failed. The government won the vote with 61 votes in favour and 50 against, along with eight abstentions and one absent.[12] To some extent, the vote itself was overshadowed by the tone of the debate. The use of fiery rhetoric was nothing new to the Knesset floor, but the insults and emotive nature of the debate did not bode well for the future of Israeli democracy.

The signing of the deal and its ratification did not lead to the end of the debate about its merits. The implementation of the initial stages of the Accords and the negotiations over the subsequent agreements provided much opportunity for the rejectionists, like Netanyahu, to make their voices heard.

5

Dangerous Games

Within the Likud, there was genuine apprehension about the Rabin government's peace process with the PLO. Divisions arose, however, over the best tactics to deal with the new political realities of the era. To some extent, the divisions reflected once again the internal challenges to Netanyahu's leadership from key alternative leaders of the party. While Netanyahu stuck to his total rejectionist position towards the deal with the PLO, his main leadership rival, Ariel Sharon, adopted a very different approach.

Sharon told his Likud colleagues that Netanyahu's policy was naïve, in that the deal with the PLO was an internationally recognized one that could not be ripped up.[1] Pacing through the corridors of the Knesset carrying large tubes containing maps of the West Bank, Sharon met with colleagues. He tried to convince them that the best strategy was to try to make sure that the next stages of the negotiations with the PLO produced deals that maximized Israel's security and gave away as little as possible to the Palestinians.

The Netanyahu–Sharon rivalry for the leadership of the party was to become central to Israeli politics during the subsequent decade. At the end of 1993, Netanyahu still believed that the obstacles that needed to be overcome if the deal with the PLO was to work in the long term would prove too great and, therefore, there was not much point in being anything but entirely opposed to it. Israel's improved standing in the world as a result of the agreement was lost on Netanyahu, as a string of meetings took place between members of the Rabin government and world leaders.

Even Israel's isolation in the Middle East appeared to be changing, with the potential for it to develop new ties with regional powers. Shimon Peres's vision of a 'New Middle East', in which the region was to adopt a European model of integration, was a tad optimistic, but things were changing fast. For a time, the youthful Netanyahu sounded like an old man who belonged to a different generation of political leaders. Rabin and Peres, who were both veteran leaders, looked more in touch with the changed new world.

That Sharon appeared to sit politically closer to Rabin than he did to Netanyahu over the PLO deal increased the impression that Netanyahu was politically isolated, and rapidly moving towards the right. In short, Netanyahu appeared the ideologue and Sharon the pragmatist.

During the course of 1994, Netanyahu's fortunes experienced a dramatic turnaround to the extent that, had elections taken place at the end of the year, he would have handsomely defeated Yitzhak Rabin.[2] During the course of the year, as the British put it, 'Netanyahu was increasingly able to probe Labour [Party] policies without exposing his own unclear policies to close examination.'[3]

The year will be remembered as the one when everybody sobered up after the euphoria of the signing of the deal with the PLO and realized that the prospects for peace between Israelis and Palestinians were cloudy.[4] It was the year in which there was a deep realization by both Israelis and Palestinians that the levels of violence would in the short to medium term worsen, and the number of casualties from it would increase.

Peace agreements were meant to end the violence, not increase it. This confusion proved difficult for Israeli and Palestinian leaders to overcome as they tried to deepen support for the agreement and the ones that came after it.

The key expression in Israeli society became 'personal security' and the perceived lack of it. In Palestinian society many were left with a sense of what improvements, if any, peace would bring in terms of the nationalistic struggle and, equally importantly, in economic terms. For Netanyahu, it was a year in which he took risks in allying himself with elements of the Settlers movement, whose noisy opposition to the implementation of the Oslo Accords verged on the unacceptable within the borders of a democratic state.

For much of 1994, there were undertones of violence within Israeli society that saw those Israelis who had originally been so vocal in supporting the agreements retreat into the comfort of their homes. The Israeli 'street' was controlled by those who opposed the deal with the PLO, and who saw their debate as a battle for the soul of the State of Israel.

In Netanyahu they found their perfect spokesman, leader and, at times, agitator. Netanyahu's conduct, for much of the year, left a lot to be desired. Sensing that it was settlers who dominated the debate both politically and financially, he sought to play to the lowest level – with use of rhetoric that fell short of acceptable to many in Israel.

To add fuel to the fires internally in Israel, Rabin was no saint either. He treated the opponents of the PLO deal as enemies of the state. Netanyahu was singled out for particular ridicule in Rabin's speeches to supporters at Labour Party rallies and events. On a number of occasions when Netanyahu rose to speak in the Knesset, Rabin made a point of standing up and walking out of the chamber.

Rabin's attitude was that it was he who, as Chief of Staff of the IDF, had been instrumental in seizing the West Bank, East Jerusalem and the rest in the 1967 Six Day War – and it would be he who would determine whether it was safe to hand over control of some, or all, of these lands to the Palestinians.

Increasingly to Rabin, Netanyahu was little more than an upstart of a captain – a reference to his army rank – versus Rabin, the general. Needless to say, the two men clashed frequently during the course of the year, with Netanyahu looking to land a knockout blow on Rabin's disintegrating governing coalition.

At a time when an Israeli government was attempting to take historic decisions about the future of the state and its relations with the Palestinians, the coalition system of government was hampering the ability of its leaders to govern effectively. Naturally, Netanyahu was happy to exploit this for his political advantage by continuing to attempt to persuade Shas, which had formally left the government, to remain outside of it.

As a result, Rabin was forced to look for new bedfellows for the coalition, and managed to attract a few stragglers who had broken away from the right-wing party Tsomet. Despite the presence of these new recruits to the coalition, Rabin still only had a minority in the Knesset (58 out of 120 seats) and had to rely on the support of the Arab parties to pass legislation.[5] Although it was only 1994, the attention of individual politicians was turning towards the 1996 elections. It became harder for Rabin to maintain party discipline and arguments on issues away from the peace process such as tax and economic policy became more divisive.

Netanyahu's plan to force early elections that had been torpedoed by the announcement of the Israel-PLO deal looked a decidedly more realistic prospect in 1994. With Rabin's coalition troubles looking impossible to resolve in a satisfactory manner, the prospect of bringing down the government in a vote of confidence increased. During the course of the year events presented Netanyahu with plenty of opportunities to inflict damage on the government and he did just that.

At the heart of the improvement in his fortunes was the increasingly pessimistic outlook of Israelis towards the deal with Arafat. The British Ambassador wrote, 'fears rose sharply about whether the price of peace was going to be too high. But the desire for it remained strong.'[6]

The transformation of the written agreement to reality on the ground reflected the worrying trait that neither Israeli nor Palestinian society had been suitably prepared by their respective leaderships for the difficult compromises that the agreement encapsulated. The British Ambassador summarized the problems:

> On 4 May in Cairo, the Gaza/Jericho agreement was signed, amidst last minute confusion as [Yasser] Arafat quibbled over the maps. The agreement took on real life as Arafat took control. The Israelis withdrew, insisting that the settlements and supporting military bases should remain until the final status negotiations. They then watched with mounting anxiety Arafat's attempt to run a competent government, capable of pressing-on with the peace process, while clamping down on anti-Israeli violence.[7]

All of this provided Netanyahu with much needed ammunition. TV pictures of Arafat arriving in Gaza on 1 July 1994 proved too much for some Israelis. The day after Arafat's arrival some 100,000 Israelis attended a protest rally in Jerusalem, on 2 July. There were no pro-Oslo rallies. Rabin's advisors did consider organizing a major rally in support of the peace process, but decided against it, fearing that few Israelis would show up for it.

The relatively poor performance of Rabin's public relations machine created a vacuum, which Netanyahu was competently able to fill.

One government official quipped when asked by the Israeli press how best to improve its PR performance, 'hire Netanyahu'. The sentiment was not lost on Rabin's advisors, who understood that the Likud leader was dominating the media agenda with his finely tuned rejectionist sound bites.

All of this added to the feeling expressed by a number of voters that the government was in trouble, and that Netanyahu was fast becoming an effective leader of the opposition in Israel. The Israeli press, however, continued to ridicule him: his style of presentation, absence of clear alternative policies and lack of leadership skills. He was still seen as too shallow to manage the complexities of running Israel.

Events on the ground have a nasty habit of hijacking negotiations in the Israeli–Palestinian conflict. For a large proportion of the year, this made it extremely difficult for the Rabin government to effectively manage the peace process, which, at times, ground to a standstill. The Hebron massacre, carried out by a Jewish settler at the Tomb of the Patriarchs on 25 February 1994, shocked Israelis and Palestinians and led to a freezing of negotiations.

Most Israelis, however, did not accept that they had to make 'substantive political or security concessions to allow negotiations to resume'.[8] Netanyahu was able to exploit this sense of injustice, citing that the government was playing politics with Israel's national security. It was a simple, yet effective message delivered to a receptive domestic audience.

Arguably the greatest driving force in the shift towards Netanyahu were the violent attacks against Israelis by Palestinian opponents of the peace process, most notably Hamas and Islamic Jihad. The fact that the government offered no clear response to the attacks added to the impression that it did not know how best to protect the personal security of Israel.[9]

The attacks increased in intensity and, in October 1994, two incidents dominated the headlines in Israel and across the globe. The first was the kidnapping of an Israeli soldier, Nachshon Wachsman, on 9 October, and his subsequent murder on 14 October during an IDF rescue operation. In this instance, Rabin had made the safe return of the soldier the responsibility of Arafat, believing (incorrectly) that he was being held in areas controlled by the Palestinian Authority.

Netanyahu backed the failed rescue attempt, but warned of the dangers that Arafat was causing by not moving against groups such as

Hamas and Islamic Jihad. In a twist of fate, 17 years later, in October 2011, Netanyahu as Prime Minister authorized the release of the Hamas driver imprisoned for the murder of Wachsman as part of the exchange deal for the release of another IDF soldier, Gilad Shalit, kidnapped by Hamas in 2006 and held captive for five years in Gaza.

On 19 October 1994, Israel suffered its first suicide bomb attack, when a No. 5 bus was blown up on Dizengoff Street in Tel Aviv. The attack, which killed 22 and injured more than a hundred, shocked Israelis. The tactic of suicide bombing was relatively new to the Middle East, and this was its first use in the Israeli–Palestinian conflict. The fact that an Israeli bus had been struck in the heart of an Israeli city, which hitherto had been considered safe, meant that the attack was particularly traumatic for Israel.

Upon hearing of the bomb attack, Netanyahu rushed to the scene and gave interviews to the press asking, 'Is this peace?' Netanyahu's conduct and the aggressive tone of his address to the media led to a wave of criticism for using the tragedy for political purposes. Yitzhak Rabin, who had been on a visit to London at the time of the attack, and was in a BBC radio studio, returned to Israel and quietly visited the scene the next day.

Netanyahu's antics on Dizengoff Street won him few plaudits in the Israeli media or pro-Oslo supporters. They did, however, resonate well with the anti-Oslo camp. The latter group was already increasing the political temperature with well-attended rallies, handing out bumper stickers at key road junctions and making as much political noise as possible.

As the British Ambassador noted, 'this was especially true in Jerusalem where the religious voters drove Likud policy and forced showdowns over continuing Palestinian political activity in East Jerusalem'.[10] One word expressed the problems across Israel at the time, and explained the rise in support for Netanyahu: fear. The increase in violence within the Green Line had led to more Israeli deaths than at any time since the start of the Palestinian *Intifada*.[11]

Rabin took the decision to effectively negotiate under fire. In the past, Israeli prime ministers had rejected any negotiations while the country was under attack. Rabin's decision was not universally welcomed in Israel. Even within his own Labour Party, there were calls to postpone the implementation of the agreements with the Palestinians until after the next election. Opinion polls started to indicate, for the first time, that more Israelis rejected the agreements than supported them.

The announcement that Rabin, Peres and Arafat had been awarded the Nobel Peace Prize illustrated the continued disconnect between the aspirations of the outside world for peace and the gloomy situation on the ground. It came as little surprise that Netanyahu, in time-honoured fashion, used the award of the prize as an indication that Rabin and Peres had lost their connection with the country and the values it supported.

While the Palestinian track of the peace process provided political ammunition for Netanyahu to attack the government, the news that Rabin and King Hussein of Jordan had concluded a formal peace treaty between their respective countries presented a different set of challenges.

Unlike the peace deal with the Palestinians, the agreement with King Hussein was widely welcomed in Israel across the political spectrum. Among the Israeli public there was also widespread support for the deal and for the efforts of King Hussein to create a warmer peace between his country and Israel, as opposed to the colder peace that existed between Egypt and Israel.

For Rabin and his government, the peace deal with Jordan brought a welcome relief during the otherwise dark month of October 1994. Rabin and the King signed the formal treaty during a ceremony at the Arava Valley, in front of President Clinton and other foreign dignitaries on 26 October 1994. For Netanyahu the deal with Jordan was a welcome development.

The Jordanians moved with speed to negotiate the deal with Israel to minimize the risks of being 'pre-empted by the Palestinians'.[12] Prior to the agreement, Netanyahu had met, in private, with Jordanian officials who were keen to sound out the leader of the opposition in Israel on issues relating to the peace process with Jordan and the Palestinians. The Jordanians were particularly keen for recognition of the ongoing Jordanian role in managing the Islamic holy sites in Jerusalem.[13]

The King included Netanyahu in the diplomatic process for a number of reasons. He wished to develop political support for the peace accord across the political spectrum in Israel. There was a feeling that the Oslo Accords essentially represented a deal between the Israeli left and the PLO. The King wished to avoid the charge that the Israel–Jordan deal was simply a deal between himself and the Israeli left.

Moreover, King Hussein's contacts with Netanyahu's predecessor as leader of the Likud, Yitzhak Shamir, in the period prior to the Persian Gulf War had created a degree of trust between the King and the Likud. Yitzhak Shamir was a notable invitee to the signing ceremony for the accord at the Arava Valley.

Put simply, the King wanted to make peace with not only the existing Israeli government, but also the major opposition party in the country. Opinion polls conducted in the autumn of 1994 indicated that Netanyahu and the Likud stood a good chance of forming the next government in Israel.

In political terms, to some extent Netanyahu and the Jordanians shared common policy objectives with regard to the Palestinians. King Hussein was concerned that the establishment of a PLO-led Palestinian state in the West Bank would destabilize the Hashemite Kingdom. The King viewed the establishment of a Palestinian state as the likely outcome from the Oslo Accords, and wanted to develop ties with the leader of the Israeli opposition who was opposed to implementing the Oslo Accords.

There was also concern in Amman that the Labour Party, especially Shimon Peres and his supporters, would be willing to concede to a PLO presence in Jerusalem that included a role for it in the management of the holy sites. For his part, Netanyahu was keen to show Israelis that there were concerns among some of Israel's neighbours about the potential destabilizing influence of the creation of a Palestinian state on the region.

From the outset, Netanyahu remained in favour of developing ties with Jordan as a counterweight to the Palestinians. His execution of this policy was far from perfect. The Jordanians often went out of their way to offer him political cover, especially during the 1996 election campaign.

Then, with the rest of the Arab world and the West lining up behind Shimon Peres, King Hussein invited Netanyahu to visit Amman, his first public trip to meet the leadership of an Arab country. By the time of his death, however, King Hussein had fallen out with Netanyahu, whom he characterized as untrustworthy. Both King Hussein and his successor, King Abdullah II, expressed a preference for dealing with Netanyahu's Likud rival, Ariel Sharon.

In retrospect, Netanyahu's management of his relationship never really recovered from his authorization of the attempted assassination of one of leaders of Hamas, Khaled Mashal, on 25 September 1997. Mossad agents poisoned Mashal, but were soon captured. King Hussein threatened to void the peace agreement he signed with Israel in 1994 if Mashal died. Israel agreed to provide the antidote to treat Mashal, who, as a result, made a full recovery. Relations between the King and Netanyahu, however, were not mended, and Israel's peace with Jordan was profoundly damaged by Netanyahu's actions. Back in 1994, King Hussein harboured hopes that Netanyahu would prove useful to thwarting the attempts of his Arab enemy, Yasser Arafat, to create a Palestinian state.

By the end of 1994, Netanyahu had, at the very least, established himself as the leader of the opposition in Israel. His popularity was on the rise, not as the result of an improvement in his image or performance; rather, the simple fact that he offered a political home to the rising number of Israelis that were unconvinced that the Israeli–Palestinian peace process would succeed. He had managed to achieve this with minimum commitments as to what he would do, if elected, to form the next government.

The strategy of evasion and zigzag that he would employ throughout his political career had come to the fore during the course of the year. Netanyahu's political vagueness was partially allowed to develop because the Rabin-led government was unwilling to publicly commit itself as to where it was leading Israel in the negotiations with the Palestinians. Netanyahu was clearly a major benefactor from this fuzziness, as he did not have to commit himself to adopting a position towards the Oslo Accords above and beyond his blanket rejection of them.

The debate within the government remained essentially one between Rabin and Peres over the nature of a permanent peace with the Palestinians, the outcome of which would set the parameters of Israeli policy towards the Palestinians in the subsequent years. For Rabin, the result of the process with Arafat was more akin to a divorce, with few opportunities for joint economic and political projects.

Essentially, Rabin viewed peace as a method of agreeing a separation between closed borders. As the number of Palestinian suicide attacks against Israel increased in early 1995, Rabin started to give serious consideration to the concept of a physical barrier to run along an agreed border between the two peoples. Peres took a view to the end product of the peace process with the Palestinians that contradicted Rabin's.

For Peres, it was all about the development of openness. He believed that a Palestinian state would only be viable if it were attached to Israel's with open access and borders. He often cited the fact that over 100,000 Palestinians crossed into Israel from the West Bank and Gaza each day for work – many more also crossed illegally.

While Rabin talked of a separation and a divorce, Peres's language was steeped in a spirit of nurturing cooperation and joint development projects. To the Europeans, Peres was seen as a visionary, Rabin as lagging behind. The British summed up this sentiment: 'But whereas Peres favoured bold moves, Rabin's instinct was to work conscientiously through the security implications of each move.'[14] President Clinton tried to persuade Rabin to adopt a more flexible approach, but largely viewed Peres's visions of a new Middle East with Israeli and Palestinian openness as a little over-optimistic.

Netanyahu watched the internal debate between Rabin and Peres with great interest, and drew his conclusions from the mixed signals coming out of the government. Despite the strong denials from Rabin, Netanyahu saw the logical outcome of the Oslo Accords as the creation of a Palestinian state in most of the West Bank and the Gaza Strip: Arafat and PLO would not accept anything less. In public, Rabin talked of the creation of a Palestinian entity and whether or not he really would have agreed to the creation of a Palestinian state remains a contentious point.

While there remains debate over Rabin's views on Palestinian statehood, at the end of 1994 the majority of Israelis still had reservations about a two-state solution to the conflict. The rise in Palestinian violence from Hamas and Islamic Jihad, and Arafat's failure to deal with it, worried Israelis – who Netanyahu continually lectured about the impending doom of statehood that lay over the horizon.

In other words, while the government got on with trying to run the country, Netanyahu did what he was arguably best at: scaring people. While this worked in winning support in the Likud base, in an increasing number of key electoral constituencies it reinforced the perception that he was not statesmanlike. Elements of the international press started to paint Israeli politics in black and white terms – as being between war and peace. This was nothing new.

Ever since 1977, the Likud and Netanyahu's two predecessors as leaders, Begin and Shamir, had received similar treatment. In Netanyahu's case there was an additional element of character assassination directed towards him. This was also present at the time in some of the coverage in the left-wing elements of the Israeli press. The net result of this was the siege mentality of 'Team Netanyahu', the small group of dedicated advisors that surrounded the Likud leader.

The central message that his team continued to transmit to Netanyahu was that in order to win the next election he would need to unify all the elements of the right in Israel behind his leadership. In terms of political positioning strategy, they tried to push to the right, and not to the centre ground of Israeli politics. This was a risky strategy, as previous Israeli elections had been won with a plurality of votes from the centre-ground voters.

As events in 1995 came to confirm, there were other risks in adopting this strategy. In terms of Netanyahu the man and politician it would also help to provide an answer to the question of whether or not he was merely a right-wing ideologue or a pragmatist.

6

Dark Nights

Prior to the murder of Rabin, Netanyahu's fortunes during 1995 continued to rise. A spate of suicide bombings throughout the year (20 January at Beit Lid, near Netanya, 24 July in Ramat Gan, and 21 August in Jerusalem) kept the spotlight on personal security. The feeling that there was no end in sight to the attacks by Palestinian rejectionists, and the atmosphere of fear, once again benefited Netanyahu who needed to do little more than recite his stump speech for his popularity to rise.

The only two setbacks for the Likud leader prior to November were his lack of success in bringing down the government to force early elections, and the inauguration of a new political movement by his Likud internal rival, David Levy. Neither of these, however, looked like derailing the Netanyahu bandwagon, which increased the momentum carried over from the previous year.

Within the Labour leadership there was a belief that the strong polling numbers for Netanyahu and the Likud were soft. When the time came, they hoped (but were far from certain) that the voters would back Rabin and Labour. Central to this hope was the strong performance of the Israeli economy, which was related to the peace process. Netanyahu countered this belief, arguing that there had been no peace dividend for the lowest earners in Israel and that the economy was in dire need of a new round of liberalization.

The key economic group that was identified by both Netanyahu and Rabin as vital to their prospects in the next elections were the ex-Soviet immigrants. The economic indicators in 1995 pointed to seemingly paradoxical findings. By and large, the immigrants were doing better economically than almost all previous waves of immigration to Israel. The level of dissatisfaction about their economic plight, however, was increasing – and they demanded that more be done to successfully absorb them into Israeli society.

If the polling data was confirmed, it looked as if this group would desert Rabin and Labour in 1996 just as they had done with Shamir and the Likud in 1992. With the new immigrants comprising nearly 20 per cent of the electorate, this represented a hammer blow to Rabin and Labour.

It wasn't all plain sailing for Netanyahu. The Likud's dream that this new wave of immigrants would settle in the Occupied Territories and change its demographic balance was not realized. Instead, the vast majority of the immigrants chose to live within the Green Line in existing communities. The lack of willing new settlers made it impossible for Netanyahu to harbour any realistic hopes of achieving a Jewish majority in the West Bank.

The second complication for Netanyahu came in the form of the announcement, on 7 June 1995, by the de facto leader of the new immigrants, Natan Sharansky, that he was forming a new political movement called Yisrael Ba'aliyah, which aimed to represent the interests of the immigrants.

Netanyahu had originally hoped to incorporate Sharansky and his supporters into the Likud, to help strengthen his connection with the immigrants group. He argued, with some justification, that the political outlook of the immigrants was more akin to that of the Likud than Labour. In general, they adopted a more hawkish position towards the peace process with the Arabs than traditional Labour Party supporters, and were keener on capitalist enterprise than the more collectivist nature that still characterized the labour Zionist movement.

At the time, Sharansky had a good relationship with Netanyahu, although the two would later fall out over Netanyahu's failure to keep the political promises he made to him. In 1995, Sharansky's decision to form what was, in effect, a political party reflected the changes in the electoral system that offered better opportunities for sectorial parties to win a greater number of seats in the Knesset. In truth, Netanyahu and his team were not over-concerned about the manoeuvrings of Sharansky and the immigrants.

In private, they understood that gaining the endorsement of Sharansky for Netanyahu in the direct election for Prime Minister was more critical than whatever the new immigrants did in the Knesset elections. In putting his own election prospects ahead of those of the Likud, Netanyahu sent a clear signal of his personal priorities. Putting his own interests above those of the party became a familiar trait in his career. Back in 1995, when the full effects of the new electoral system were not fully understood, the implications of this prioritization were far from clear.

What Netanyahu did clearly envisage was that his route to victory in the direct election for Prime Minister lay in winning the support of the religious voters and a plurality of votes from the new immigrants. He worked hard in honing his message to these key groups, making promises in the socio-economic and secular/religious areas of his embryonic policy platform.

It was largely, however, for external consumption that, in 1995, Netanyahu published his second book in English with the slightly pretentious title, *Fighting Terrorism: How Democracies Can Defeat Domestic and International Terrorism*. This short book was a reworked collection of past essays, stitched together with a new extended section on the (negative) implications of the Oslo Accords along with the lessons that needed to be learned.

There was nothing new to be gleaned from this work that hadn't already been said by Netanyahu in Hebrew. The true intention of the book was to help further internationalize 'Brand Netanyahu' and to further associate his name with the fight against terrorism.

His previous book, published in 1993 and entitled *A Place Among Nations: Israel and the World*, had been intended to set out his agenda and vision for Israel. The book constituted a narrative of a very select history of Israel's conflict with the Arabs and the present-day and future implications. Naturally, the reviews of this work in the United States and Europe were coloured by the political persuasion of the reviewer and the publication.

In truth, the book served as little more than a policy road map, published at the outset of a future leader's career. The world of politics is full of examples of similar works by young and ambitious leaders, with few selling well or being fondly remembered. The key point about Netanyahu's work was that many people outside of Israel paid a great deal of attention to it.

Political enemies and allies, scholars and journalists read the book in expectation that it would outline the policies, ethos and vision that would come to constitute 'Netanyahuism'. Instead, they found a strangely impersonal book in which the sole chapter that offered any meaningful insight was the ninth, entitled 'A Durable Peace'.[1] Even in this chapter Netanyahu clings to what he sees as the injustices suffered by the Israeli state at the hands of the Arabs and the international media.

The one clear message it presents is that peace would only be on (as defined by Netanyahu) Israel's terms. The book is steeped in a tone of victimhood and loss. It fails to deliver any set of indicators as to where, if elected, he would take Israel. Looking back, it is a strangely dated book, even by Middle Eastern standards.

The book belongs to a bygone era and lacks the depth of understanding, compassion and forwardness. Its main interest remains in its relevance as a snapshot of the Netanyahu mind, if only fleeting, with a smokescreen of pseudo-intellectual camouflage. What is clear is that the book is merely a reflection of Netanyahu's politics. The words on the page indicate an author who is trying to portray himself as an ideologue, but whose overtly pragmatic instincts are never far from the surface.

To this extent, the book has been used to support two distinct takes on his early career: the first, characterized by his strong sense of traditional Revisionist ideology, and the second, by his overarching degree of pragmatism. Needless to say, the book sold well in the United States, but did poorly in European markets.

Of Netanyahu's two books, the one on terrorism did at least contain an erudite section on his opposition, in which he revealed for foreign consumption what he saw as the tragic mistakes of the Rabin government. In operational terms he argued that the government had impaired Israel's capacity to successfully deal with terrorism by making six major mistakes with the Oslo Accords. It is worth noting down the six in Netanyahu's own words:

1. It tried to subcontract the job of fighting terrorism to someone else – in this case to the terrorists themselves.
2. It tied the hands of its security forces by denying them the right to enter or strike at terrorist havens, thus creating inviolable domains for terrorist actions.
3. It released thousands of jailed terrorists into these domains, many of whom promptly took up their weapons and returned to ply their trade.

4. It armed the terrorists, by enabling the unrestricted flow of thousands of weapons into Gaza, which soon found their way into the hands of the myriad militias and terrorist gangs.

5. It promised safe passage for terrorists by exempting PLO VIPs from inspection at border crossings from Egypt and Jordan, thus enabling the smuggling of terrorists into Gaza and Jericho, and from there into Israel itself.

6. It betrayed its Palestinian Arab informants, many of whom were murdered by the PLO, leaving Israel without an invaluable source of intelligence against terrorist operations in the evacuated areas.[2]

At the time of the book's publication point six of the above was arguably the most discussed within the Israeli security services. The loss of Israeli 'eyes and ears' in areas controlled by the Palestinians meant that Israel was essentially blind in these areas. When the suicide attacks in Israel started in the autumn of 1994, Israeli forces found it difficult to disrupt the bombers' support networks, due to a lack of reliable intelligence emanating from Palestinian-controlled lands. It would take Israeli intelligence services the best part of a decade to rectify this problem.

What is perhaps most interesting and revealing about Netanyahu's comments is that his criticisms and concerns about the security implications of the Oslo Accords might have been written by Yitzhak Rabin and his team of writers. The Prime Minister was still known in Israel as 'Mr Security' and he was acutely aware of the security shortcomings caused by the Oslo Accords.

The difference between his viewpoint and that of Netanyahu was that the loss of security would be short-term, and that once a permanent agreement was in place the levels of violence would drop. A constant theme employed by Rabin against Netanyahu was that the Likud leader could offer no viable alternative to the Oslo Accords.

From Rabin's perspective, Netanyahu was merely a younger model of his predecessor, Yitzhak Shamir. Rabin, in short, saw Netanyahu as an ideologue whose policies of rejection would put the country on a collision course with the United States – just as Shamir had done from 1991 to 1992. Rabin's view of Netanyahu was flawed and mixed with a dose of realpolitik.

In order to attack Netanyahu, Rabin highlighted his lack of government experience and his inflexibility in accepting the deal with the PLO as evidence of his unsuitability for government. What Rabin and many failed to detect in 1995, however, was that it was the forthcoming election, and not ideology, that dictated Netanyahu's position towards the Accords. Netanyahu opposed the Accords, but his guiding light was putting in place the correct strategies and tactics in order to win the election.

In executing his carefully laid plans, Netanyahu spent much of 1995 speaking to the right and the Settlers movement. For its part, the Settlers movement was leading a vocal, highly organized and dangerous campaign against the Oslo Accords. The campaign at times verged on the unacceptable for the norms of a democratic state. The demonization of Rabin was intolerable, as were the similar attacks on Shimon Peres, Yossi Beilin and the others responsible for framing or supporting the Oslo Accords.

It was Rabin who bore the brunt of the attacks. Some anti-Oslo campaigners believed that Rabin would see the error of his ways and be forced back on to a more centrist track. Rabin's predecessor as Prime Minister, Yitzhak Shamir, was not one of the hopeful. He thought that the Rabin of the era of the Oslo Accords was politically unrecognizable from the Rabin who had served as Israel's Minister of Defence from 1984 to 1990.[3]

On his part, Netanyahu was not totally convinced that Rabin had passed the point of no return in implementing the Oslo Accords. He was aware of the internal pressure on him from the centrist parts of the Labour Party to postpone the implementation of the Accords until after the election. Netanyahu feared that Rabin would shift back to the political centre on the peace process to take the votes of this important constituency.

He was also aware that the Israeli economy, while showing signs of overheating, was by and large in good shape.[4] As the British Ambassador noted, 'Living standards [in Israel] continued to rise fast to levels greater than those of several EU member states.'[5] If Rabin, with Arafat's tacit help, could keep the violence in check around election time, the government would be able to focus the campaign on the economic improvements that the peace deal had brought much of the country. This was exactly how Netanyahu saw himself potentially losing the election.

On 18 July 1995, the Knesset formally swore in two new Labour Party ministers. The first was the main Israeli architect of the Oslo Accords, the ex-deputy Minister of Foreign Affairs, Yossi Beilin, who was close to Shimon Peres. The second was the ex-Chief of Staff of the IDF, Ehud Barak, who was appointed as Minister of the Interior.

Both appointments represented an effort on the part of Rabin to promote generational handover. The timing of Barak's appointment was particularly interesting, given that he and Netanyahu were from the same generation and that Barak was widely viewed (not least by himself) as Rabin's chosen successor when he eventually stepped down.

Barak's reputation was of being one of Israel's finest generals and bravest soldiers. Intriguingly, Barak had been Netanyahu's commander when the two men had served in Israel's elite commando unit, *Sayeret Matkal*. Israeli political commentators predicted a rosy future for Barak, who had been parachuted into a top cabinet job after his retirement from the IDF. Cast in a similar mould to Rabin, Barak was widely trusted as an expert in Israeli security.

The message his appointment sent to Israelis was that another expert in security was saying that it was all right to continue with the peace process with the PLO. Indeed, Barak, and the IDF, had been heavily involved in negotiating the security aspects of the Accords. Rabin's clear intention was to undermine Netanyahu – the so-called security expert – by appointing the man who was the real thing in this area.

It also made for good press coverage for Rabin and Barak, as Israelis were reminded that Netanyahu had only been a junior officer in the IDF. Over the years, Netanyahu's rivalry with Barak would become one of the central features of Israeli politics with their careers seemingly intertwined.

Over the hot summer months of 1995, while Rabin hosted a number of foreign leaders, and was welcomed in overseas visits around the globe, Netanyahu travelled throughout Israel continuing to build his personal election machine and attending anti-Oslo rallies. As a result of the heat, at the beginning of July the country experienced some of the worst forest fires in Israel's history, which destroyed nearly 5,000 acres of forest in the area of the Jerusalem corridor.[6]

The political temperature was fast rising in the country as well. With the government negotiating the interim agreement with the Palestinians that would lead to a further handover of land in the West Bank to the Palestinians, the tone of political debate in Israel further deteriorated.

Violence at political rallies was nothing new in Israel. The 1981 election campaign, widely regarded as the most polemical, was characterized by political attacks on both Labour and Likud leaders.

At the start of the autumn of 1995, the levels of threat and actual instances of political attacks were getting out of hand. Some commentators argued that Israelis needed to let off steam and that Israeli democracy was strong enough to withstand the stormy and bitter debate about the implementation of the Oslo Accords.

Netanyahu continued to act as if this was the case. His attacks on the government grew ever more emotive, and his language nastier, sometimes pushing the boundaries of acceptability. He sensed that the decisive battle over the Accords was taking place as Rabin and Peres negotiated Israel's further withdrawals from the West Bank.

Like most Israelis, Netanyahu believed that once the land had been handed over Israel would never get it back. From his perspective, he felt that he needed to act before it was too late. While the Oslo Accords were officially classified as interim agreements to be superseded by the outcome of the final status talks, few believed that any land Israel handed over during the implementation of the first stages would be returned.

Like most political leaders who were reliant on popular support, Netanyahu needed an audience. In Israel, the one on the street was increasingly controlled by elements linked to the extremist part of the Settlers movement, and political parties that were far to the right of the Likud.

Netanyahu's fears were further fuelled by the news on 24 September 1995 that Shimon Peres and Yasser Arafat had initialled an Interim Agreement in Taba. Four days later, on 28 September, amid much fanfare, Yitzhak Rabin and Yasser Arafat formally signed the agreement in Washington. For the anti-Oslo camp in Israel, the agreement came as a hammer blow. The British summarized its impact:

> The Interim Agreement gave the Palestinians control over about 30% of the West Bank. The Zionist dream of suzerainty over Eretz Israel, the undefined area of biblical Israel, was over . . . Rabin was content to give the Palestinian population of the West Bank responsibility for running much of its own affairs. The pull out from the West Bank was real.[7]

On 5 September, the Knesset started a two-day debate on the Interim Agreement to be followed by a vote on its ratification. The debate was one of the stormiest and bitterest in the relatively short history of the Knesset. Every Knesset member was offered the opportunity of making a short speech, and almost all spoke.

The realization that the Oslo Accords were no longer merely about a withdrawal from Gaza and a tiny area of the West Bank, rather about an eventual Israeli withdrawal from almost all of the West Bank, brought a cold reality to the debate. The British pointed out that a pull-out from the West Bank, which for a generation of Israelis had been unthinkable, was happening before their eyes.

On the first night of the debate, Netanyahu made one of the biggest mistakes of his political career up to that point. It was an error of judgement that would be used by his Israeli political enemies and international detractors alike to seemingly place him well and truly in the camp of the extremists.

Netanyahu attended a rally of around 30,000 anti-Oslo protestors in Zion Square in the centre of Jerusalem. Emotions were running high and many of the demonstrators had been bussed in from settlements in the West Bank. There was also the usual mixture of diehard *Likudniks* and the supporters of far-right parties demonstrating against Rabin and the Interim Agreement.

In the weeks leading up to the rally, the Israeli internal security services, Shin Beth, and the Israeli media were investigating reports that some Orthodox rabbis and scholars had been making pronouncements that, as Rabin was willing to hand over the West Bank to the Palestinians, it was permissible to kill him.[8]

At the rally, protestors carried placards with pictures of Rabin that had been modified to dress him in an SS uniform. The crowds chanted 'Rabin is a traitor', 'Rabin is Arafat's dog' and, ominously, 'Death to Rabin'.

Netanyahu was on a balcony overlooking the square, along with other opposition leaders, watching the demonstration and waiting for his turn to address the crowd. In the television broadcast of the event, he appears content, pleased with the turnout and the noise that the crowd were making. Netanyahu later denied that he heard the chants of 'Death to Rabin', and argued that had he done so he would have disowned them when he eventually spoke.

For a leader who was a grand master in the use of the television interview and image to further his career, it was a calamitous mistake. The fact that neither he nor his supporters around him condemned the images of Rabin in SS uniform and the chants against Rabin's life cast a deep shadow over their judgement.

A more experienced and wily politician than Netanyahu would have left the rally when he realized its timbre and radical overtones. Instead, he was introduced to the crowd as the next Prime Minister of Israel and gave his fiery anti-Oslo speech to a highly receptive audience.

Television images of the crowd waving pictures of Rabin in SS uniform, and chanting 'Death to Rabin' were broadcast in Israel and across the world. The impression that the television images and photographs published in newspapers gave was of the Likud leader standing shoulder to shoulder with those who were calling for the use of extremist means to rid the country of the government.

Netanyahu's detractors talked not only of his poor political judgement, but also of his total inability to absorb what was going on in Israel at the time. Members of Shin Beth had allegedly spoken to Netanyahu about the worsening political situation in Israel, and asked him to tone down his anti-government rhetoric.

The Minister of Housing and Construction, Binyamin 'Fuad' Ben-Eliezer, a close ally of Rabin, and who had been attacked at the rally, recalled years later in a media interview:

> One month before the assassination there was the big demonstration in Jerusalem's Zion Square, at which all the heads of the Likud party spoke. By chance I happened on the back end of the demonstration, near the Knesset. Suddenly, I found myself surrounded by thousands, the subject of cursing and swearing.[9]

Ben-Eliezer then went on to describe what happened next.

> A young man, who later turned out to be the brother of [Rabin assassin] Yigal Amir, climbed onto my car. The amount of cursing and swearing to which I was subjected was unbelievable and at the lowest levels, including spitting in my face. Luckily for me the police were called and they extricated me in quite a state. I was very agitated.[10]

As soon as he got back to the Knesset, he went to find Netanyahu to remonstrate with him. He still remembers what he said when he caught up with him: 'Listen closely, we're going to have a murder here.'[11] Netanyahu reassured him that nothing was going on. The next day, when Ben-Eliezer recalled the events to Rabin at a cabinet meeting, saying, 'I was almost murdered last night and there is going to be a murder here', Rabin ignored his warnings and continued with the meeting.[12]

Netanyahu failed to understand the bigger picture. Lost in his strategies and tactical planning to bring down the government, he missed the simple point that leaders – even opposition heads – have a civic duty to rein in extremists. Unbeknown to Netanyahu there were individuals who were willing to take the rhetoric to heart and carry out an attack on the Prime Minister.

On this point, despite briefings from Shin Beth to the contrary, Rabin also believed that there was little threat from these radicalized Jews. In the wake of the attack on Ben-Eliezer, Shin Beth ordered that security be stepped up for government ministers, especially Yossi Beilin and Shimon Peres who were the two members of the government most associated with having started the Israel–PLO negotiations.

It would be unfair on Netanyahu not to mention that he never endorsed the comments and slogans directed against Rabin by the protestors. On occasions, in the Knesset, he derided the opponents of the Accords who called Rabin a traitor. He described Rabin as a political rival, and during at least one Likud rally reminded his supporters that Rabin was not a traitor. He also spoke on the floor of the Knesset and denounced the posters and placards claiming that Rabin was a Nazi collaborator.

Where he lost his way was in not distancing himself far enough politically from those extremists whose opinion he did not share, and who were using him to gain political legitimacy. His mistakes were not those of a malicious nature, rather they were caused by his inexperience and lack of understanding of the dangerous political temperature in Israel at that time.

In retrospect, he and Rabin should have sat down privately and worked out an agreement to lower the political temperature that would have allowed for a rigorous, cool-headed debate on the Interim Agreement. Such a move would have constituted leadership by both men and sent a clear message that extremist views and actions would not be tolerated in Israel.

In the end, after two days of stormy debate in the Knesset, Netanyahu and the other opponents of the Interim Agreement lost the vote, but only by a whisker. The agreement was passed by 61 votes to 59 with all 120 members of the Knesset casting their votes on this crucial agreement. As a result of the vote, four days later, on 10 October, 950 Palestinian prisoners were released as part of the opening phase of the implementation of the Interim Agreement.

For many Israelis, the release of prisoners was too much to take, with Netanyahu reminding Israel and the world that many of them would, as he had put it in his book, 'promptly take up their weapons and returned to ply their trade'.[13] The release of the prisoners further increased the political temperature in Israel between those politicians who saw it as a price Israel had to pay for peace, and those who viewed it as essentially surrender to Arafat and the PLO.

On 25 October 1995, the IDF started its redeployment from Jenin. It looked at the start of November 1995, as if, following months of political stalemate between the Rabin government and the Palestinian Authority – that resulted in a series of missed deadlines – the peace process was getting back on track. Netanyahu, for one, was not so sure. He sensed that the country was heading more and more towards his way of thinking regarding the Interim Agreement.

In essence, Netanyahu still believed that major problems lay ahead in implementing the agreement, with further Israeli pullbacks to be finalized and implemented, amidst a potential increase in attacks against Israelis by Palestinian rejectionist groups. Riding high in the opinion polls, and with only a year to go until elections, Netanyahu still felt confident that it would be a government led by him that would soon be responsible for dealing with any future implementation of the Accords.

The increasing domestic political violence had shocked many left-wing Israelis out of their overtly defensive political malaise. The absence of large-scale, widespread centre-left political rallies had been a feature of Israeli politics since the signing of the Oslo Accords over two years earlier.

The organizers of the rally in the King of Israel Square in Tel Aviv wanted to make a stand against worsening political violence in Israel. The message of the rally was that enough was enough. The political agenda of the rally was an attempt to take the Israeli streets back from the anti-Oslo protestors, whose huge rallies over the previous two years had dominated news headlines.

At first, Rabin was set to decline an invitation to address the rally. Previous attempts at putting on a pro-Oslo demonstration had attracted small crowds. Once, when told there was a pro-Oslo demonstration at the Prime Minister's office in Jerusalem, Rabin had rushed outside to discover that it comprised only a couple of dozen people.

He feared the same for the 4 November rally in Tel Aviv, despite a high-profile team of organizers and the presence of Shimon Peres and leading figures from the Israeli music world. In the end, he changed his mind and went to the rally, which was attended by some 100,000 people.

The rally was larger than any anti-Oslo gathering, and Rabin uncharacteristically appeared to let down his guard a little and enjoy himself. As he was leaving the rally, he was shot and killed by a fellow Israeli Jew. What shocked Israelis the most was that his assassin, Yigal Amir, was not a settler, but a middle-class law student from the coastal plain.

'Rabin was murdered because Israeli opponents of the peace process realised that he meant it when he said he was willing to trade land for peace,' wrote the British Deputy Head of Mission in Tel Aviv, John White.[14] Amidst all the Israeli, Arab and international tributes, White offered a sober addition to his own tribute:

> He was insensitive to the fears (and aspirations) of settlers and many on the religious right during and after the negotiation of the Interim Agreement. This helped create a sense of desperation among some individuals, given expression by increasingly violent rhetoric about the peace process that seems to have influenced Rabin's assassin.[15]

The 80 heads of state and government, and royalty, who attended Rabin's funeral echoed *Shalom, Haver*, goodbye, friend – the memorable phrase used by President Clinton during his eulogy for Rabin. The attendance at Rabin's funeral was a sign of how far Israel had come internationally since 1993, and a show of support for the continuation of the peace process. The Interim Agreement had become his legacy. White summed it up:

Rabin in his death had secured a depth of affection and under-standing from the Israeli public which he did not enjoy in life. His murder broke the quiet of the silent (just) majority. It energised a new generation to political activism.[16]

For Netanyahu, the assassination of Rabin represented a disaster on multiple fronts. His position wasn't improved when Rabin's griev-ing family accused him of helping to create the conditions that led to the murder. After he had recovered from the initial shock of what happened, he did what he could to try to repair the damage.

He announced that he and the Likud would not oppose the forma-tion of the new government, led by Rabin's successor, Shimon Peres. 'In Israel, governments are changed at ballot boxes, and not by guns,' he proclaimed. It was a powerful sound bite, and he meant it.

The news did not immediately get any better for Netanyahu and the Likud, as the polls indicated that his lead had evaporated, and that Peres looked a shoo-in for victory in the next election, due to be held in 1996.

PART THREE

Arrival

7

Election Night

As the polls closed across Israel on the evening of 29 May 1996, Israelis, and much of the rest of the world, waited with bated breath to hear the results of the exit polls, which were broadcast on Israeli television channels at 10.00 p.m. local time. It was to prove to be another decisive moment in the career of Benjamin Netanyahu.

Earlier in the day, he had admitted to feeling nervous as he cast his vote. 'Butterflies in my stomach? Well, I had moments of hesitation, but I'll tell you who I voted for. I voted for Netanyahu,' he had told the gathered media scrum.[1]

'Too close to call,' announced the presenters on Israel's Channel 1 and Channel 2 at exactly 10.00 p.m. Then a picture of the Prime Minister, Shimon Peres, flashed on the screen – both networks were calling the direct election for Prime Minister for Peres, but by a margin of error of 1 per cent.

The exit poll put Peres on 50.7 per cent with Netanyahu on 49.3 per cent.[2] The television coverage then cut to the Labour Party's election headquarters where there were muted cheers. At the Likud election headquarters there was a feeling that the night was young and that the official result would be different.

Both Netanyahu and Peres were nervously watching the coverage, trying to catch key official results as they were announced. What struck both candidates was the exit poll for the Knesset, which indicated that both the major party lists – Labour and Likud – had done badly, and the religious parties and other smaller parties had picked up a large number of seats.

Netanyahu and Peres both understood immediately that whoever won the race to become Prime Minister would face major obstacles in putting together a winning coalition of 61 seats in the Knesset. The intention of the supporters of the new electoral system of strengthening the executive over the legislature had failed.

Yossi Beilin, one of Shimon Peres's closest allies and a minister in the outgoing government, did a brief round of local and international interviews. 'A win is a win,' he told journalists.[3] Likud politicians were sceptical of Beilin's comments, describing them as premature. Netanyahu's choice for Minister of Defence, Yitzhak Mordechai, was sent out to reassure the Likud faithful and brief the international press. 'This is just an exit poll. We will wait for the results.'[4]

Locked away in his private suite, Netanyahu remained confident. He and his small electoral team understood two important precedents that would impact upon the results. The first of these was the unspoken truth of Israeli politics: Israelis do not always reveal their real voting intentions to pollsters. Moreover, the majority of those who were less than truthful about how they voted on election day more often than not favoured the Likud over the Labour Party. There appeared to be a stigma for some centre-ground voters to admit to supporting the candidates of the right at any given election.

Netanyahu's opponent in the 1996 race had a painful personal experience of this phenomenon. In the 1981 election, Peres was humiliated when Israeli television announced the exit poll results giving Labour the lead – defeating the Likud, led by the then Prime Minister Menachem Begin.

Peres triumphantly appeared before jubilant Labour Party supporters to celebrate the victory, only to learn later in the night that the television exit polls had been wrong.[5] In 1996, Peres wasn't going to make the same mistake again and stayed safely locked away from his supporters and the gathered press, waiting for the official results to start to come in.

Netanyahu's second reason for confidence was that the exit poll did not include the 150,000 absentee ballots, most of them cast by serving members of the IDF. In previous elections, the majority of the soldiers had taken a hawkish view of the peace process and supported the Likud. Given his strong emphasis on security over peacemaking, Netanyahu believed that he would gain enough of the soldiers' votes to see him over the line.

With this in mind, at 1.00 a.m. Netanyahu appeared in front of his supporters at election headquarters. 'The race is very, very close. Do not lose hope,' he told his hushed supporters, who were still trying to understand the tightness of the Prime Minister's race and the poor result of the Likud in the Knesset elections.[6]

Prior to going to the stage, Netanyahu's aides had told him that barring anything unexpected among the absentee ballots he would be Israel's next Prime Minister. Netanyahu was set to become Israel's youngest Prime Minister, and would achieve this without having previously occupied any of the senior political offices in the country.

In the end, Netanyahu's margin of victory over Peres was narrow, but decisive. He won 50.4 per cent of the vote to Peres's 49.5 per cent and in terms of actual votes 1,501,023 to Peres's 1,471,566.[7] Netanyahu's victory revealed another characteristic that came to serve him well, namely his resilience. Largely written off, including by many in his own party, after Rabin's assassination, Netanyahu – with the help of events and mistakes made by Peres's campaign team – had become Israel's very own 'comeback kid'.

Netanyahu's victory was no accident. He had run a futuristic twenty-first-century campaign against a twentieth-century one of Peres and the Labour Party. Ignoring the issues, events and Netanyahu's own performance for a moment, there were two reasons for his victory: the huge amount of campaign funds he raised, and his appointment of an American election strategist to oversee his campaign.

Israeli elections, as a result, would never be the same again. Peres and Labour could not match the funds raised by Netanyahu, and his campaign manager, Chaim Ramon, overruled Peres's calls for the appointment of an overseas campaign strategist. Ramon was also one of the potential successors to Peres when he stood down.

The message that Netanyahu put over in his campaign was simple: security was more important than peace. Critics rightly tried to pin him down on the issue, arguing that the two were interrelated, in that you couldn't have security without peace.

It didn't matter. Netanyahu's message was slickly presented and appealed to the constituencies he was targeting to secure his victory. It would be unfair to suggest that his campaign represented a simple case of spin over substance. It did not. What it did reveal was that

Netanyahu's American style of politics worked with Israelis, and future elections in Israel would reflect this change.

On 30 May 1996, Israelis awoke to the news that they would have a new Prime Minister, but wondered what type of government he would be able to put together. For the moment, Benjamin and Sara Netanyahu basked in the glow of victory. Sara would be given a prominent role in public life, an American-style first lady. This starkly contrasted with Shimon Peres's wife, Sonia, who had remained in the background. The how-to-handle-Sara question was discussed by Netanyahu's aides soon after his victory was confirmed.

Political honeymoons in Israel tend to be short-term affairs, and even before he entered what were to become tortuous negotiations over the formation of his coalition government, Netanyahu had work to do to reassure the divided nation, and a sceptical world, that he was a statesman.

In what amounted to his victory speech and coronation rolled into one, he addressed a packed audience at the International Convention Centre in Jerusalem on 2 June 1996. His message was simple: the need to unify the divisions in Israel (both Jew and non-Jew) and to reassure the outside world, specifically the Clinton administration, of his intentions regarding the peace process.

Bristling with the confidence of victory, the transformation of Netanyahu from rabble-rousing opposition leader to statesman was almost complete. His speech was delivered in a tone that indicated he was the father figure of the nation. As he put it:

> The State of Israel is embarking on a new path today, a path of hope and of unity, a path of security and of peace. And the first and foremost peace we must make is peace at home, amongst ourselves.
>
> This is our most important task because in recent years the polarization in Israeli society has deepened, the gaps have become larger, and the tension has increased.
>
> Dear friends, I see my first task as Prime Minister to mend the rifts, to reduce the tensions and to strengthen the unity and the sense of partnership, which is the basis of our existence. And I want to tell you: the first peace is peace at home.
>
> Israeli society is blessed with many shades and persuasions. Our unity is not based on blurring the uniqueness of each group. It is

expressed by nurturing tolerance and mutual respect while maintaining the religious status quo.

I am talking about a coming together of all the sectors in Israeli society, while maintaining the delicate balance between differing worldviews. This is our way and we will pursue it.[8]

That he talked of healing the wounds of Israeli society was lost on the Israeli left, who argued that he had been the principle cause of the polarization of society. On the peace process his words were carefully chosen to try to provide reassurance to groups with differing views on it:

The government we will form in a few days, with God's help, will act to strengthen ties of peace which have already been forged with Jordan and Egypt. We will continue the negotiations with the Palestinians. And we will work to further peace Accords and coexistence with other Arab countries. I call upon them too: join the circle of peace.

I see our friend, the United States of America, as a true partner in this process of making real peace. The relations between the U.S. and Israel are rock solid, and I am certain they will remain that way in the next four years. Our relations are built not only on common interest. They are founded on the shared values of democracy and human dignity.[9]

The section contained one of the buzzwords that would be much employed during Netanyahu's tenure as Prime Minister, namely democracy. In this respect, Netanyahu once again shifted the goalposts of Israeli politics. He was essentially a strong believer in American-style democracy over its European form. Like a man taking a new car out for a spin, Netanyahu wanted to remind the world that democracy was to be aspired to, and that making peace with the Arab world would be much simpler if the Arabs embraced democracy.

The speech in Jerusalem was Netanyahu's coming of age. The election had provided his greatest challenge to date and his victory arguably represented the most decisive moment in his career to that point. It is worth highlighting the counterfactual to the electoral victory. If Netanyahu had lost the election, even by a small margin, he would have faced within days a challenge to his leadership of the

Likud from Ariel Sharon, David Levy and one or two of the Likud Princes such as Benni Begin.

Deserted by many of the supporters who had originally backed him as the best bet of beating the Labour Party, it would have been difficult to see his leadership of the Likud surviving the onslaught from his party rivals. In all likelihood, the name of Benjamin Netanyahu would have been consigned to the dustbin of political history. Not content to play a secondary role in political life, Netanyahu would have become a successful businessman, making his fortunes in trade deals between Israeli and American companies.

The premature ending of his political career following his electoral defeat would have been harsh. His rival in the direct election for Prime Minister, Shimon Peres, had previously been unable to form governments after the 1977, 1981, 1984 and 1988 elections. Peres's political career had not been terminated after continuous electoral failure, but there was something unique about Netanyahu that made it difficult to envisage him surviving politically after an electoral defeat in 1996.

His margin of victory in 1996 was small, but it really was the difference between being crowned king and being exiled into the political wilderness. As he looked out over the cheering masses of Likud supporters chanting 'Bibi, Bibi' at the International Convention Centre, he was aware just how narrow the margin was between victory and defeat, success and failure.

The long dark nights of November and December 1995 appeared a lifetime away to him, as they seemingly did to most Israelis. Back in 1995 all had appeared lost, and it had been his deep sense of optimism that things would change for the better for him personally that had kept him going.

Following the assassination of Rabin and the formation of a new government led by Shimon Peres, the first task for Netanyahu had been to convince those close to him, and in the wider Likud, that he could still win the next election. This was no easy task. In doing this, Netanyahu argued that the assassination had actually changed very little in Israeli politics.

The issues remained much the same: implementation of the Interim Agreement, personal security for Israelis, dealing with Hamas and Islamic Jihad. As the implementation of the Interim Agreement called for Israeli withdrawals from the West Bank, something Netanyahu sensed that many Israelis were not fully prepared to accept, he saw opportunities that lay ahead for him to recover politically.

Although opinion polls conducted by the Israeli media in the months following the assassination (in November and December 1995) indicated that Netanyahu and the Likud would be trounced at the next elections, he believed the numbers to be soft. In other words, the assassination did not change the deep-rooted opinions of Israelis towards the peace process. The polls reflected an emotional response to the assassination that would pass as the political agenda of the country moved on.

Netanyahu and his team argued that there was still a paradox in the mindset of Israelis towards the peace process. The 60:60 formula, as David Levy labelled it, was characterized by the two paradoxical polling numbers: 60 per cent of Israelis wanted peace and 60 per cent did not want to give up land.[10] This was true for both the Syrian and Palestinian tracks of the peace process. Levy reminded everybody, including Netanyahu, that the politician who could bridge these two conflicting polling findings would win the elections in 1996.

On this score, Netanyahu was proved correct. Israeli opinion towards the Palestinian peace process was soft and did eventually return to its pre-assassination position. In order to have a chance of winning the election, Netanyahu had first to see off an internal challenge in the Likud to his leadership.

The Israeli media ran one story after another about plots within the Likud to remove Netanyahu from the leadership. His alleged indirect complicity in the assassination, articulated by members of the Rabin family, tainted him among some *Likudniks* as being politically unelectable.

In the end, this did not prove as difficult as first thought. In this respect, Netanyahu got the first piece of luck in the early months. The name mooted as the alternative leader in both the press and inside the Likud was that of Dan Meridor. A fellow Likud Prince, Meridor was viewed as politically clean, had a strong record in defending minorities during his stint as Minister of Justice in the previous Likud government and, crucially, was seen as a moderate.

Those in the Likud who supported a Meridor coup (and they were numerous) were aware that, given the changes made to the party's constitution by Netanyahu, it would be difficult to replace the incumbent without his agreement. Plans were hatched for a group of party elders to approach Netanyahu to ask him to stand down for the good of the party. It was to be made clear to Netanyahu that Meridor enjoyed strong support among many in the party, and that he should exit gracefully.

Netanyahu got wind of the plot – this wasn't difficult as the details of the potential challenge from Meridor were splashed over the newspapers and openly discussed on television news programmes. Smartly, and employing the carrot and stick approach, Netanyahu convinced Meridor not to run against him.

The carrot was the promise of a major cabinet position in any Netanyahu-led government. The stick amounted to a veiled threat to marginalize Meridor in the party by not offering him help in the Likud primaries for its Knesset list. It worked. Meridor announced that he would not run for the leadership of the Likud and the press soon lost interest in the story.

Although he didn't realize it at the time, the 'Meridor Plot' was not the serious challenge to his leadership that he had presumed it to be. It transpired that Meridor had hesitated to fully commit himself to the challenge. While he dithered, Netanyahu had made his move. Netanyahu's promise of a future senior cabinet post for Meridor would not be the last one he made.

In seeing off the challenge of Meridor, Netanyahu had achieved the first part of his political rehabilitation. He would remain as the leader of the Likud and be its candidate in the direct election for Prime Minster against Shimon Peres. Those *Likudniks* who had wished to get Netanyahu out had missed a golden opportunity that would not present itself again for quite some time.

With the internal challenge to his position behind him, Netanyahu was able to focus on the forthcoming election. There were concerns that Peres might try and cash in on his large lead in the polls and call early elections for the first part of 1996. For Peres, this was arguably his safest option to retain power. The timing of the election became a vitally important decision for Peres as he prepared his peacemaking strategy.

While Peres had been fully in the loop on the Palestinian track, Rabin had kept his talks through the Americans to Syria close to his chest. When Peres was informed of the negotiations after succeeding Rabin, he indicated a strong desire to try to rekindle the negotiations with the Syrians.

All of this was factored into Peres's decision about the timing of the elections. The essence of the decision that Peres faced was whether to try to make as much peace as possible before the election, or to move the poll date forward and secure a new mandate for his policies.

In the end, afraid that any move towards early election would give the impression of cashing in on Rabin's assassination, Peres chose not to call elections for the first part of 1996 but to try to get as much peace-making completed before going to the polls. It was a brave choice, but it turned out from his perspective to be the wrong one. Netanyahu – although he did not realise it at the time – had just got his second big break since the Rabin assassination, following on from the failed Meridor challenge.

At the end of 1995, lagging well behind in the polls, and with the stigma of the accusations of his role in creating the political climate that led to Rabin's death proving hard to shake off, Netanyahu took what was for an Israeli politician a revolutionary decision. Without discussion with his close set of advisors, he decided to hire an American strategist to oversee his campaign. Today, almost every political campaign in Israel comes with American spin doctors and strategists representing the candidates. This was not the case in the mid-1990's.

The appointment of Arthur J. Finkelstein turned out to be one of the most important and astute that Netanyahu had made up until this point in his career. Finkelstein was to take the Netanyahu political machine to new heights of efficiency in getting over his message to the Israeli public. Finkelstein's appointment was kept secret for a long time: Netanyahu did not want to alert Peres and the Labour Party. Finkelstein checked into the King David Hotel in Jerusalem under a false name and commuted back and forth from the United States.

Finkelstein's track record in the United States in getting Republican candidates elected was extremely impressive. He was experienced, ruthless, demanded total control over campaigns he worked on – and he was expensive. Netanyahu resolved the money issue by tapping one of his American donors, Ronald Lauder, the cosmetics billionaire, to foot the bill. It was Lauder who had recommended Finkelstein to Netanyahu, and Lauder was happy to pick up the tab.

With Lauder effectively bankrolling his campaign for Prime Minister and one of America's most effective election strategists at his side,

Netanyahu, unbeknown to Peres, was very much back in the political frame. After meeting Finkelstein for the first time, Netanyahu understood exactly what he needed to do to win the election in terms of positioning strategy and for him personally. The good news for Netanyahu was that, despite his lowly poll ratings, Finkelstein believed the forthcoming election to be highly winnable.

Any concerns that Netanyahu might have had over the reaction of his own team of advisors to his appointment of Finkelstein, and the handing over of total control to him, soon evaporated. Netanyahu's close advisors such as Eyal Arad and Limor Livnat welcomed the arrival of Finkelstein, whom they viewed as having come to Israel on a mission to win.[11]

While Netanyahu was busy fending off an internal challenge to his leadership of the Likud and subsequently putting together what he viewed as a winning team for the forthcoming election, the Peres-led government moved quickly to try to implement as much of the Interim Agreement as possible before going to the polls. This proved easier than under Rabin, with the agreement very much perceived by Israelis as Rabin's political legacy. The opposition to the agreement from Netanyahu and other opponents was toned down. This was a tactical retreat by Netanyahu who needed to rehabilitate his image with centrist parts of the Israeli electorate.

Peres made good on his word to complete as much of the implementation of the agreement on schedule – unlike the previous stages of the Oslo Accords. The planned Israeli withdrawals from West Bank cities and towns covered by the agreement were completed on time by the IDF. The exception to this was Hebron where Peres decided to postpone a partial withdrawal until after the elections.[12] As Netanyahu would one day discover himself, Peres had good reason to leave the religiously sensitive Hebron until later.

Peres's decision was largely motivated by his desire not to offend the religious parties in Israel prior to the election. It might appear strange that a leader who had been abandoned by Shas during his attempt to form a government in 1990 could believe that he stood a chance of wooing the religious voters six years later.

The Labour Party saw Netanyahu's personal weaknesses as opening the gates of opportunity for Peres to make inroads into this constituency. More centrist elements in the party thought this all rather fanciful, arguing that Netanyahu already had the religious vote wrapped up.

With the exception of Hebron, the Peres-led government could point to major progress in the peace process with the Palestinians. The withdrawal of the IDF from key Palestinian cities and towns in the West Bank meant that the Palestinian election could go ahead in January 1996. The Israeli left and the outside world viewed this important development as proof that the implementation of the Interim Agreement was progressing well.

The Palestinian elections were held on 20 January 1996, with the presidential election won by Yasser Arafat with a resounding 88.2 per cent of the votes. Arafat's Fatah movement secured 55 of the 88 seats and also won the legislative elections, which were held on the same day.

It was hoped that the achievement of a higher level of political legitimacy by Arafat would increase his scope and willingness to deal with the Palestinian rejectionist groups to the Oslo Accords. Netanyahu argued that it would make little difference and that Arafat would not offer full security cooperation with Israel. Whatever Netanyahu's viewpoint, it was abundantly clear that Arafat's victory in the elections – described by observers as generally fair and open – did enhance his international standing.

Unbeknown to Netanyahu, although he did suspect it, Peres, as well as pushing the Palestinian track forward, was also involved in secret negotiations with the Syrians. Peres had succeeded in getting the talks restarted by agreeing to discuss not only security-related issues, but a wide range of subjects, including water rights.

The talks that took place in Washington were led from the Israeli side by Yossi Beilin, and were thought to be making some progress. Peres, however, was unable to translate this into either an agreement or even the holding of a summit meeting with President Assad.

In the end, with the Syrian track unlikely to produce a quick breakthrough and with final status talks with the Palestinians due to start in May 1996, Peres was left with little choice but to bring the elections forward from November to the end of May.

Netanyahu, Finkelstein and the rest of team were prepared for the new date and ready to execute the closely guarded plans the American had made for the campaign. While the Israeli press still labelled Peres the favourite to win the race, there was a quiet confidence in the Netanyahu camp that, if their candidate did not make any mistakes, he would be victorious.

8

Campaign

Almost as soon as Peres announced the election date, all hell was let loose in Israel. With a wave of suicide bombings by Hamas and Islamic Jihad, in February and March 1996, progress in the Israeli–Palestinian peace process was jeopardized.

President Clinton tried to intervene to help the government. He arranged an anti-terrorism summit of world leaders in Egypt, and the United States supplied Israel with additional bomb-detecting equipment and counter-terrorist assistance. Clinton also visited Israel – meeting both Peres and Netanyahu – and addressed the Knesset on 14 March.[1] President Clinton, Peres and Netanyahu all understood the political impact of the attacks.

Soon enough, the polling data revealed that Netanyahu's ratings had climbed and Peres's had fallen. Within the margins of error of the polls, Netanyahu and Peres were running neck and neck. There was a sense of near-panic in the Peres camp, with some Labour Party leaders claiming that Netanyahu was the major beneficiary of the horrendous attacks.

Netanyahu's response was much more restrained than in the past. Finkelstein told him to restrict his comments to promising to prioritize 'personal security' over the peace process. It was a simple message, but from his perspective an effective one.

The February and March attacks ensured that the election would be fought on the issues of peace and security. Economic issues were all but ignored: an own goal by Peres. Several Labour Party strategists argued to the contrary, that the best way of defeating Netanyahu was to highlight the economic improvements for Israelis that had resulted from the peace process.

Peres and his campaign manager, Chaim Ramon, chose to ignore this line of thinking, opting instead to go head-on with Netanyahu on peace and security. This suited Netanyahu perfectly well. Peres had chosen to fight the election on Netanyahu's strongest areas.

The core issue that Finkelstein identified as being Netanyahu's weakest area was his perceived lack of statesmanlike skills. This, Finkelstein argued, was both a physical and character issue – and he made plans to age Netanyahu superficially using make-up and by whitening his (already greying) hair.

A studio set was built that resembled the White House Oval Office, and Netanyahu's speech writers were instructed to compose campaign messages lasting no more than 30 seconds. Netanyahu was advised against giving impromptu interviews, and from visiting the sites of suicide bombings. Discipline and repetition became the two key words in the campaign.

Compared to the sleek Netanyahu campaign machine, the Peres and Labour Party campaigns were in disarray. Peres appointed the two men who viewed themselves as his potential successors to key positions within the campaign team. Chaim Ramon and Ehud Barak did not get along well during the campaign, nor did their respective staffs.

Petty jealousies, along with an eye on the future, prevented both men from working efficiently together. The central thrust of the campaign was that Peres could be trusted on security. The sense in the campaign was that, if the security services could prevent another Palestinian suicide bombing, then Peres and the Labour Party would win.

Netanyahu's campaign counter-message was threefold: Peres was planning to divide Jerusalem; Peres was going to give up the Golan Heights; and Netanyahu would bring not only peace, but security. The message was to be repeated over and over again, simply, clearly and concisely. Simplicity of message had been a characteristic of Finkelstein's previous campaigns in the United States.

Due to personal and professional commitments, Finkelstein was not based in Israel for the whole campaign. Instead, Netanyahu often communicated with him by car phone. All of this added to the mystique of the strategist. The television advertisements that were directed around his threefold message appeared to be working, with more Israelis inclined to take Netanyahu's leadership skills more seriously. This happened, despite a strong attack on Netanyahu from Ehud Barak at the end of the campaign.

As Barak put it, 'An Israeli Prime Minister needs to take instant decisions that could affect lives and could not afford to consult with advisors beforehand.' He went on to add that Netanyahu had served under him in the army and clearly did not have what it took to be Prime Minister.[2] Barak's comments reflected the increasing nervousness of the Labour Party as polling day approached. The attack on Netanyahu was widely published in Israel and disseminated in the international press.

At the outset of the campaign, Finkelstein had convinced Netanyahu not to respond to attacks from the Labour Party, and this policy remained in place even after Barak's attack. The question that much of the press tried to focus on was along similar lines to that of Barak, namely question marks over Netanyahu's judgement. Many of the old chestnuts were brought up, particularly 'Bibi-gate', which was used – once again – as evidence to suggest that he panicked when under pressure.

In the end, with the polls indicating a slight lead for Peres (but within the margins of error), it all came down to the television debate between Netanyahu and Peres. The election teams eventually agreed to a single debate in which Netanyahu and Peres would face questions from a moderator. This was Netanyahu's last chance to come across as statesmanlike and convince Israelis to trust him with the leadership of the country. Peres and Labour saw it as an opportunity to expose Netanyahu as a lightweight whose position was based on his telegenic rather than his political skills.

The Netanyahu team worked especially hard to prepare their candidate. He was told to keep his answers short and precise: Peres, they presumed, would ramble and talk in generalities. Netanyahu wrote comments and short answers on crib cards that he stuck to his practice desk. Time and time again his team honed his message. Once again, he was told not to enter into direct or heated arguments with Peres. The main aim was to make Netanyahu look prime ministerial.

While Netanyahu practised his responses to the likely questions, Peres concentrated on running the country. His attention was divided between taking measures to prevent another Palestinian suicide attack that might have doomed his re-election chances, and preparing for the debate that would also make or break his campaign. For a man who was already in his seventies, this proved to be no easy task.

To add to Peres's difficulties, there were strong indications in the polls that Israeli Arabs, who had traditionally cast their ballots for the Labour Party, were not going to vote – in protest against an Israeli military operation in Lebanon. Operation Grapes of Wrath was launched by Peres in April 1996 in response to the heavy shelling of northern Israel by Hezbollah. The Israeli operation resulted in the deaths of more than 150 Lebanese, as well as the temporary displacement of nearly half a million. In one attack, more than one hundred Lebanese were killed in the shelling of a UN compound at Qana.

At the time, Peres was accused of initiating Operation Grapes of Wrath to indicate that he was resolute in defending Israeli security interests. Given the attack from Hezbollah, however, Peres's options for an Israeli response were limited. What surprised many was the scale of the Israeli military operation, with Israel mounting more than a thousand air raids during the operation. The Israeli Arabs blamed Peres for the casualties and vowed to make their feelings clear at the polls.

So as Netanyahu arrived for the television debate, he faced an incumbent Prime Minister who was losing votes to his left through Israel's actions in Lebanon, and from centre-ground voters – as the result of the suicide attacks in Israel by militant Palestinian groups. While Netanyahu was generally supportive of Peres's efforts in Lebanon, he did not think that Peres had done enough to ensure the personal security of Israelis from attacks by the militant Palestinian groups.

Netanyahu's aides reported that he was nervous prior to the debate. For a man who appeared a natural on television, this might seem strange. He understood that his political career would largely be determined by the thirty-minute debate, the only time that the two candidates would appear together. Unlike most election debates, which go out live, this one was pre-recorded and aired later the same day, in the evening. This helped international news networks, such as CNN, to broadcast the debate at the same time as Israeli television with accurate subtitles or translated voiceover.

At the start of the debate, Netanyahu wanted to make sure that he was seated, so that viewers would not see the scar on his lip. Peres was surprised when he raised the question of the seating arrangements, and said, 'Sit wherever you want.'³ Prior to the recording, Netanyahu cleverly stuck his preparation notes on his podium so that he could see them, but the camera could not. The notes contained specific reminders on how to behave, statistics and other evidence to support his arguments.

Throughout the debate, Netanyahu looked straight at the camera when giving his allotted 90-second replies to questions. Peres chose to treat the debate more like a traditional television political interview by looking at the moderator, Dan Margalit, when replying to his questions.[4] Peres also did not look at Netanyahu during the debate, trying to avoid giving any additional attention to the challenger.

As the debate progressed, it was soon apparent that Netanyahu was speaking faster than Peres, uttering an extra 300 words more than Peres in the first ten minutes of the debate. Finkelstein had prepared Netanyahu well in using the questions as a mechanism for getting over his message in a simple and erudite manner. Peres offered long, rambling answers and struggled with the 90-second format, often running out of time.

Netanyahu's tactics of referring to Peres directly in a negative sense also paid off. Peres talked in the collective – 'the government' and 'the party' – while Netanyahu used the first person singular when replying. By the end of the debate, Peres looked tired. In truth, he was worn out, having endured a sleepless night before the debate. Netanyahu looked just as his team had hoped he would – energetic and with a good grasp of the issues.

Arguably the best part of the debate was when Dan Margalit asked both candidates a question about their weakest personal areas: Peres on his age and Netanyahu on his extra-marital affair. Peres replied with humour:

> If you had to elect a male model and not a Prime Minister, then the age would be an issue. I feel great. My ability to work is excellent. I know a lot of people who are young, but their thoughts are very old.[5]

Netanyahu's reply to Margalit's question attempted to take a personal negative directed at him and turn it around into an attack on Peres:

> Concerning this matter that you bring up now, I expressed a lot of sorrow. It hurt me. It hurt my wife. It hurt my family. It was a mistake. But the mistake that Mr. Peres made, that he is making

now, that he made in the last four years, hurts the whole people of
Israel. People here live in fear.[6]

Margalit then probed Netanyahu over the question of his application to
change his name to Ben Nitai while he was living in the United States
during the 1970s, and whether this meant that he had considered staying there. The subtext to the question was whether or not Netanyahu
was a true Israeli – or merely 'a stranger in a strange land'. Netanyahu
still held American and Israeli citizenship.

Netanyahu responded in a manner suggesting he was hurt by this
question before suffixing his comments with another attack on Peres:

> Not for a single moment. I come from a Jewish, Zionist family,
> with roots here for 100 years. It is not enough, Mr. Peres, to pose
> with children. You have to insure their security.[7]

When the single election debate of the campaign was aired, around 70
per cent of Israelis tuned in to watch it. Several international media
outlets called the debate a draw, with Peres having the better message
and Netanyahu the better presentation. This was not the case in Israel:
when the audience for the debate was polled, the majority believed
that Netanyahu had won. Israeli newspapers called the debate for
Netanyahu, and so too did the voters.

The report of the Labour Party enquiry into its electoral loss
stated that Peres and the Labour Party lost 60,000 voters that night.[8]
Netanyahu either matched or defeated Peres in the three key areas:
best candidate for Prime Minister; credibility; and offering hope. Peres
offered a Richard Nixon in the 1960 debate with John F. Kennedy-style
explanation for his loss. He blamed the lack of correct make-up and the
studio lighting.[9]

After the debate, a confident Netanyahu told his aides that he had
won it, and would win the election. His confidence was well placed.
Prior to the debate, Netanyahu was trailing in the polls; after the
debate he was either tied or ahead. This simple piece of polling data
was confirmed by his own polls, as well as in internal polls for the
Labour Party and in surveys conducted by the Israeli media. One
short, half-hour debate had effectively changed the face of Israeli
politics.

Several local journalists accused Netanyahu of being an actor during the debate, of conducting an elaborate role-play. There was a sense of surprise among the foreign commentators that he had been able to do so well against an experienced, wily old political operator like Peres.

In the final days of the campaign, Netanyahu attempted to convince a sceptical outside world of his good intentions towards the peace process.[10] At the start of the campaign, he had shifted his hawkish position on the Oslo Accords to a slightly more centrist one, arguing that the agreements were signed and therefore binding to the new government. In other words, accepting the facts on the ground. He argued that he would attempt to renegotiate parts of them and would not offer the same concessions as a Peres-led government.[11]

He returned again to his comparison between the Oslo Accords and the British appeasement of Nazi Germany. As he put it:

> Britain understands that the peace does not come at any price. With a dictatorial regime peace can endure only if it is coupled with security. This is a very simple lesson which most Westerners remember well for themselves, but forget for Israel.[12]

This message that Netanyahu continued to put out was that, while he believed the Oslo Accords to be a historic mistake, he would try to make the best of a bad deal.

As the campaign ended and Israelis prepared to go to the polls, it marked the end of an extraordinary six months for Netanyahu. At the end of May 1996, the Rabin assassination had not been forgotten by Israelis, but it appeared to belong to an era that was more distant than the six months that had passed since it took place. During this period, Netanyahu had been able to recover his position from rock bottom to standing on the verge of becoming Israel's youngest Prime Minister.

The 1996 election, like many before it in Israel, was dominated by violence and this fear factor in Israel played into Netanyahu's hand. With Final Status negotiations due to start for real (there had been a largely insignificant opening session prior to the election), Israelis had an eye on the future. Who they wanted to lead the country into these talks with Arafat was central to the thinking of many Israelis. Netanyahu's promise to be tough on Arafat was taken to mean that he would not be willing to offer the same range of concessions as Peres. This went down well with a number of voters.

Above all, and what was most interesting about the campaign, was the change in the political culture of campaigning in Israel. Netanyahu revealed himself, once again, to be hugely influenced by the American-style election culture of fundraising and television politics. The television spots, his theatrical performance in the debate, the hiring of one of the top guns of American right-wing political strategy and the sound bites, all left their marks on Israeli politics.

At times his campaign resembled that of an outsider running for office in Israel. The concentration of the 'I' over the 'We' was an ever-present part of the campaign, which to all intents and purposes took on the characteristics of an American presidential race. Netanyahu had few qualms about planting the flag of American political culture firmly into Israeli soil. It was, after all, what he knew and understood best. Few, if any, other Israeli politicians would have dared to do this in 1996. After 1996, however, this American-style campaigning became the norm in Israel.

As Israelis went to the polls, the two candidates still believed they would win the election. Netanyahu's comeback was impressive, although largely built on present-day fears and concerns about the future.

9

Cheques

In terms of electoral arithmetic Netanyahu's victory in 1996 was based on the failings of the Labour Party. The old adage 'governments lose elections, and opposition don't win them' was never truer. As threatened, thousands of Israeli Arabs failed to show up to vote for Peres; some stayed away from the polls, but others deliberately spoiled their ballot papers in protest over Operation Grapes of Wrath.

By the time Labour Party officials understood the scale of the electoral rebellion on the day of the election, it was too late. Despite frantic helicopter trips to try to convince the leaders of Israel's Arab communities, Peres and Labour failed to get out the vote. For leader and party this represented total disaster.

Netanyahu's careful wooing of Israel's religious leaders proved successful. With the help of Ariel Sharon, Netanyahu devoted considerable energies to convincing them to support him. A number of political cheques were written to these groups, especially the ultra-orthodox Shas movement, pledging more funds for religious schools – and promises of cabinet portfolios.

At the start of the campaign, Peres and Labour had largely ignored the requests of the religious community. The belief was that Peres was a long way ahead in the polls and didn't need them. Late efforts by Peres to repair this political snub fell on deaf ears. Peres's campaign strategy had been on his winning the election from the left and centre-ground secular voters in Israel (including the Israeli Arabs).

The basic reason for his defeat was that he failed to win enough of the centre-ground voters who had backed Rabin in 1992 – many of the new immigrant voters who had supported Rabin in 1992 backed Netanyahu in 1996. Although Peres's margin of defeat appeared small, he lost out in most of the key constituencies that win Israeli elections.

As a result, Netanyahu was elected Prime Minister, without having given major commitments on the peace process. It was a completely different case in internal politics and in putting together his first cabinet, which because of the need to include a large number of small parties in his coalition, would not have as many Likud ministers as the party had hoped.

Netanyahu had a long list of potentially tricky situations to resolve that resulted from the political cheques – also known as promises – he had issued to key senior members of the Likud. At the head of the queue were Dan Meridor and Ariel Sharon, both of whom had proved to be extremely useful to Netanyahu during the campaign. Within the Likud, Meridor and Sharon had large followings and therefore needed to be handled with care.

The left and centre-ground voters saw Meridor as the most credible Likud leader, and so during the campaign he was ushered in to speak to this audience. His most telling intervention in the campaign was his comment arguing that Peres and Labour were becoming more left-wing. 'If you want to know what Labour will really do in the future, we only have to listen to what Meretz is saying today – this is what happened in 1992,' he said.[1]

His comments stuck in the mind of centre-ground voters who were reluctant to openly back Netanyahu, but who were afraid that Peres and the Labour Party would offer too many concessions to Arafat. Meridor acted as Netanyahu's centrist wingman, putting out fires for Netanyahu and emphasizing that the peace process would move forward under a Netanyahu government, albeit at a slower pace. What is more, centrist Israeli voters believed this to be the case when they heard it from Meridor's mouth.

In 1996, the relationship between Netanyahu and Meridor was complicated. Despite his electoral victory, Netanyahu still sensed that there were those in the Likud who might be tempted to dump him in favour of Meridor, if things did not go well for the government. He also believed, correctly, that the Americans preferred Meridor to him as Prime Minister. In truth, by this stage, there was little chance that

Meridor would mount any credible challenge against Netanyahu. Still the idea stuck in the back of Netanyahu's mind.

In the end, Netanyahu gave Meridor the Ministry of Finance. Meridor was not Netanyahu's first choice for the post: he himself harboured hopes of offering it to Yaakov Frenkel, the Governor of the Bank of Israel. Towards the end of the campaign, Netanyahu had outlined an ambitious programme of economic reforms for the Israeli economy and wanted a technocrat such as Frenkel to implement the plan.

Netanyahu's concerns about Meridor were mirrored in his staggeringly poor treatment of Ariel Sharon. During the campaign, Sharon worked energetically to help Netanyahu to secure the religious constituency. He met religious leaders, assured them of Netanyahu's credibility to represent their interests and helped to put a gloss on elements of Netanyahu's private life. In return, Sharon wasn't even offered a cabinet post. Only after the intervention of David Levy was he offered the lowly Ministry of Energy and Water Resources.

In truth, Netanyahu never stopped running for elections. Once an election was out of the way, his attention and strategic antennae turned to the next one. His treatment of Meridor, to whom he would have liked to offer only a junior portfolio, and of Sharon, was based on his political planning for Likud leadership elections, scheduled for the year 2000. Similar treatment was dished out to Moshe Katsav and Benni Begin, both of whom Netanyahu viewed as potential challengers for the leadership in 2000.

On a deeper level, Netanyahu was attempting to illustrate that, having been elected in direct elections for Prime Minister, his mandate was stronger than those of previous leaders who had not been elected in this way. The introduction of the direct election was meant to strengthen the executive, and Netanyahu was attempting to test the boundaries of this new strength.

In his head, Netanyahu envisaged transforming Israeli politics along the lines of the American model. He wanted to create a powerful Prime Minister's office that would include its own national security advisor and powerful teams of advisors – answerable to him. What Netanyahu wanted was, in effect, to create a presidential style of government in Israel with enhanced powers for the executive and less power for the cabinet. As he was soon to discover, this would prove to be impossible. Instead of increasing the power of the Prime Minister, the new electoral system had made it harder for him to form a coalition and to govern the country.

Netanyahu's first job as the winner of the direct election for Prime Minister was to put together a majority of at least 61 members of the Knesset. He approached this task in the spirit of having just been elected 'Emperor of Israel'. In trying to bring some order to what is usually a highly fraught process of forming a governing coalition, Netanyahu and his team imposed a deadline on the negotiations of 17 June.

The process in 1996 had been complicated by the election results for the Knesset that saw the Likud list win only 32 seats, the religious parties doing well, along with a number of smaller parties establishing themselves. On top of this – under new rules – Netanyahu was only allowed to appoint 18 ministers to the cabinet. He understood from the very start that, given the relative number of parties that were required to form a coalition, he would have to give up a lot of these cabinet posts to non-*Likudniks*.

At the outset of his premiership, Netanyahu had to say no to a large number of *Likudniks* who had previously believed they had been in line for a senior position in the government. This did not bode well for him in the future. Netanyahu tried to smooth it over as best he could with key supporters of his who failed to get a job. This did not always work to quell the sense of rebellion in the party.

Some of the *Likudniks* who were overlooked for a cabinet post were promised chairs of the major committees in the Knesset, others key ambassadorships, but many were simply left out in the political wilderness. Resentment, envy and a sense of betrayal characterized the feelings of the disgruntled *Likudniks*, many of whom vowed to plot against their leader at the earliest opportunity.

Netanyahu revealed his political inexperience at almost every juncture of the process in forming his government. His seeming over-generosity to the religious parties in offering a large number of cabinet portfolios to them at the expense of his Likud colleagues was a bridge too far for many in his own party. The National Religious Party (NRP) was singled out for particular generosity as Netanyahu felt the need to reward the Likud's true coalition partners. The NRP had openly called upon its supporters to vote for Netanyahu.

Netanyahu defended his coalition policies to his Likud colleagues, arguing that he had ensured that members of it would occupy the top three ministries in the government: defence, foreign affairs and finance. The Ministry of Defence went to Yitzhak Mordechai, whom Netanyahu had selected for the job after Mordechai retired from the senior ranks of the IDF. Shimon Peres had tried to persuade Mordechai to join the Labour Party, but was unwilling to offer him the promise of a top job in a Labour government.

As a result, Mordechai opened negotiations with Netanyahu who offered him more favourable terms, which Mordechai quickly accepted. In the Likud primaries prior to the start of the official election campaign, Mordechai finished top of the list (as leader, Netanyahu did not have to run). This high poll finish helped confirm that Mordechai would be Minister of Defence in the Netanyahu government. During the election campaign, the presence of Mordechai on the Likud ticket helped deflect attacks from the Labour Party about Netanyahu's lack of experience on security issues.

Netanyahu was generally content with his appointment of Mordechai, but he had considerable qualms about making David Levy the Minister of Foreign Affairs. In reality, in 1996 Netanyahu had few alternatives other than to appoint his old political nemesis. Prior to the election, Levy and Netanyahu had publicly buried the hatchet. Levy's Gesher movement joined the Likud list along with another party to the political right of the Likud, Tsomet.

The agreement, between Likud–Gesher–Tsomet and signed on 12 March 1996, was self-serving for Netanyahu. It had removed the two alternative right-wing candidates from the race for Prime Minister (David Levy and the leader of Tsomet, Rafael Eitan). It also meant that it added to the number of seats the joint list could win in the Knesset elections. The 32 seats it eventually won was considered by all to have been a major disappointment.

The agreement did help give the impression of a unified Likud camp, in contrast to the 1992 election – in which the divisions on the right helped give Rabin and the Labour Party its narrow victory, at coalition level. Many in the Likud, however, had flagged concerns as to what Netanyahu was willing to give to Gesher and Tsomet in order to reach the electoral deal.

The agreement led to 14 safe slots in the Likud lists being handed over to Gesher and Tsomet. Several national Likud leaders recorded their unease at the move. Netanyahu brushed off the criticism.

His supporters reminded the Likud that if Netanyahu were not elected Prime Minister there would be nobody from the Likud in the government.

Gesher and Tsomet were much happier. They both received good slots for their candidates on the Likud list and the price of the withdrawal, of Levy and Eitan from the race to be Prime Minister, was not high. Neither candidate looked likely to make it past the first round of voting.

The agreement revealed the lengths to which Netanyahu was willing to go to secure his success, even if this meant damaging the prospects of members of the Likud. Indeed, despite his lofty rhetoric on the values and history of the Likud, Netanyahu viewed the party as little more than a vehicle to the premiership.

The pre-election deals with Levy and Eitan, and the post-election process of forming the governing coalition, exposed his intention to circumvent the interest of the parties for his own agenda. At the time this was something quite new in Israel and many people, *Likudniks* among them, hoped he would fail in this project.

Whatever the motives of Netanyahu in his electoral coalitions, he found himself in what was essentially a marriage of convenience with Levy as Minister of Foreign Affairs. It was a flashback to the end to the Madrid Peace Conference, in that Netanyahu feared Levy would be too soft on the Palestinians. In planning for future talks with Arafat and the PLO, Netanyahu told his advisors he wanted to make sure that all substantive decisions and policymaking in this area emanated from the Prime Minister's office.

With almost all of the governing coalition jigsaw pieces in place, Netanyahu was faced with having to smooth over things with Levy as he once again threatened to resign if the deal to bring Sharon into the government was not fully implemented. There had been a slight delay, but Levy's actions were a crisp reminder of the problems that lay ahead for Netanyahu.

While Netanyahu was conducting his complex coalition talks, a joke circulating in the Labour Party had it that Netanyahu had asked Peres to continue to run Israel until he had figured out what to do with the country. It was based on an old joke from 1977, when the Labour Party had made a similar quip about Menachem Begin. There were, however, increasing concerns as to when all the electoral politics would finish and the world would see what Netanyahu was like as a leader, rather than merely a person who knew how to get himself elected.

For Netanyahu, the period following his election victory could be summed up by the phrase 'lurching from crisis to crisis'. Surely his government would fare better. Or would it?

PART FOUR

Power

10

Arafat's Hand

On 4 September 1996, in a small, plain room in a nondescript office block at an Israeli army base at the Erez Checkpoint in Gaza, Benjamin Netanyahu met Yasser Arafat for the first time. Netanyahu arrived for the meeting looking tense and was greeted by a small, but vocal demonstration from members of Peace Now, an Israeli activist group. Arafat soon followed and both men, along with their respective teams, sat across the table from one another. The room was eerily quiet except for the noise of cameras clicking and the murmur of Palestinian security officers.

On the Israeli side, Netanyahu's foreign policy advisor, Dore Gold, who sat two places to the right of Netanyahu, didn't know where to look. He glanced nervously across the table before looking back at the Prime Minister. Eventually, as if to try to end the unbearable tension, Netanyahu and Arafat stood, extended their arms and shook hands. Netanyahu looked directly at Arafat and then turned his head to the camera and with a slight frown on his face sat down.

After the cameras stopped clicking there was silence, which was only interrupted by a mobile phone ringing. Netanyahu once again turned his head and looked directly towards the TV cameras with a vacant, distant expression as if to suggest that he would rather be anywhere else in the world than in this room.

Cynics, critics and political enemies of Netanyahu accused him of play-acting for the cameras: a theatrical performance to match those from earlier in his career. There was speculation as to whether he had rehearsed the handshake, his body language and the frown to make sure that his performance set exactly the tone he wanted to transmit to the watching world.

No matter how pre-planned or otherwise, the handshake with Arafat was a decisive moment in his life. Nothing for him would be the same again, and everything that had happened to his family in the past would need to be looked at through a new reality.

As the meeting broke up, Netanyahu gave a very run-of-the-mill statement to the waiting world press:

> After my talks today here I can observe that both parties reiterate their commitment to the interim agreement and their determination to carry out its implementation. However, I would like to emphasize that we have to take into account the needs and the requirements of both sides on the basis of reciprocity and the assurance of the security and well-being of both Israelis and Palestinian alike.

He then went on to try to reassure the Palestinians (and through them the Clinton administration):

> I have heard in the Palestinian press and Palestinian quarters that my intention is to fragment, to break up the agreement. This is not true. This is not our intention. We want to advance the issues of concern to all of us and we want to do so in such ways to facilitate negotiations on the final status.
>
> I also want to make clear that our position is to not only move on the peace process but to also improve the prosperity and economic conditions of the Palestinian population.
>
> We think that prosperity and peace go hand in hand and I believe that we can advance to achieve both goals for the benefit of both peoples.

The link between peace and economic advancement was a nice touch. One of the major complaints of the Palestinians was that the peace process had not improved its economic wellbeing; rather, the economic difficulties had got worse. Arafat and the PA blamed this on the closures imposed by the Rabin and Peres-led governments on the Gaza Strip and West Bank that followed attacks on Israel by Palestinian groups.

The ice had been broken, the taboo ended, and for Netanyahu he would no longer have to try to dodge the Arafat question.

It had been the question that almost every journalist had asked him since he had taken office on 18 June 1996: would he meet with the head of the Palestinian Authority, Yasser Arafat? During the election campaign, Netanyahu had stated that he would avoid meeting Arafat unless absolutely necessary. The ambiguity of the statement lay in the fact that an Israeli Prime Minister who wished to continue with the implementation of the Interim Agreement would have to meet with Arafat.

Given the obsession of the media about the potential for a meeting with Arafat, Netanyahu had decided to arrange it sooner rather than later. During his first visit to the United States as Prime Minister at the start of July 1996 Netanyahu met with President Clinton on 9 July. Clinton was keen to hear Netanyahu commit himself and his government to fully implementing the next stage of the Interim Agreement, which centred on Hebron.

At the press conference that followed their lunchtime meeting, the first question Netanyahu received focused on the land-for-peace formula, a withdrawal from Hebron and the possibility of a meeting with Arafat. Netanyahu answered the first two parts of the question, but chose to ignore the third. The journalist repeated the final part of the question: Are you willing to meet with Mr Arafat? Do you plan to meet with Mr Arafat soon?

Netanyahu replied evasively:

Well, as you know, we have on-going contacts with Mr. Arafat and with the Palestinian Authority. I have my own representatives who have been meeting with him on a regular basis. And we'll expand these contacts, both in frequency and the level of the personnel involved. I said that if I deem it necessary for peace or for the interest of Israel to meet Arafat, I won't rule it out, and I have not changed my position.[1]

The 'will he, won't he' question refused to go away over the summer holiday season. For the international journalists, the question of a potential meeting led to huge coverage about the issue in the media during the relatively quiet news cycle of August.

Privately, Netanyahu had long made up his mind that he would meet with Arafat, but he liked the drama. In building the suspense, Netanyahu hoped that his eventual meeting with Arafat would be perceived by the Clinton administration as an Israeli concession in the Palestinian peace process. It proved to be a not wholly unsuccessful strategy.

Throughout the period from the start of the Netanyahu government up to the handshake with Arafat, the world's media had been full of the bite-size chunks of the Netanyahu life story. It resembled a 'Netanyahu made simple' guide or an 'everything you wanted to know about the Prime Minister of Israel, but were afraid to ask' session. To some extent, the international press was still playing catch-up with the personal narrative and character of the man most had written off less than a year earlier.

Over and over again the journalistic profiles published at the time focused on the impact on Netanyahu of the death of his older brother Yonatan (Yoni) – killed during the Entebbe raid in 1976. Benjamin Netanyahu's tough line against terrorism, and Yasser Arafat in particular, was said to have originated from his brother's death.

The reality of the impact of Yonatan on Benjamin, however, is much more complex than first meets the eye. It was not only in the area of terrorism that Yoni's death became linked to the development of Netanyahu's philosophy and outlook on the world.

As is the case with many families with two or more boys, Netanyahu worshipped his older brother, who was the son that the family felt was most likely to succeed. Benjamin was the middle brother, with Iddo the younger brother. As the middle brother, Benjamin did not feel as pressured to succeed as Yonatan. For Yonatan the route to military, academic and political advancement was clearly laid out.

In Israel success is measured in a different way from the United States or Europe. In Israeli terms, it meant enjoying a successful career in the IDF before completing a postgraduate degree overseas, and then going into national politics or senior management in a business corporation. Those who served in the senior ranks of the army were often offered top level positions in the major political parties and in the government. The Israeli expression 'political parachuting' essentially meant being given a senior political role soon after leaving the IDF.

The Netanyahu family hoped their eldest son would one day be promoted to the rank of general, potentially then to become the Chief of Staff of the IDF, before transferring into politics and becoming Prime Minister. Far-fetched ambitions perhaps, but Benjamin Netanyahu believed that everything could be achieved by his brother. The career path of one of Yonatan's contemporaries, Ehud Barak, followed this exact route.

The young Benjamin Netanyahu was happy to share his family's hopes for his elder brother. His own interests were being drawn in different directions such as architecture and subsequently business. He hoped that his success would be measured by his wealth. Given his early acquired taste for top-notch restaurants and his enjoyment of a more materialistic, American lifestyle, his financial ambitions were not surprising.

With Yonatan identified as a rising star in the ranks of the IDF – along with Ehud Barak – the pressure and the spotlight were off Benjamin, who made the most of his time studying in the United States and starting to develop a career in business management. Possessed of good organizational skills, the determined and hugely ambitious middle son looked set for a successful career in business ventures that spanned the United States and Israel.

As Yonatan fought in the front line against the Syrians in the 1973 Yom Kippur War and Palestinian terrorism, his younger brother never matched his exploits in the army. By normal Israeli standards of military success, however, Benjamin was no failure. He served in the most prestigious commando unit, *Sayeret Matkal*, and took part in one of its most famous rescue operations.

On 9 May 1972, 16 members of *Sayeret Matkal* took part in the operation to end the hijacking of Sabena flight 571. Led by Ehud Barak, the commandos, disguised as technicians and wearing white overalls, stormed the aircraft at Lod Airport (later renamed Ben-Gurion Airport). Netanyahu was wounded in the exchange, when the gun of one of his fellow commandos went off by mistake. The passengers were rescued (although one, Miriam Anderson, later died from wounds sustained during the exchange of fire). The hijackers were either killed or arrested.

Despite this stunningly successful rescue operation, Benjamin Netanyahu's army service remained overshadowed by his big brother's. In truth, the younger Netanyahu had little problem with this. He was proud of Yonatan's military service and wanted to emulate him and to serve Israel, but he didn't display any signs of jealousy or demand greater recognition from his family for his own military record.

Instead, Benjamin tried to learn everything he could from his older brother. This was not confined to military matters. Considered by some to have been something of a philosopher and deep thinker, Yonatan passed on his knowledge to his brother either while he was home on leave or in letters.

Central to his thoughts was the feeling that it was better to live continually by the sword than to lose the State of Israel, a loss that would have meant the Jews becoming once again a stateless people wandering from country to country.

Fundamentally, Yonatan believed that you should never give in to terrorism. There could be no compromise with those who wished to destroy the nation. The young Benjamin was in complete agreement with his brother, and believed that a strong and robust system of deterrents was crucial to Israel's survival. Events in 1973 confirmed their belief.

When the Yom Kippur War started on 6 October 1973 with the surprise attack by Egyptian and Syrian forces on Israel, Benjamin Netanyahu was studying in the United States. According to Israeli sources, Yonatan telephoned him to tell him that there was heavy fighting in the south along the Suez Canal area and in the north on the Golan Heights.[2]

Like many Israelis based in the United States in 1973, Netanyahu rushed to try to get back to Israel. This was no easy task, with thousands of Israelis at the airport in New York. Amid chaotic scenes, Netanyahu managed to board a flight for Tel Aviv. Back in Israel he found much of the country in a state of shock.

Questions about how the Egyptian and Syrian forces had been able to mount a coordinated attack on Israel without Israeli intelligence seemingly getting wind of it would come later. For now, it was clear that Israel was involved in a battle for its survival, and that the first days of the war had not gone well.

Benjamin Netanyahu played a minor role in the war. Yonatan, on the other hand, was in the thick of the battles on the Golan Heights. His reputation as a brave and tenacious fighter, and good leader of men, was further enhanced in the battles he fought on the Golan. For much of the time, Syrian forces intent on taking back the land they had lost in the 1967 Six Day War heavily outnumbered Yonatan's men.

Eventually, the tide of the war turned in Israel's favour and, with the help of military equipment flown in from the United States, the IDF was able to push the Egyptians and Syrians back before a UN ceasefire brought an end to the war. Although Israel emerged victorious, few Israelis recall the war in that light. Israel paid a high price to secure its survival: approximately 2,500 dead and more than 7,000 wounded. The lessons of the war would eventually be learned, but the impact on the politics of Israel was felt almost immediately.

In the Netanyahu family the very different war experiences of Yonatan and Benjamin arguably confirmed the belief that it would be the highly decorated eldest son who would go on to become a senior officer in the IDF, and from there parachute into national politics. It was also clear that if Benjamin ever wanted to enter politics, he would do so by more traditional civilian routes.

At this stage, however, Benjamin showed little interest in joining the political fray. At the end of the war he returned to the United States to finish his studies. After this, his aim was a very American one: to make money in business. Despite fulfilling his patriotic duty to Israel during the war, his mindset and career objectives were much more American-centric than Israeli. To all intents and purposes, he appeared to have settled for a life and a career in the United States.

Netanyahu's main connection with his homeland was in his efforts to defend Israel and its policies in campus debates and later in the local media. From the outset, it was clear that he was something of a natural, engaging in debates with students and academics (including, on one occasion, the eminent Palestinian scholar Edward Said).

The local Israeli organizers of the debates could see straightaway that Netanyahu was in his element. He was also apparently without nerves. What Netanyahu refused to do was to be an effective spokesman for the Labour Party-led Israeli government. He objected to many of the policies of the government, believing them to be too soft and out of touch with reality.

With his family's close connection to the revisionist Zionist movement along with the hawkish rhetoric he employed in debate, it was clear that Benjamin Netanyahu was a disciple of Menachem Begin and the Likud. The Likud had been formed by an alliance of several right-wing parties prior to the 1973 Knesset elections: Herut, the Liberal Party, the Free Centre, the National List and the Movement for Greater Israel.

The merging of these parties into one single party was seen as the best opportunity of challenging the Labour Party which had ruled Israel (in various guises) since 1948. This was soon put to the test in the 1973 Knesset elections which had originally been postponed because of the Yom Kippur War. When the rescheduled elections eventually took place on 31 December 1973, the Likud won 39 seats, which represented a significant increase from the combined number of votes the parties that eventually made up the Likud gained in the 1969 election. Although the Alignment (Labour Party and Mapam) won 51 seats, this total was down five seats from the previous election.

The results didn't represent an electoral earthquake, but they did indicate that one day, perhaps soon, it was possible that Menachem Begin, who had been leader of the opposition in the Knesset since 1948, would become Prime Minister. There were many complex, long-term reasons for the decline of the Labour Party, but its apparent failure to successfully manage the Yom Kippur War and Israel's security was at the forefront of people's minds.[3] In simple political terms, the fortunes of the Likud were on the up, and those of the Labour Party were in decline.

Benjamin Netanyahu shared the feelings of many Israelis that the government had let down the nation in the period prior to and during the Yom Kippur War. In his debates, he called for clear Israeli responses to the status of the Occupied Territories. With the political process of change back in Israel starting to gather momentum as the Labour-led government lurched from one crisis to another, opportunities would soon present themselves for the young Netanyahu.

Ben Nitai, as he preferred to call himself in the United States, was still undertaking all of these political activities as something of a hobby when, on 27 June 1976, an Air France aeroplane was reported to have been hijacked en route from Athens to Paris. The plane had originally departed Tel Aviv with a stopover in Athens before flying on to the French capital. The hijackers were from the Popular Front for the Liberation of Palestine (PFLP) and from German revolutionary groups.

After being diverted to Benghazi in Libya, it flew on to its final destination, Entebbe in Uganda. As was the norm, the hijackers demanded the release of pro-Palestinian militants, many of whom were held in Israeli jails. Despite Israel's policy of not negotiating with terrorists, Israeli Prime Minister Yitzhak Rabin authorized negotiations to be opened – in order to gain an extension of the deadline before the hijackers started killing the hostages. That extension, from 1 to 4 July, helped give the IDF time to put together a daring rescue plan.

Operation Thunderbolt was a bold attempt to rescue the hostages by flying a unit of Israeli commandos to Uganda who would storm the terminal and free those being held. At the same time, another group of commandos was to disable the Ugandan Air Force planes that might have provided a threat to the Israeli aircraft. In the complex plan, which featured many of the top Israeli soldiers of their generation, Yonatan Netanyahu was put in command of the reconnaissance unit. His men were given the responsibility of storming the airport terminal where the hostages were being held.

With time running out for the hostages, the Israeli government gave the green light for the operation to go ahead. As Yonatan Netanyahu was sitting in an Israeli Air Force plane making its way down to Entebbe, Benjamin was in the United States continuing his studies. The contrast between the two couldn't have been greater: Yonatan making final preparations for operations; Benjamin, thousands of miles away, with no idea that the Israelis were about to undertake a last-minute rescue mission.

The rescue operation went better than the IDF and the political leadership had dared hope. Three hostages were killed and several injured: a much lower figure than the planners of the operation had feared. The sole fatality among the Israeli forces was Yonatan Netanyahu, who was killed by a shot from a Ugandan soldier stationed in the control tower. The loss of Yonatan overshadowed a hugely successful military operation that became one of the most famous in Israeli history.

The death of his older brother remains to this day the worst thing to have happened to Benjamin Netanyahu, who took it upon himself to inform his parents of the news of Yonatan's death. It is sometimes a little simplistic to suggest that the death of a close family member is life-changing for the family, but for Benjamin Netanyahu this was very much the case. There are two quite distinct Benjamin Netanyahu characters: the one before his brother's death and the one after it.

In the aftermath of his brother's death, Netanyahu vowed to achieve everything that Yonatan had been destined to do. Gone was the slightly goofy wanderer who sought a career in business management; now Netanyahu's ambitions shifted to protecting his brother's legacy.

The importance of legacy is something that Netanyahu has always had one eye on. From there, he wished to develop Yonatan's legacy into something practical that could serve Israel and the world. Lofty ambitions indeed, but Netanyahu had a clear plan and a vision as to how to make it happen.

His plans involved the setting up of the 'Jonathan Institute' in memory of his brother. The work of the institute focused on research on counter-terrorism strategies and the dissemination of this work within Israel and to international audiences. The institute became internationally known when, in the summer of 1979, it hosted its first international conference on terrorism, which Netanyahu had energetically organized.

In retrospect, the list of speakers makes for impressive reading. Netanyahu had pulled out all the stops, using his contacts from the United States to draw in big names: George H. W. Bush, George Shultz, Jeane Kirkpatrick, Ed Meese and William Webster all came from the US to attend the conference.[4] From Israel, Yitzhak Rabin and Moshe Arens were present, and the Israeli Prime Minister Menachem Begin addressed the conference.

From the American side, the list read like a who's who of the era of the administration of President Ronald Reagan. For Netanyahu, the conference – and others he subsequently organized – offered an excellent networking opportunity for him to further develop contacts with the Republican Party in the United States.

Almost everybody who attended the initial conference had heard of Yonatan, and knew the story of the Entebbe raid. Few of them, however, knew much about his younger brother, Benjamin Netanyahu. All of this was about to change.

Netanyahu's attitude towards terrorism was born out of the death of Yonatan. His writings and speeches on the topic pointed to a deeply held belief that it was morally wrong to talk to terrorists. Even after he was elected Prime Minister in 1996, his position on terrorism had still not undergone any revision.

In essence, he still believed that a military and economic solution was possible for ridding the world of terrorist organizations. Militarily, this meant attacking the infrastructure and personnel of those organizations; economically, it meant stopping the supply of funds to them.

So, as Netanyahu stood up and reached out to shake Arafat's hand on 4 September 1996, he still felt that he was letting his family down by shaking the hand of the man he regarded as the godfather of international terrorism. To some extent Netanyahu was acting for the assembled Israeli and international press, but his loathing of Yasser Arafat was very real.

This did not bode well for the peace process, and specifically for the negotiations that were due to start concerning an IDF withdrawal from Hebron.

Hebron

Busy, noisy and a vitally important centre of Palestinian trade, Hebron, the largest city in the West Bank, is considered by Jews and Muslims alike as holy. As a result, the city has a long history of violence between the religious groups fighting for control of its holy sites and the rest of the city.

In 1996, a complex deal needed to be negotiated over its status by the Israeli government and the Palestinian Authority as part of the implementation of the Interim Agreement. Hebron was a present from Peres and the Labour Party to the Netanyahu government. Peres's decision to postpone the withdrawal was a sensible move on his part prior to the elections, but it put Netanyahu in a markedly difficult position.

Still finding his feet as Prime Minister, and with his almost daily mistakes being gloated over by a hostile Israeli press, Netanyahu tried to set the parameters of future negotiations in an extended interview in the Israeli daily newspaper *Haaretz*, which was published on 22 November 1996. In response to a question about Hebron from the journalist Avi Shavit, Netanyahu attempted to put the best possible gloss on the prospect of leaving Hebron:

> We are not cutting ourselves off from Hebron. We are redeploying there. What I have been working hard to achieve over the past few weeks is precisely to ensure that we protect the lives of the Jews in Hebron and maintain our holy sites in the city.[1]

This was followed by a familiar tactic, the use of historical and personal references to the place which was a hallmark of Netanyahu's tactics with the press:

> Nevertheless, the arrangement in Hebron is extremely difficult for me since I have a deep bond to these places. They speak to me. Every stone, every terrace, every tree and every hill raises memories, connects me to a very real historical experience of which I feel an inseparable part.
>
> I cannot understand why we tend to have great respect for the Arabs' bond to the land, which is relatively recent, while at the same time disparaging our own bond to the land, which goes back thousands of years.[2]

Despite Netanyahu's apparent personal connection to Hebron, the biggest problem he faced was not over the future of the city. Indeed, the problem could have been applied to his policies towards the peace process as a whole, Palestinian and Syrian. In essence, Netanyahu had to please two masters who were demanding very different things from him: his cabinet and the Clinton administration in the United States. Netanyahu spent much of his first period in office trying to balance these conflicting demands.

With a party, a cabinet and a wider coalition that were widely opposed to making any additional territorial compromises with the Palestinians, and who didn't like the idea of handing over to Syria even a single part of the Golan Heights, Netanyahu found himself in something of a political jam. Given the importance of Hebron to Judaism, Netanyahu was particularly keen not to be seen to give it up without a fight.

Although only just elected as Prime Minister, Netanyahu already had one eye on the next elections, scheduled for 2000. He was aware, from electoral data from the 1996 election, that the religious votes had been instrumental in giving him his victory over Peres. The last thing he wished to do was alienate this constituency, the leaders of which have long memories.

To complicate matters over Hebron, Netanyahu showed his political inexperience in making a series of mistakes and misreading key situations. In the initial stages of his premiership he looked like a bull in a china shop, who didn't fathom the extent of the damage he was about to cause, not least to his own prospects. Dealing with Hebron would have been difficult enough for Peres and Labour, but for Netanyahu it came close to terminally damaging him.

The negotiations over Hebron were protracted and characterized by a deep feeling of distrust between the parties. It was soon apparent that the negotiators whom Netanyahu dispatched to the talks were not experts in the Oslo Accords, and specifically the Interim Agreements.

Many of the Palestinian delegation were veterans of the original negotiations in Oslo and all the subsequent stages of implementing the agreements. To some extent, this provided the Palestinians with an early advantage as the Israeli delegation struggled to get up to speed.

Several members of the Israeli delegation initially regarded their Palestinian counterparts as essentially unrepentant and unreformed PLO terrorists. The Israelis were curt, dictatorial and suspicious. All this reflected Netanyahu's unease at having to continue with the implementation of an agreement, which he believed in terms of its security provision for Israel contained as many holes as a Swiss cheese.

If Netanyahu had harboured any hopes of being able to renegotiate parts of the agreement he was soon disappointed, as both the Palestinians demanded, and the Americans requested, that he continue where Peres and Labour had left off. It was at this point that Netanyahu found himself having to work overtime on his speeches and comments to please his two paradoxical masters: his cabinet and the United States.

In Jerusalem, the Likud remained in a state of dazed confusion and was slowly coming to terms with the price the party had paid in getting Netanyahu elected as Prime Minister. Those few *Likudniks* who held cabinet positions made it clear that they would not be bound by collective responsibility and would reject an Israeli withdrawal from Hebron. Other Likud MKs paced the Knesset's corridors plotting their strategies for undermining Netanyahu if he brought a bad deal on Hebron before them.

In Washington, the Clinton administration remained deeply uneasy and uncomfortable with the Netanyahu-led government. President Clinton, however, did not want to overplay his hand and apply too much pressure on Netanyahu, which the administration argued could be counter-productive. Instead, Clinton tried to quietly chaperone the two parties and encourage them to come to an agreement over Hebron.

Netanyahu's stalling tactics became a major facet of the negotiations. His motives in doing this were twofold: to try to garner support for a deal among his sceptical cabinet and party, and to limit the amount of land that Israel would have to redeploy from as part of any deal over Hebron. Needless to say, his tactics frustrated and then infuriated the Clinton administration which was hoping that the Israelis and Palestinians would soon be able to move to the final part of the peace process, namely final status talks.

In the meantime, Netanyahu saved his hard-line statements on the peace process for meetings of the Likud Central Committee. There he spoke with passion, and articulated Israel's claim to the lands. In doing this, he was trying to present himself to the party as much more hawkish on the peace process than his actions as Prime Minister indicated. These speeches would often focus on Jerusalem, and Israel's right to build wherever it wanted in the city.[3]

Eventually, a deal was reached on Hebron and initialled by the chief Israeli negotiator, Dan Shomron, and his Palestinian counterpart, Saeb Erekat, on 15 January 1997. The next day, the Knesset approved the Hebron Protocol by 87 to 17 (with one abstention). The opposition Labour Party provided a political safety net for Netanyahu by voting in favour of the Hebron Protocol. The IDF completed its redeployment from Hebron on the same day as the Knesset vote.

Questioned about the agreement, Netanyahu was keen to downplay its historical significance for the Likud and to offer assurances that it would not have ramifications for settlement building. In response to a question on this topic from a journalist, Netanyahu gave an intriguing and, in the second part of his answer, highly misleading reply:

> I've said that it is not the Likud that has changed, it is the reality that has changed. We've found, on the eve of the elections, a different reality, facts on the ground that were created by the previous government, and agreements that were reached by the previous government.
>
> We said that we would honour these agreements, providing of course, the other side honours them as well, and we recognize the facts. We cannot put our head in the sand and say, well, they're not in Kalkilya, or the Palestinian Authority is not in Jericho, and so on.

We have sought, as we promised, to fashion a different reality and a different outcome from these distressing conditions. I think the Hebron Agreement proves that that is possible, because we modified it, or rather modified it through implementation, through the details, to be a safer and better agreement.

And I think the post-Hebron agreement, in particular, where we, I think, received degrees of freedom of negotiation that were not present there before, proves that we can achieve a better result towards the end. So I wouldn't go through this line that is now very fashionable [about] the end of the Likud, the end of ideology.

Leadership always is the meeting ground between vision and reality. Between ideology and practicality. It is not something that is new in the world. It's not something that is new to us.[4]

On the question of settlement expansion, he said:

We have a declared policy on the Jewish communities in Judea and Samaria. We have said that we would enable them to grow and prosper. We have not said that we would build additional settlements. We have said that we would consider that if the issue became appropriate.[5]

The figures appeared to indicate a job well done by Netanyahu in getting the deal over Hebron and the IDF redeployment passed. With the Labour Party promising to support the ratification, the Knesset was the least of the problems for Netanyahu. In cabinet, he had struggled to convince his colleagues about the merits of the deal, only winning the vote by ten to seven after a marathon session.[6]

The stick with which Netanyahu threatened his government and the Likud was the prospect that he could dissolve the government and form a national unity government with the Labour Party. The Israeli media was full of speculation that Netanyahu was tempted to look towards a new coalition with his old army commander, Ehud Barak, who had succeeded Shimon Peres as leader of the Labour Party.

Netanyahu tried to remind everybody that as the first directly elected Prime Minister he should be able to exert more power over the cabinet and the coalition than previous Israeli prime ministers. This may have been the intention of those who had favoured the shift to the direct election of Prime Minister (including Netanyahu), but the end result was very different.

Two developments in the first quarter of 1997 confirmed the difficulties that Netanyahu faced, and the problems he confronted in balancing the conflicting demands of his government against the continued pressure from Washington – who were calling for the pace of the peace process to pick up. As Netanyahu sat at his desk on the top floor of the Prime Minister's office in Jerusalem, he decided to use a very simple political tactic to reassure his hawkish supporters that he was still their man.

A deal to hand over additional land to the Palestinians in the West Bank was agreed as part of the implementation of the Oslo Accords. Netanyahu, however, agreed to hand over only 9 per cent, and not the 25 to 39 per cent that the Palestinians were expecting.

Netanyahu's move was aimed at appeasing his cabinet and the Likud. It signalled his intention to continue with the implementation of the agreements with the Palestinians, while at the same time trying to hand over as little as possible additional land to them prior to final status talks.

His plans to appease the cabinet and the Likud almost came unstuck. Once again, he had misjudged the political temperature of the cabinet in particular. As a result, Netanyahu was forced to endure a series of hostile cabinet sessions with many of his minsters leaking details of the meetings to the Israeli press.

Ariel Sharon led the cabinet rebellion to the handover, arguing that no land from Area C of the West Bank (under Israeli rule and where most of the Israeli settlements were located) should be handed over to the Palestinians prior to final status talks. Eventually, Netanyahu limped over the finish line and won cabinet ratification for the withdrawal by ten votes to six. This was the end of this particular story, but the beginning of an even bigger one that threatened Netanyahu and some of his closest political colleagues.

In order to win the cabinet vote, Netanyahu had been forced to buy the support of some of the religious ministers by agreeing to a package of measures. The price that Netanyahu was willing to pay for their support was, in retrospect, quite shocking. It was a clear indication of just how politically weak and isolated he was at the time.

The package included his support for the construction of a new Jewish housing project (meaning settlement) in East Jerusalem. With his efforts at appeasing the right-wing in Israel by only handing over

9 per cent of the West Bank having backfired, he viewed Jerusalem as a safe bet to reassure the constituency. He understood that the majority of the opposition Labour Party would also support the building of 6,500 new homes. In terms of Israeli internal politics it would not cause him many problems.

Outside of Israel, it was a very different story. When the ministerial committee approved the decision to start construction at Har Homa on 26 February 1997, the Palestinians were furious. There were violent demonstrations and Arafat effectively froze the peace process with Israel. The Clinton administration were publicly dismayed about the decision, particularly its timing. In private, President Clinton increasingly questioned Netanyahu's commitment to the peace process.

To complicate matters, a political scandal broke in what became known as the Bar-On Affair. During this dismal and murky episode, Netanyahu, the director of his Prime Minister's office, Avigdor Lieberman, and the Minister of Justice, Tzachi Hanegbi, were all placed under investigation over an alleged plea-bargain deal concerning the leader of Shas.[7]

The deal would have seen Shas ministers supporting or abstaining in the cabinet vote on the Hebron deal from earlier in the year, in exchange for a plea bargain for Aryeh Deri, the leader of Shas, who was eventually convicted of corruption charges in 1999. For a time, it looked like Netanyahu was in deep trouble with the police.

Both the Israeli and international media provided detailed coverage of the investigation. The key decision centred upon whether Netanyahu would be indicted and face criminal charges. In such a scenario, he would have had little choice other than to resign, and if convicted by the courts his political career would have been over.

In reality, any case against Netanyahu was shaky. There was little evidence to link him to the deal. On 21 April 1997, prosecutors dropped the investigation into the Prime Minister, but only after he was questioned at length by police officers.

The period of the investigation had been one of the darkest of Netanyahu's career, with a hostile press using alleged leaks from the investigation to stir anti-Netanyahu sentiments. The lasting impression of the affair was that Netanyahu wasn't corrupt, but that the lines between legitimate political bargaining and criminal activity were becoming more blurred.

The Bar-On Affair also provided tangible evidence that the Netanyahu administration was lurching from one crisis to another. Everything Netanyahu did appeared to go wrong. A hostile press, which hoped his fall from power would be imminent, fuelled the sense of crisis. More often than not, Netanyahu's wounds were self-inflicted: a product of his inexperience and lack of clear strategic thinking and planning. He increasingly appeared to be reacting to events rather than setting the agenda.

The election of Ehud Barak as leader of the Labour Party presented Netanyahu with additional problems. Without ever saying as much, since assuming office Netanyahu had tried to position himself as the natural successor to Israel's first Prime Minister, Ben-Gurion, and Yitzhak Rabin, albeit the pre-Oslo version of the murdered Prime Minister. Central to Netanyahu's path was his attempt to outline a vision of what in effect was 'Netanyahuism'. Rather than use a clumsy 'ism' suffix, however, Netanyahu preferred to call it 'the third way'.

The closest he came to outlining this pathway was in an address at the National Defence College on 4 August 1997. The annual speech to the graduates of the defence college is seen as an opportunity for Israeli leaders to outline their vision and hopes for the future. Netanyahu concluded his remarks with the following vision:

> Between 'rose garden' dreams on the one hand, and paranoia and isolation on the other, there is a golden path of realism, of realpolitik. This is the path that Israel chose beginning in the Ben-Gurion era, and this must be our choice today. If we know when to compromise, when to grasp opportunities and when to display determination and decisiveness, we can bring peace with security to our country and our people.[8]

Earlier in the speech Netanyahu had talked of Rabin's demands of the Palestinians:

> The late Yitzhak Rabin made it clear, even before signing the Oslo Agreements, that the Palestinians must vigorously battle terrorism and amend the Palestinian Charter, before Israel can undertake withdrawals from territories. For the past four years, our partners have completely ignored these commitments.[9]

A third way, clearly identified with Ben-Gurion and Rabin, was the political ground that Netanyahu wanted to occupy. With the entry of Barak into the fray, this became all the more difficult than when the more dovish Shimon Peres led the Labour Party. As was evident later, from their time working together in government, there was not much political difference between Netanyahu and Barak in key areas of foreign policymaking.

The entry of Barak caused overcrowding in the centre ground in Israeli politics, for Barak also viewed himself as the natural heir to Rabin and the notion of the third way. The trouble for Netanyahu was that much of Barak's party were quite content with Barak's outlook on the peace process.

Netanyahu himself did not enjoy such a luxury. Many of the senior leaders and much of the rank and file of the Likud were far from reconciled to any third way pragmatic policy. From their perspective, they wanted Netanyahu to stop making worthless concessions to Arafat and the Palestinian Authority.

Netanyahu was faced with having to match his pragmatic third way approach with the need to speak to his political base. A perfect example of this took place a month after his speech to the National Defence College. On 5 September 1997, Netanyahu gave an aggressive speech to the Central Committee of the Likud. The key sound bite from his address was his vow to oppose the creation of a Palestinian state. The speech made headlines across the world, and was used as evidence that he was not serious about advancing the peace process.

To Netanyahu, the seeming incompatibility with his comments to the National Defence College and the Central Committee of the Likud were not important. He was essentially telling everyone what they wanted and needed to hear. It appeared that the world took Netanyahu's comments more seriously than he did.

The lasting impression this created was of a leader who was untrustworthy and who was starting to sound like a local American-style politician saying anything to get elected. The only trouble was that he was running Israel and not some run-of-the-mill mid-sized American state.

By the end of 1997, the lack of trust in Netanyahu was becoming a significant factor and one that threatened the continuation of the government. Rumours of plots and internal coups remained part of

Israeli political culture, but there was a growing feeling from the right that anyone might be better than Netanyahu. This was the case even if it meant bringing down the government.

During 1998, all this came to a head as the conflicting demands on Netanyahu from the Clinton administration and his own political constituency grew too great for even Netanyahu to manage successfully. The catalyst was the invitation of President Clinton to Netanyahu and Arafat to attend a summit at Wye in the United States in order to put the peace process back on track.

As he prepared to leave for the United States, Netanyahu feared that this summit would neither end well for himself personally, nor for the State of Israel.

Wye

Netanyahu's single biggest success during his first two years of office was his own survival. The catalogue of events, scandals, revolts and intrigues during this period would have proved sufficient to end most premierships. Not so Benjamin Netanyahu. He viewed his first two years in office as a qualified success. Others begged to differ on Netanyahu's self-assessment, but he was having none of it.

His instincts told him that he had essentially put off what he dreaded most: the choice between land and peace. True, he had handed over a part of the West Bank, but the 9 per cent represented a much smaller slab of land than he had feared would be required. The situation on the ground in Hebron remained a mess, but the security arrangements to guard the tiny number of Jewish settlers had not completely broken down.

Netanyahu's day of decision on the peace process was something that he hoped to avoid for as long as possible: at least, potentially until he was in his second term as Prime Minister. The strategy of stalling, hoping for better political conditions in the future, and putting as many facts (settlements) on the ground was nothing new. Netanyahu's predecessor as leader of the Likud, Yitzhak Shamir had attempted to do just this in 1991 leading to arguably Israel's biggest diplomatic crisis with the United States.

The signals from Washington in 1998 were not looking good for Netanyahu. In January 1998 details of the Monica Lewinsky sex scandal were published in the *Washington Post*. To an extent, this brought the second term of President Clinton to a shuddering halt, as the political investigation into it came to dominate the agenda. No stranger to scandal himself, Netanyahu watched events develop in Washington as a curious bystander.

Soon after the news of President Clinton's difficulties broke, Netanyahu was bidding farewell to Madeleine Albright, the US Secretary of State, at Andrews Air Force Base when he surprised her by expressing concern: 'I have been through the experience of having my personal life raked over,' he said. He went on to ask if he should call the President to express his sympathy. Albright suggested that this gesture would be very much appreciated by the President.[1]

Despite their different political backgrounds and colours, Clinton impressed Netanyahu as a political operator and in his ability to withstand past scandals. Clinton's strong emotional and political commitment to Israel, which had been a feature of his presidential campaigns in 1992 and 1996, as well as his peacemaking efforts when in office, were highly commendable from Netanyahu's perspective. Although personal relations between the two men were never genuinely warm, they did have a relatively good, if complicated, working relationship.

Initial speculation that events would distract Clinton from his attempts to increase the political pressure on Netanyahu turned out to be unfounded. In the wake of the scandal, President Clinton upped his efforts to achieve Israeli–Palestinian peace, and, later, an Israeli–Syrian agreement. As time went on, Clinton appeared to want an Israeli–Palestinian peace deal to be the legacy of a presidency that many feared would be characterized only by the scandal.

Beset by time constraints and frustrations, and fearing a potential total breakdown of the peace process, the Clinton administration decided to invite the Israelis and the Palestinians to Wye in order to try to add a memorandum to the peace agreements that would help get the process back on track. This was an ambitious and risky move by the Americans. Netanyahu had seen it coming and had already made his preparations.

The American plan was based on using a similar formula to the Camp David Summit between Israel and Egypt, which had been hosted by President Jimmy Carter. That summit was held for similar reasons to the one in Wye, namely the peace process had reached an impasse that seemed impossible to break.

In 1978, the summit led to the Israeli Prime Minister Menachem Begin and President Anwar Sadat of Egypt signing the peace treaty between their two countries. The formula of high stakes summit diplomacy was not without risks.

Madeleine Albright wrote about the potential dangers of a summit:

> The question we faced was whether to risk the prestige of the
> Presidency by inviting Arafat and Netanyahu to a summit remi-
> niscent of the 1978 meetings at Camp David that produced
> Egyptian-Israeli peace.
>   I supported the summit but with reservations . . . If we convened
> a summit that failed, we would look impotent, and people would
> blame the Secretary of State for misjudging the odds. We didn't
> however, have many alternatives.[2]

She went on, however, to suggest that a summit was needed sooner rather than later as the situation on the ground was worsening.

> For the first time since Oslo had been signed in 1993, some polls
> showed a majority of Palestinians so frustrated that they favoured
> using terror to force Israel to withdraw to 1967 borders. Israel had
> also uncovered evidence that the military wing of Hamas was plan-
> ning a new round of attacks. So while we were talking, the clock
> was ticking.[3]

In reality, the Americans were worried about Netanyahu's and Arafat's ability to keep control of the increasingly volatile situation in which extremists from both sides appeared to be making daily gains. The crux of the situation was that neither Netanyahu nor Arafat wanted to be blamed for the breakdown of the peace process, but both feared the domestic fallout from reaching a deal. Neither leader wanted to be seen as having essentially given in to pressure from Washington.

For Netanyahu, the problem remained his cabinet, the coalition and the Likud. He understood that if he made concessions to the Palestinians in order to get a deal, the Labour Party would support him in the Knesset and therefore ratify the deal. He also had one eye on the next election. At the time of the preparatory stages for the summit, his coalition was already showing signs of unravelling, and it looked a fair bet that the elections might need to be brought forward from their scheduled date of 2000.

David Levy, the Minister of Foreign Affairs, resigned and left the government. He acted not over the government's handling of the peace process, rather over the state budget. As he said in his resignation statement:

> It [the budget] is not good for the country, it's not good for the public, it's not good for the government, and so I have no choice but to do the responsible thing – and from a moral standing the government's policy does not promote the partnership, the promises, nor a common point of view.
>
> There is one conclusion which is to resign from the government, and I intend today, after this meeting, to send the Prime Minister a letter of resignation, and with all due respect and manners I am no longer a member of this government.[4]

Levy's resignation was important for Netanyahu for two related reasons. By resigning, this populist politician believed that elections were coming over the horizon and did not want to be associated with the economic hardship that the budget would cause to his mainly lower-income Sephardic-origin constituency.

The second important lesson for Netanyahu was that, as elections approached, other coalition partners would find reason to leave the government. Unless Netanyahu could do something to stem this tide, he would need to put together an alternative coalition, or more likely to call early elections.

Any possibility of broadening the coalition into a national unity government with the Labour Party receded in 1998. Secret negotiations that took place on several occasions between representatives of Netanyahu and Barak produced agreed policy deadlines for a unity government, but made little progress over the thorny question of the division of cabinet portfolios.

In reality, Barak and the Labour Party had few reasons for joining a unity government. Barak's thinking was based on a number of factors, most of which centred upon the perceived weakness of Netanyahu at the time. Barak did not want to serve as number two to Netanyahu, and did not need the Labour Party to be in power to protect his position as leader. Barak concentrated his strategy on preparing for early elections, which he believed could be called sooner rather than later.[5]

In light of his lack of options, Netanyahu moved to essentially kill two birds with one stone. He appointed the hawkish Ariel Sharon as his Minister of Foreign Affairs. At the time, it appeared a smart choice, but Netanyahu would come to regret it as Sharon became his biggest rival in the Likud. However, the appointment of Ariel Sharon as Minister of Foreign Affairs on 3 October 1998 appeared an essentially win-win situation for Netanyahu.

The Americans noted that Netanyahu would not in all probability sign a deal without Sharon's consent. There was another precedent here from the Camp David Summit of 1978. Before Menachem Begin agreed to sign the deal with Sadat, he had first checked if Sharon supported the decision to withdraw from the Sinai, and uproot the Jewish settlements that were based in the area. Netanyahu was essentially asking Sharon to play the same kingmaker role for a deal with the Palestinians.

Netanyahu was wily enough to know that any deal signed at Wye would involve some level of difficult compromise, and Sharon was the man to sell the deal back home to the cabinet, the coalition and the Likud. With Sharon on-board, Netanyahu's room for manoeuvre to agree a deal increased. If no deal was struck with the Palestinians, Netanyahu could blame Sharon for obstructing or derailing a potential agreement.

For his part it was a good deal for Sharon, who had been shunned by the US and European leaders since the Lebanon War of 1982, and the massacres in the Sabra and Shatila Palestinian refugee camps in Beirut. The Kahan Commission set up by Israel to investigate events in Beirut said Sharon was indirectly, but personally, to blame for the massacres.[6]

The report of the Kahan Commission concluded that Sharon had made a grave mistake in failing to order 'appropriate measures for preventing or reducing the danger of a massacre' at the camps. It went on to state that Sharon should have foreseen what the Phalangists would do when they entered the camps. The massacre had occurred after Bashir Gemayel, the Christian Lebanese President-elect and leader of the Phalange party, was assassinated.[7]

For years, Sharon had been looking for international rehabilitation, and Netanyahu's offer of the foreign ministry was a perfect opportunity for him to build up his international credentials. At the time, the Americans found Sharon both difficult and direct. He lectured President Clinton and stuck to his articulation of the Israeli hardline position.[8]

If the Americans thought that Netanyahu had appointed Sharon as part of a good cop/bad cop routine, they were soon disappointed.

In the period running up to the summit, Netanyahu spent much of the time talking to his hawkish base in Israel. In attempting to reassure them, he talked of the need to forget trying to implement any further stages of the Interim Agreement that involved Israel handing over more land to the Palestinians.

His preference was if (and it was 'if' as far as he was concerned) Arafat could prevent new terrorist attacks, dismantle the Hamas infrastructure and stop Palestinian incitement, then he would be willing to open final status talks. He argued that the Interim Agreement with its phased pullbacks merely encouraged rejectionist groups such as Hamas to launch attacks against Israel.

During the summer of 1998, Israeli and Palestinian mediators had met secretly on several occasions to try to narrow the gaps between them on key issues. The meetings had not proved wholly successful, but they did sow the seeds of a draft outline that the Americans felt they could use at Wye. Given the high degree of mistrust between the parties, the Americans saw the summit as essentially a means to close the deal with the help of the direct mediation of President Clinton.[9]

The Americans chose the Wye River Conference Center in Maryland to host the summit. It was an idyllic setting that was both large enough for the participants to relax in and close enough to Washington, should the need arise to return to the capital. The conference room was big enough to host the opening session, and there were plenty of other smaller rooms for more intimate discussions. To help try to focus minds, the Americans set a three-day deadline for the summit. In retrospect, this proved to be a little overambitious.

The summit began on 15 October 1998, with Netanyahu making a point of shaking the hand of Yasser Arafat at the plenary meeting on the first day. American officials described the mood as good, as the two sides parted to meet independently with the Americans. The summit had been set up so that, while President Clinton met with Netanyahu, Secretary of State Albright met with Arafat, and vice versa. The President wasn't at Wye for the entire time, so when he was back in Washington, Albright took command.

According to Dennis Ross, President Clinton's Special Envoy to the Middle East, the first day had been all about psychology: 'making each

Benjamin Netanyahu (LEFT) as Deputy Foreign Minister during a meeting with Foreign Minister Moshe Arens and Eduard Shevardnadze at the Soviet Embassy in Cairo, 22 February 1989.

SA'AR YA'ACOV

During a flight to New York, 5 April 1989, Netanyahu (SEATED) going through papers with Government Secretary Elyakim Rubinstein. SA'AR YA'ACOV

On the White House lawn, 6 April 1989, Deputy Foreign Minister Benjamin Netanyahu (SECOND FROM LEFT) stands behind Israeli Prime Minister Yitzhak Shamir and US President George H. W. Bush.
SA'AR YA'ACOV

As Opposition Leader, Netanyahu addresses the Knesset during the debate on the agreement with the PLO on 21 September 1993. OHAYON AVI

Celebrating his 1996 election victory with David Levy (CENTRE AT PODIUM) and Yitzhak Mordechai (LEFT OF PHOTO). OHAYON AVI

Prime Minister Benjamin Netanyahu, in a more relaxed moment in the Knesset, 18 June 1996.
OHAYON AVI

Benjamin Netanyahu and his wife, Sara, with their two children, Yair (LEFT) and Avner (RIGHT), aboard an IAF flight to Israel after their first official visit to the United States, 14 July 1996. SA'AR YA'ACOV

En-route to Amman, Jordan, 5 August 1996. Netanyahu and his wife, Sara, look out from their helicopter at the Jordanian Air Force escort. OHAYON AVI

Prime Minister Benjamin Netanyahu strolls in the garden with King Hussein of Jordan.
OHAYON AVI

A visit to one of the IDF forward posts on the border with South Lebanon, 19 August 1996.
SA'AR YA'ACOV

US President Bill Clinton and Israeli Prime Minister Benjamin Netanyahu in close conversation in the Oval Office at the White House, 9 July 1996. SA'AR YA'ACOV

US Secretary of State Madeleine Albright during her visit to Jerusalem in January 1998 at the home of Benjamin and Sara Netanyahu. AMOS BEN GERSHOM

On 4 September 1996, at an IDF facility at Erez Checkpoint in Gaza, the first public handshake between PLO Chairman Yasser Arafat and Benjamin Netanyahu. MILNER MOSHE

leader feel comfortable'.[10] Ross wasn't sure if this was an altogether good sign. He argued that agreements emerged from 'high-stakes settings where each side felt uncomfortable'. He went on to warn, 'no one made hard decisions unless they had to'.[11]

On the score of feeling comfortable, Ross needn't have worried. The comfort factor rapidly disappeared as the talks on substantive issues got underway. Smiles were replaced by frowns, grimaces and shrugs. In other words, it was a return to the norm that, according to Clinton, included, 'the posturing and pettiness that are a usual part of all such negotiations'.[12]

As many of the participants had feared, the talks did not progress as well and speedily as the Americans had initially hoped. Netanyahu did not want to retreat from his demands in the area of Palestinian assurance on Israeli security, and on a range of other issues.

It became apparent that Netanyahu was not moving from his rigid and specific security demands, which included the arrest of named Palestinian militants, weapons collection points and plans to stop mosques being used by the militant Palestinian groups. The Palestinian responses were vague and general in nature.

At this stage, the Americans suspected that Netanyahu was overplaying his hand a little. Every step he took and in every move he made, Netanyahu had at least one eye on the domestic political situation in Israel and the next election. He did not want to have to go to the polls with a half-baked agreement that unravelled and led to a further increase in violence in Israel.

On the Sunday, scheduled as the last day of the summit, Netanyahu had all but given up any hope of a comprehensive agreement. Therefore he suggested a partial deal to President Clinton. In essence, Netanyahu proposed that Israel withdraw from a further 13 per cent of the West Bank in exchange for complete Palestinian cooperation on security issues. The rest of the remaining issues he proposed to leave to another day, by which Netanyahu meant preferably at final status talks.

President Clinton rejected Netanyahu's partial deal on the grounds that they had come so far, and that they were close to a more comprehensive agreement. In his heart, Clinton understood that the partial deal proposed by Netanyahu would be viewed as a failure by the outside world which was waiting on the doorstep for news of the summit. With his domestic problems increasing over the sex scandal, Clinton needed something more than a partial agreement to help lift him out of the political doldrums.

The next day, Clinton made it clear that he felt a more comprehensive deal was much closer than the parties (as well as several members of the American team) felt. He cited examples from the peace process in Northern Ireland and looked at focusing on what was already agreed. Netanyahu listened intently, but still refused to be swayed by the President's apparent optimism.

Ariel Sharon had been hovering in the background of the negotiations, and the Americans decided it was now time to move the political bulldozer to the centre of the stage. The American thinking was that Netanyahu would accept a deal that Sharon accepted, but would say no to a deal if Sharon rejected it.[13] To this extent, they were correct.

The trouble with Sharon, from an American perspective, was that he had still not been broken into the niceties of the peace process. Brash, arrogant, charismatic and populist, Sharon had boasted that he would never shake the hand of Yasser Arafat. True to his word, Sharon did not shake Arafat's hand at Wye.[14]

Sharon found himself at the same dinner table as Arafat. The conversation was not of a light nature. Sharon talked at the Palestinian leader rather than to him, in the tone of a rancher to his farmhand. In between Sharon's outbursts, President Clinton did his best to fill the silence. Sharon attacked Arafat's claim that Palestinian farmers were broke. The dinner was not a social success and increased the tension between the delegations.

Netanyahu was much more comfortable in the company of Arafat and the other Palestinian negotiators. Prior to Wye, he had even enjoyed his favourite pastime, a post-meal Cuban cigar, with the Palestinians. Madeleine Albright recalled that Netanyahu asked Arafat if he minded if he smoked a cigar. One of the Palestinians then pulled out a box of Cohibas which they and Netanyahu enjoyed together.[15]

In contrast to Sharon, there was an air of sophistication about Netanyahu. His American education made him culturally more akin to a native of the east coast of the United States. Albright told Clinton that she sometimes had to remind herself that Netanyahu wasn't in fact American. Netanyahu spoke like an American, Sharon like a veteran Israeli farmer, but neither appeared to be able to get through to Arafat and the Palestinians.

At the end of the scheduled talks, the major achievement of the hard work of the American team was that nobody had walked out. Indeed, both parties agreed to extend the talks in the hope of reaching the comprehensive deal that Clinton was aiming to achieve. The extension was only achieved after the intervention of Clinton, who would have to leave the talks to return to Washington, but would return when developments required his presence.

With the summit apparently in trouble, Clinton decided that the presence of King Hussein of Jordan would help focus the minds of the delegations. The King was being treated for cancer in the Mayo Clinic in Rochester, Minnesota, and had offered to visit the summit if Clinton felt his presence would be useful. There were obvious concerns that his health was too frail for him to be able to attend, but Queen Noor assured Clinton that the King wanted to come to the summit and contribute what he could to the negotiations.

King Hussein's arrival on 20 October gave the summit the drama that it had hitherto lacked, in contrast to the Camp David Summit of the Begin and Sadat talks which had been packed with personal dramas and tantrums. The impact of the King's arrival at Wye was hugely important to the chances of success in reaching an agreement.

The King's cancer treatment had led to the loss of his white hair and beard, and he had lost a great deal of weight. Mentally, he was still very much his old straight-talking self, and he spoke with both Netanyahu and Arafat and the members of the two delegations.[16]

As President Clinton recalled, the two parties had still only managed to strike a deal on the security aspect of the negotiations. Clinton feared, as a result, that Netanyahu would celebrate his forty-ninth birthday by exiting what would have been regarded as a failed summit. Instead the parties eventually came to a complex understanding on the second issue at stake: getting the Palestinian Council to change the parts of its charter that still called for the destruction of Israel.[17]

The charter issue had become an important part of Netanyahu's reciprocal approach to the peace process with the Palestinians. To the Israeli right it had been a glaring oversight of the previous Labour-led governments not to demand that this issue be resolved before moving forward with the peace process. Given the centrality of the issue to Netanyahu's approach, it would have been extremely difficult to make any further concessions at the summit without a deal on the charter issue.

In order to resolve the issue, Clinton agreed to go to Gaza to address the Palestinian Council along with Arafat – asking that he delete the offending articles about Israel from the charter. Arafat would then ask for a show of support for the move, and then the changes would be made. To some extent, it was a risk for Clinton that could easily have come undone. Clinton was willing to take that risk in order to try to close the comprehensive deal that he had hoped for at the outset of the summit.

The major remaining issue to be solved was the release of the Palestinians from Israeli jails. Of all the issues this was arguably the most difficult one for Netanyahu to sell back home. His preference was that a large number of the Palestinian prisoners to be released should be criminal offenders rather than security prisoners with blood on their hands. There were also disagreements over the numbers of prisoners to be released, with Netanyahu stating no more than five hundred – and Arafat demanding a thousand.

The fact that Netanyahu, the self-proclaimed expert on anti-terrorist strategies, found himself in tense negotiations over releasing a number of prisoners with Israeli blood on their hands was evidence of his more pragmatic instincts and policies in office. The Netanyahu at Wye was almost unrecognizable from the fiery opposition candidate from the 1996 election campaign. The perceived change in Netanyahu's outlook would come to damage his short- to medium-term political prospects.

PART FIVE

Decline

13

Deal Breaker

Nobody was more aware of the potential political damage of an agreement at Wye to Netanyahu than Netanyahu himself. He had known from day one that he might need an effective get-out-of-jail card from the Americans to help sell any agreement to his political colleagues back in Israel. There were a number of requests that Netanyahu could have made to Clinton to help him on this score, but he chose the most difficult one for the President to deliver successfully.

During the course of a late-night private meeting with the President, Netanyahu had apparently secured a promise from Clinton that the United States would free Jonathan Pollard, an American citizen who had been convicted of spying for Israel and sentenced to life imprisonment. His case had been taken up with the United States by several Israeli prime ministers and by various Jewish groups. In Israel, the freeing of Pollard had become a high-profile issue, particularly among voters who supported the Likud and other parties in the governing coalition.

As Dennis Ross explained to the President, after Netanyahu had first broached the news of his demand for the release of Pollard to him, Ross believed it would be seen as a great help to the Prime Minister. Ross reminded Clinton, 'he [Pollard] is considered a soldier for Israel and there is an ethos in Israel that you never leave a soldier behind in the field'.[1] In looking at the issue, Ross took a strategic – rather than moral – approach to a potential release of Pollard.

Ross advised Clinton against releasing Pollard, not on the grounds that his crimes against the United States were of too serious a nature for him to be released, rather because he thought the timing of the release was wrong. As Ross told the President:

> It would be a huge pay off for Bibi [Netanyahu]; you don't have many like this in your pocket. I would save it for permanent status [negotiations]. You will need it later, don't use it now.[2]

For once, Clinton disagreed with Ross and replied:

> This stalemate has lasted so long that it has created a kind of constipation. Release it and a lot becomes possible. I don't think that we can afford to wait, and if Pollard is the key to getting it done now, we should do it.[3]

Whatever the internal American debates about Pollard, Netanyahu was given the clear impression from Clinton that the release of the convicted spy would happen if a comprehensive deal was agreed and signed.

With time fast running out, and Clinton needing to join the campaign trail for the mid-term elections, the sides accelerated the pace of the negotiations. The words that the ailing King Hussein had spoken to the parties were also helping to focus the minds of the leaders. In referring to the differences that remained between the two parties, the King said:

> These differences pale in comparison with what is at stake. After agreement both sides will look back and not even recall these issues. It is now time to finish, bearing in mind the responsibility that both leaders have to their people and especially the children.[4]

The King's unspoken message was, equally, not lost on Netanyahu and Arafat. Clinton summed up the King's message as 'I might not have long to live; it's up to you not to let the peace die.'[5]

Eventually, a deal was reached, or so the Americans thought. The prisoner release number was set at 750, the halfway point between Netanyahu's and Arafat's demands. Netanyahu agreed to accept the proposal to release security prisoners, provided they did not have Israeli blood on their hands.

Of the 750 prisoners, 340 would be security prisoners and the rest common criminals. President Clinton described the deal over the prisoners to his team as the good news. Albright, Ross and the rest of the American team understood from the President's words that there was bad news to follow.

In a return of actions in the aftermath of the Hebron Agreement, Netanyahu told the President, 'I will have to do the Har Homa tenders.' The proposed construction of housing units would begin, as the clearing of the land was complete.

Ross reminded everyone that Har Homa was the reason that the peace process had been stalled for the previous 18 months, and why they were at Wye desperately trying to save it.[6] The Palestinians were quick once again to point out that the creation of this new Jewish neighbourhood would effectively cut off Bethlehem from Arab East Jerusalem.

Clinton and Ross met with Netanyahu, in order to try to convince him to drop the start of the construction phase. Netanyahu held his ground: 'I will not initiate this, I won't rush into it. Politically I have no choice.'[7] The best the Americans could get Netanyahu to agree upon was an informal delay in starting the process for around eight months, which would give them eight months to try to advance final status talks. Not perfect by any means, but Netanyahu would at least be able to sell this to his right-wing constituency in Israel.

Netanyahu's second demand was that President Clinton request the Egyptians to release an Israeli Druze, who had been arrested for spying. President Clinton agreed to telephone President Hosni Mubarak of Egypt to try to persuade him to authorize the prisoner's release. In the end, Mubarak rejected the plea from Clinton and a similar one made in a phone conversation with Yasser Arafat.

Everything else came together with surprising speed, thanks in the main to some creative mediation by the Americans. President Clinton summarized the agreement:

> The agreement provided the Palestinians with more land on the West Bank, the airport, a seaport, a prisoner release, safe passage between Gaza and the West Bank, and economic aid.
>
> In return, Israel would get unprecedented cooperation in the fight against violence and terror, the jailing of specific Palestinians whom Israelis had identified as the source of continuing violence and killing, the change in the Palestinian covenant, and a quick start on the final status talks.

The United States would provide aid to help Israel meet the security costs of redeployment and support for Palestinian economic development, and would play a central role in cementing the unprecedented security cooperation the two sides had agreed to embrace.[8]

As the American officials were celebrating and being informed of how the deal was going to be presented to the media, Ross noticed Clinton and Netanyahu sitting alone with no smiles on their faces; Netanyahu looked genuinely angry.

From his perspective, Netanyahu had good reason not to join in the premature celebrations. Clinton had just walked over to him and quietly informed him that Pollard would not be released as part of the overall deal. Netanyahu responded by stating that he would not sign the agreement unless Pollard was released.

Clinton headed to the bathroom and signalled to Ross to follow him there. The outcome of high-stakes diplomacy was to be sealed in the men's room with Clinton sitting on the sink. Clinton recounted his conversation with Netanyahu to Ross explaining that Netanyahu had said:

> He'd made concessions on the prisoners based on the assumption
> that he would have Pollard and on that basis could sell the prison-
> ers, indeed, could sell the whole deal. He couldn't sell the agreement
> otherwise and he had been counting on Pollard and that's why he'd
> consented to the things he'd agreed to.[9]

Ross then sought clarification from Clinton if he had promised Netanyahu that Pollard would be released as part of a final deal. Ross told the President that if he had promised Netanyahu this then he had to honour the deal. Clinton replied, denying that he had promised Netanyahu anything other than that he would try to include it in the deal. He was telling the truth, but had not passed on the bad news to Netanyahu that it would be impossible to do this until after the final status agreement was reached.

Clinton had discussed the potential release of Pollard with his staff and the Director of the CIA, George Tenet, who participated in the summit to help with the security aspects of the agreement. When in the presence of the President, American officials explained to Director

Tenet that the President might have to agree to the release of Pollard in order to help persuade Netanyahu to sign an agreement, Tenet had responded angrily, 'You can't do this.'[10]

Tenet didn't stop there. After a lengthy explanation of the damage the release would do to the American intelligence services and its deterrents to prevent the sale of classified information, he concluded by informing Clinton that he would have to resign if Pollard were to be released.

Secretary of State Madeleine Albright agreed that it was a mistake to release Pollard, as did key Clinton aides. Later, Clinton claimed that he too had not wanted to commute Pollard's sentence, so it was never in reality going to happen.[11]

For Netanyahu the omission of Pollard's release from the deal was a crushing blow. The master political operator, President Clinton, had outwitted Netanyahu, the prince of Machiavellian politics.

Feeling betrayed and hurt, Netanyahu informed the Americans that he was returning to his quarters at Wye in order to get some much needed sleep, after which he would decide what to do. He departed, leaving the President in little doubt that as things stood there was no agreement.

Sleep was, however, the last thing on Netanyahu's mind. He immediately called a meeting of the senior members of the Israeli delegation to go over their options in light of the absence of Pollard from the deal.

Dennis Ross, who sensed that the Prime Minister would not be sleeping, headed over to the Israeli quarters. Ross believed that Netanyahu was bluffing. Netanyahu, he felt, would not dare sacrifice the deal over Pollard, and his bluff should be called by the Americans.[12]

Ross met with Netanyahu's officials and made his hardball pitch to get the Israelis back on board. He admitted that there appeared to have been a genuine misunderstanding between the President and Netanyahu over Pollard, but reminded them that Clinton had not made any direct promise on the case. Before he departed, Ross tried to give the Israelis a reality check to report back to their Prime Minister. He said:

> The president won't budge now. Tell Bibi [Netanyahu] he will
> lose everything if this collapses over Pollard. You can evaluate the
> damage to him in Israel, but I can tell you he will kill himself here.[13]

Netanyahu appeared to have got the message. He met alone with Clinton one more time and agreed the deal. He told the President that he had considered reducing the number of prisoners to be released from 750 to 500, but, in hindsight, felt that the Palestinians should not lose out on account of a US–Israeli issue.

He did, however, inform the President that he would alter the ratio of the third phased release of prisoners to include more common criminals and fewer security prisoners. The Americans cleared this with Arafat, in the belief that they would be able to work on this later to get the original ratios reinstated.[14]

On this occasion, in an act of repayment over Pollard, it was the student teaching the master a lesson. As it later transpired, what Netanyahu meant by changing the mix of the prisoners, was that no prisoners with blood on their hands would be released. Ross would later kick himself for not pressing the President further on the details of his conversation with Netanyahu.

As he admitted later, the ambiguity should have been cleared up before the deal was signed. Clinton needed and deserved the ceremony at the White House, and time restraints meant that the deal could not be reopened. As they drove to the White House, Ross turned and said to another American official, 'Bibi has already robbed us of the joy of reaching agreement.'[15]

The deal was sealed with handshakes before everybody rushed back to the White House to formally announce it to the outside world ahead of the start of the Jewish Sabbath. The ceremony took place in the East Room of the White House at 4 p.m. on 23 October 1998. The list of speakers in addition to Netanyahu included Albright, Vice-President Al Gore, President Clinton, Arafat and King Hussein. Netanyahu spoke briefly, in what Clinton rather flatteringly called very upbeat and states-manlike language.[16]

During the course of his address, Netanyahu singled out Clinton for special praise:

I want to especially thank President Clinton. He is, if I can
borrow a cliché, he is a warrior for peace. I mean; he doesn't stop.
He has this ability to maintain a tireless pace and to nudge and
prod and suggest and use a nimble and flexible mind to truly
explore the possibilities of both sides, and never just on one side.

That is a great gift, I think a precious and unique one, and it served us well.

So I thank you, Mr. President, for serving us, and the cause of peace well. And I thank you, too, for your boundless optimism, without which these qualities cannot come into effect. You needed a lot of optimism.[17]

Rarely has there been such a strong disconnect between words and the reality of the situation. Netanyahu remained distrustful of Clinton as a result of their misunderstanding. In due course, as Netanyahu and Clinton's second misunderstanding came to light, this time over prisoner releases, relations between the two leaders would further deteriorate. In the meantime, Netanyahu headed home to face the fight of his political life: to sell the agreement to his cabinet, coalition and party.

14

Home

An already exhausted Netanyahu worked on the political spin on the plane almost all the way back to Israel. On a positive note, at least his Minister of Foreign Affairs, Ariel Sharon, would try to sell the agreement that he had helped negotiate.

As soon as his plane touched down in Tel Aviv on 25 October 1998, Netanyahu put forward his best salesman's pitch to the gathered press. He concentrated on the three pluses for Israel: a promise of better Palestinian commitment to security; a reduction in their territorial expectations; and the deepened involvement of the United States in all parts of the peace process with the Palestinians.

Amid all the detailed analysis of the negotiations, what was most revealing was how he concluded his statement to the press. Netanyahu understood more than most on how to speak to the base, but his message was clear to the settlers and the rest of his right-wing constituency: the deal was the best we could get and no government would have represented you better than this one.

> I met at Wye Plantation in a field. I came there with my wife, Sara, and I met some of the settler representatives. We sat there in chairs in the field. It was kind of a surrealistic site, a group of people sitting on chairs, in a field. I told them, and I say this now: you are the same, we are part of the same people. We love you. We are fighting this battle for you.
>
> There is no other government that will fight for you like this. We've already seen that. We know what was, and you know very

well there is no possibility that there will be any other government that will fight the way we did after receiving the agreement from the previous government, in order to reduce the damage and to close the holes.

These were very, very difficult negotiations. These were very, very difficult days and nights for me, and my ministers. There were radical demands by the Palestinians that we rejected, and there were demands that we made, and we didn't agree to give them up. What we have achieved is the best that could have been achieved. We've done something very good and something very important for the State of Israel.[1]

The mention given to Sara Netanyahu was meant to help reinforce the Netanyahu family's credentials as the keeper of the Settlers flame. The trouble for Netanyahu was most of the more vocal, radical settlers didn't believe a word he said.

For them the Wye Memorandum, as the agreement was known, represented capitulation by a right-wing government in Israel to the political needs of President Clinton and the Palestinians. While Netanyahu had suspected that this would be the initial reaction of these groups, he hoped to be able to convince enough Israelis from the centre-right that his third way was the best way forward.

In this respect, Ariel Sharon had become an indispensable political ally for Netanyahu. As soon as he arrived back in Israel with the Prime Minister, Sharon got to work adapting a philosophical approach in his comments to the press:

A peace process is nearly as difficult as war. In a peace process, one is compelled to make concessions. Here, we are talking about relinquishing parts of our homeland, the cradle of the Jewish people. We have decided, however, despite the pain, to make every effort to achieve peace, while ensuring maximum security for the State of Israel and its citizens in every place – and let me emphasize: in every place. Bearing in mind the agreement that the government inherited, the agreement that has now been achieved is a good one.[2]

Sharon's final sentence was uttered in the manner of a schoolchild trying to convince himself that something he said was true by repeating it over and over again, until he believed it. The simple truth was that the Wye Memorandum was not a good agreement. Indeed, it had achieved something almost unique in peacemaking: a bad deal for both sides in the conflict, as well as for the well-intentioned mediator.

From day one it would prove to be near-impossible to implement the deal that was meant to, as Netanyahu had put it, 'close the holes' in the previous agreement, but instead created new, gaping holes that proved difficult to fill.

A smart and savvy politician such as Netanyahu understood that he would not want to go to the polls highlighting his record in government with only the Wye Memorandum to show for his time in office. It looked unlikely that domestic politics would produce much that could be held up as being successful. His rainbow coalition with its diverging economic interests meant that any meaningful economic reform came a poor second to getting the annual budget passed in the Knesset.

Netanyahu's inability to introduce major economic reforms disappointed him as much as the daily frustrations of dealing with the peace process. He had hoped that, when he was elected as Prime Minister, he would be able to use the so-called new strength of the executive to impose his plans for the economic liberalization of the economy on the cabinet.

His Likud political rival Dan Meridor had resigned as Minister of Finance after only a year in office. Netanyahu had eventually replaced him with Yaakov Neeman, a political ally of the Prime Minister, and in the final months of his government Netanyahu took over the portfolio himself. This arrangement suited Netanyahu best. He needed to be in charge of the purse strings for political reasons.

An ever-increasing problem for Netanyahu to have to contend with was the link many members of the coalition made between voting to support the Prime Minister's policies towards the peace process and their demands for a greater slice of the national economic cake for their respective constituents.

With the perception that elections would be held earlier than scheduled, this additional pressure on Netanyahu grew by the day. To make matters worse, there was a queue of coalition members coming to the Prime Minister to ask him to make good on promises he had still not delivered on from the start of his administration.

With all the constant noise from his coalition partners, Netanyahu became trapped in the everyday battle for political survival and, with his attention on the short term, his vision for the medium and long term suffered. As he prepared himself and the Likud for the possibility of going to the country earlier than scheduled he spent an increasing amount of time addressing his political base in Israel.

This led to another disconnect with the Clinton administration in Washington which was trying to ensure that the Wye Memorandum was fully implemented, and that final status talks eventually got underway. In this regard, President Clinton misread and misunderstood Netanyahu as well as the political situation in Israel.

Within the Clinton administration the belief was that, after signing the agreement at Wye, Netanyahu would have to move towards the political centre ground in Israel. In the weeks and months that followed the deal at Wye, the Clinton administration thought that the most likely scenario in Israeli politics was that Netanyahu would confirm his move to the centre ground by establishing a national unity government with Ehud Barak and the Labour Party.

The rationale for the formation of a new broad-based government would be to deal with the difficult issues that would need to be resolved in the final status talks. At this stage, Israel (and the Palestinians) would be called upon to make difficult concessions to the other side. A broad-based Israeli coalition would stand a better chance of reaching a final deal with the Palestinians – and of getting it ratified. Netanyahu conceded that making the additional concessions would cause problems for the management of his right-wing coalition.

The Americans did not know that Netanyahu had reached out to Barak to form a national unity government prior to Wye, and that his efforts had proved unsuccessful. Ehud Barak appeared in no hurry to offer Netanyahu a political safety net that would have prolonged Netanyahu's time in the Prime Minister's office. Ambitious, arrogant and self-important, Barak viewed himself as the Prime-Minister-in-waiting.

The fact that around 80 per cent of Israelis initially supported the agreement that Netanyahu had reached at Wye did not derail Barak's political ambitions. Nor did it lead to any change in his strategy of attempting to replace the government as soon as possible, by trying to advance the date of the elections. In other words, Barak didn't want to cooperate with Netanyahu, he wanted to replace him.

Dennis Ross felt the mistake that Netanyahu made at this crucial juncture was his decision not to go on the offensive and try to sell the agreement at Wye to as many Israelis as possible; rather, to go defensive and retreat back into his right-wing shell. It was, as Ross put it:

> The strategic mistake, which ultimately cost him his job . . . Bibi [Netanyahu] was in a very powerful position with the agreement . . . Bibi chose to see Wye as a problem not an asset.[3]

From Netanyahu's perspective, there was a very clear problem in trying to move towards the political centre: Ehud Barak already occupied the ground. Netanyahu's old army commander, who during the 1996 campaign had declared Netanyahu unfit for high political office, had mapped out his own political strategy which focused on occupying the centre ground in Israeli politics. It was a smart move on the part of Barak, as that was the position from where Israeli elections were won.

The Rabin II candidate, Barak, would have proved difficult for Netanyahu to dislodge from the centre. Running against the more left-wing-leaning Shimon Peres in 1996 was a much easier task for Netanyahu, whose advisors plotted a centrist approach to that campaign. Deep down, and ignoring all the commentary written about his relationship with Barak, Netanyahu felt that his best chance of defeating him came from the right.

This was a miscalculation, and even Netanyahu himself suspected it, as he attempted to hold on to power long enough to try to change the political dynamics in Israel. His trouble was that his continued management of his difficult coalition was pushing him further to the right, as he tried to please his partners. It became a catch-22 for Netanyahu, and there appeared to be no easy way out of it.

The implementation of the Wye agreement, which the Americans had hoped Netanyahu would drive through, did not go well in Israel. With Netanyahu's credibility within his own cabinet crumbling, a number of ministers asked for clarification on the prisoner releases, and other issues from the Americans.

Natan Sharansky for one, whose support for Netanyahu in 1996 had been an important factor in his election, sought clarification about the planned arrests by the Palestinian Authority. Each of the requests made by the various members of the cabinet reflected the growing consensus that the government did not have long to live, and ministers, as a result, had one eye on the next election.

The Americans felt that Netanyahu was attempting to renegotiate parts of the agreement. Netanayahu said that he was merely seeking additional political cover. The game went on with Netanyahu drawing President Clinton more and more into the process. There was a feeling in the Prime Minister's office that the President was, for his own reasons, more open to Netanyahu's requests than some others in the American team.

When Netanyahu eventually brought the agreement to the cabinet for approval there was strong opposition from several ministers. As they started debating the merits of the agreement, there was a bombing in Jerusalem. The only fatalities were the bombers themselves, but it was a timely reminder of the difficulties that lay ahead. Fearing that if he continued with the meeting he would lose the vote at end of it, Netanyahu suspended the meeting.

In light of the bombing, Netanyahu called the President one more time to try and extract another concession from the Americans. The Prime Minister came straight to the point. He now needed to put out the tenders to start the construction at Har Homa. He argued that this would help him win the vote in the cabinet.

Clinton's advisors who were listening in on the conversation made frantic gestures to the President to point-blank turn down this request. 'We have given Bibi enough,' said Ross, who thought the Prime Minister was still playing political games over bringing the agreement to the cabinet.[4]

President Clinton chose to overrule the strong advice of his team and said to Netanyahu, 'Is this really necessary to get it through the cabinet?' Netanyahu replied in the affirmative. The Americans thought they could just about get this by Arafat without him walking away from the process.

So, ironically, the very issue that had caused the peace process to break down, and that had led to the summit of Wye, was to go ahead after all. In retrospect, Clinton felt it a price worth paying to finally close the deal that seemed to keep reopening.

For all his efforts to shore up support for the agreement, the cabinet meeting and vote was a humiliation for Netanyahu. After the usual round of fiery, impassioned speeches in favour and against the agreement, on 11 November 1998 the Israeli cabinet approved the agreement by eight votes to four, with five abstentions. Much to the horror of the Americans, the cabinet did add new conditions to the agreement.

At the insistence of Ariel Sharon, Netanyahu agreed that he would bring each phase of the agreement back to the cabinet for its approval once again. In reality, the cabinet agreed to the Wye Memorandum, but made it clear that they would potentially withhold the implementation of each stage of it if the Palestinians did not keep their side of the bargain.

Netanyahu's Minister of Foreign Affairs had effectively just confined another agreement to the dustbin of history. There was a double humiliation at the meeting for Netanyahu. He was forced to agree to the demands of Sharon, and the five ministers who abstained in the vote constituted all the Likud ministers who had not attended the summit at Wye.

Even with the Har Homa card to play, Netanyahu was abandoned by the right-wing he had tried so hard to keep on his side. It is always difficult to highlight an exact moment when a government starts to crumble beyond repair, but the cabinet meeting and vote represented a point of no return for the administration.

It also marked the point when even the patience of the Clinton administration started to run out on Netanyahu. Although neither man knew it at the time, it was also the beginning of the handover of the leadership of the Likud from Benjamin Netanyahu to Ariel Sharon. The right had lost its trust in Netanyahu, and was starting to turn to its old torchbearer to represent their interests.

The Americans were left, however, with little choice, given their intense involvement in mediating and framing the deal at Wye, but to send their special envoy to Israel to once again, as Dennis Ross, put it, 'hold Bibi's hand'.[5]

The Americans still appeared not to fully appreciate the extent of Netanyahu's internal political difficulties, and the likelihood that his government would fall sooner rather than later. The Palestinians were not as slow on the uptake as the Americans, understanding that it was unlikely Netanyahu would lead Israel when the final status talks eventually got underway.

In the meantime, with the help of the votes of the opposition Labour Party, the Knesset adopted the Wye Memorandum by 75 votes in favour to 19 against, with nine abstentions, on 13 November 1998. With each stage of the agreement having to win cabinet approval before being implemented, few lawmakers felt that the agreement would be fulfilled, and fewer still thought that the Netanyahu-led government would survive.

15

End

The last throw of the dice by Netanyahu took place in the autumn of 1998, when he entered into secret negotiations with the Syrians aimed at securing a peace agreement that would potentially be the crowning achievement of his time in office. It would also represent something more tangible with which to go to the country, rather than the problematic Wye Memorandum.

During the initial stages of his government, Netanyahu adopted the same hawkish position towards Damascus as his previous writings and speeches had suggested he would. To a certain extent, he used the Syrian track of the peace process to flex his hawkish credentials to his party and coalition, at the same time as making difficult concessions to the Palestinians. This strategy was not altogether convincing, but it did provide Netanyahu with some breathing room.

The central feature of Netanyahu's policy towards Syria appeared to be robust and consistent: he would not resume negotiations with the Syrians on the basis of carrying on from where they had ended with the previous Peres-led Labour government.[1] Here his argument was simple: Syria had not signed an internationally binding agreement with Israel and, therefore, he was not obliged to continue the policies of the previous government. Both Rabin and Peres had been willing to return most, or all, of the disputed Golan Heights area in exchange for peace.[2]

Within both the Likud and the coalition there were strong internal restraints on Netanyahu over the Syrian track of the peace process. So-called security experts in the Likud rejected the formula of a total return of the Golan Heights for a total peace. Netanyahu was advised by members of his party to seek a different formula from that employed by the Likud with Egypt and the Camp David Agreement, which saw all of the Sinai returned to Egypt in exchange for peace.

Netanyahu tried a number of different versions of the formula – none of which proved to be of much interest to Syria – that demanded, as a minimum price for peace, the return of 100 per cent of the Golan Heights. At first, Netanyahu tried to propose confidence-building measures such as asking Syria to restrain Hezbollah from mounting attacks against Israeli forces in southern Lebanon. This was rejected outright in Syria. Other schemes included proposed discussions on water rights and high-level military contacts to prevent any misunderstandings on the Golan Heights.[3]

The Syrians steadfastly stuck to their position that any new negotiations must start from the point at which those with the old government had finished. This was taken to mean that unless Netanyahu was willing to honour the commitments of the previous Peres government to withdraw from all of the Golan Heights, he was wasting his energy trying to move the Syrian track of the peace process forward.

With time running out for his government, Netanyahu made a stunning U-turn, one that was further evidence of his pragmatic, rather than ideological, approach to the peace process. Through private intermediaries in the United States, Netanyahu made contact with the Syrian leader, President Hafez al-Assad, and reportedly offered him a full Israeli withdrawal to 4 June 1967 borders in return for peace.[4]

In terms of selling an agreement, Netanyahu planned to do exactly what Dennis Ross and the rest of the Clinton team had hoped he would do with the Wye Memorandum, namely attempt to bypass the internal restraints imposed upon him by the Israeli right. His strategy was straight out of the manual that Ross had pleaded with him to follow with the Palestinians. Netanyahu intended to take any deal over the Golan Heights to the Israeli public, either as the central part of his election manifesto or in a separate referendum on the agreement.

In the end, all the plans for selling the agreement became redundant as President Assad rejected the offer. A number of explanations were put forward as to why he turned down Netanyahu. It was suggested the Syrian leader considered that the Netanyahu government was likely to collapse at any time. Another theory was that Assad simply wasn't interested in making peace with Israel, or preferred the status quo of no war, no peace, which suited his domestic political needs.

In Israel, there was speculation in the media that President Assad turned down the deal because Ehud Barak and the Labour Party were offering him better terms than Netanyahu. Hang on and wait for us, was the alleged message from the Labour Party. Whatever the real explanation for Assad declining the offer – and in all probability it was a mixture of the reasons mentioned here – it removed Netanyahu's last chance of pulling off a 'political spectacular' that would have shaken up Israeli politics.[5]

The Syrian issue was not a stand-alone one; it was heavily related to Lebanon – and specifically for Netanyahu – on how to extricate the IDF from the self-proclaimed security zone in the south of the country. Israel had found it much easier to invade and conquer Lebanon in 1982 than to withdraw from the country. It was an issue that had vexed all Israeli prime ministers since 1982, and one that Netanyahu was left to try to clear up.

Israel's predicament in Lebanon had all the intricacies of a Federico Fellini film.[6] Israel wanted to leave Lebanon, but Syria didn't want to let Israel leave, so encouraged Hezbollah to promise attacks on northern Israel even if the IDF departed from Lebanon. Syria's intentions were to make Lebanon as painful as possible for Israel, by keeping it locked into a protracted low-intensity war with Hezbollah that resulted in, on average, two dozen Israeli deaths each year.

Like all his predecessors, Netanyahu wanted to leave Lebanon 'yesterday'. He was aware, however, that security arrangements would have to be agreed to prevent attacks on Israel's northern towns, such as Kiryat Shmona. It was widely anticipated that Hezbollah would take over all the territory that Israel withdrew from, bringing the group right up to the fence along the Israeli–Lebanon border.

Initially, Netanyahu had proposed what he termed a Lebanon first plan. This would have seen an agreed Israeli pull-back with Syria consenting to an exercise of restraint over Hezbollah. While Netanyahu thought the plan was good, the Syrians showed no interest in it. Instead, the Syrians made it clear that they would use Lebanon as a means of increasing the pressure on Israel to agree to a full withdrawal from the Golan Heights. Even when Netanyahu seemingly agreed to a full withdrawal from the Golan Heights, the Syrians proved reluctant to give up their Lebanon card.

In truth, Netanyahu had a difficult time trying to manage Israel's Lebanon policy. At times, he appeared to be over-reliant on the advice of the General Staff of the IDF, whose policy was to accept the status quo. There was a noticeable lack of alternative policies emanating from the Prime Minister's office along with a flat rejection of the idea of a unilateral Israeli withdrawal (without Syrian agreement). 'Grin and bear it' best characterized Israeli policy towards Lebanon under Netanyahu, but nobody from his cabinet or party offered any better alternatives.[7]

By December 1998, Netanyahu had used up all his political lives. His crude argument to the right-wing in Israel: 'if you think I am bad, wait until you see the next guy', had lost much of its impact. In the corridors of the Knesset, Likud MKs, along with their coalition partners, were openly talking of anybody but Netanyahu.

His personal aura was diminished. Politically, his position had been weakened by an electoral system that reduced the ability of the Prime Minister to lead the country, and an inability to commit to implementing the deal he had signed at Wye. Netanyahu's term in office, as a result, was threatening to end in abject failure.

The timing of the demise of the government was the only factor left over which Netanyahu could exercise some control. His advisors argued that he needed to take decisive action to control this, as the opposition had put down a motion of no confidence in the government in the Knesset.

The opposition appeared, to all intents and purposes, to have the necessary number of votes for the motion to succeed. If it did, it would have meant new elections for Prime Minister and the Knesset within 60 days.[8]

With the opinion polls at the time indicating apparent low levels of support for Netanyahu, the last thing he wanted was a snap election. Instead, on 21 December, with the reluctant support of Netanyahu, the Knesset voted to dissolve the government (81 in favour with 30 against and four abstentions), which, in turn, meant the dissolution of the Knesset. The date for new elections was later set for 17 May 1999. It was to be one of the longest election campaigns in Israeli history.

The biggest victim of the extended election campaign was the peace process, especially the implementation of the Wye Memorandum. As is the case in most Israeli election campaigns, the peace process was put on hold. Arafat and the Americans would have to await the outcome of the election in May 1999.

Immediately prior to the vote on 21 December, Netanyahu had made a last-minute appeal to Barak to form a national unity government. Against the advice of several leading members of the Labour Party, Barak rejected the offer and the Knesset vote went ahead. The fear in the Labour Party, at the time, was that Barak and the party would lose the elections in May.

Despite his coalition difficulties, there were no major signs that religious Soviet immigrants and Sephardic voters were willing to abandon Netanyahu for Barak and the parties of the left.[9] Barak needed to secure at least one of these key constituencies if he were to beat Netanyahu in the race to become Prime Minister.

Netanyahu's last act, before becoming the caretaker Prime Minister, was to set the electoral clock as far back as possible. He believed that his electioneering skills would come to the fore during this extended campaign, and that he would be able to inflict political damage on his rivals who were running against him for Prime Minister.

At the centre of his strategy was his deeply held belief that much of the Israeli electorate had not really connected with Barak. The other candidates, in his eyes, had still not been subjected to the levels of scrutiny that came with national campaigns.

From Netanyahu's perspective, the plan made good sense. He was a natural at campaigning, enjoyed the challenge of electioneering and understood how to win elections. Barak was stiff on the campaign trail and at times looked as if he wanted to be somewhere else.

On television, Barak could not stop speaking like the ex-general he was. Barak's answers were too detailed, his analysis too deep for the average Israeli to understand. His tone was characterized by a slight 'know it all' streak, and he spoke as if he were talking to a class of IDF officer cadets rather than an electorate.

So, far from being downhearted, Netanyahu hit the campaign trail in an upbeat mood. He genuinely believed that he would win the election. His team told him to focus on his security record, and the fact that the number of attacks against Israelis was much lower when he was at the helm than in the Rabin–Peres era. Concessions to the Palestinians were to be put down to appeasing American pressure.

In a surprisingly candid interview with *Time* magazine in January 1999, Netanyahu attempted to set the record straight about his government, its mistakes and downfall, as well as to make a case for his re-election. The interviewer started by asking Netanyahu if he regarded his government as a failure because he had been forced to go to early elections. Netanyahu offered a robust defence:

> It's a failure of the coalition. It was just a question of time before it fell because of a challenge from the right flank. I could have kept the government had I submitted to the terms posed to me from my right wing, which said that if I tore up the Oslo and Wye Accords, they would stay. I refused, and equally I refused subsequent conditions from the left that said I should go ahead and implement Oslo regardless of Palestinian violations and no matter what violence the Palestinians perpetrate on us.[10]

When asked what he would do differently in a potential second term he responded defiantly:

> I wouldn't do anything differently on the political side. Where I would do things differently is in the management of egos. I would say the Prime Minister has to devote equal time not only to the tasks of security and peacemaking and economic reform, all of which I did to my utmost, but to the maintenance, shall we say, of personal relationships.[11]

The message here from Netanyahu was clear: he felt that any failure attributed to his government did not originate from its policies, rather from his management of the key politicians in the coalition. In electoral terms, he was saying, 'vote for me and you'll get more of the same in the peace process, but this time I will manage the coalition in a better manner'.

The answer revealed Netanyahu's strange disconnect from Israeli politics at the time. His failure to deliver the workable third way that he had outlined at the outset of his government was glossed over.

Where Netanyahu was more in tune was in understanding the sea change in Israeli politics that had shifted away from ideological and political parties to a concentration in personality politics. In Israeli politics the personality and credibility of the leader had become the most important factor in determining the outcome of elections.[12]

While Netanyahu remained popular among the rank and file members of the Likud, many of whom had been recruited to the party by the Prime Minister, he remained almost universally unpopular among fellow politicians. When asked about this polarized opinion of him by *Time*, he offered a curious response:

> It's the physics of the record disk. Those in the outer circle move
> with greater speed, and the closer you get to the pivot the slower
> they turn. So it's the same thing. Those who are closest to the
> hub of politics move the slowest. It may take them a few years to
> accept the leadership. There's a cadre of people who were ahead
> of me when I entered the Likud, who never really accepted my
> leadership.[13]

A common theme of his premiership was the charge made by members of the cabinet and the coalition that he was untrustworthy. When politicians came to cash the political cheques that Netanyahu had written, he simply refused to honour them. On this Netanyahu tried to turn the argument around:

> Every time somebody does not receive from you what they want,
> they say, 'Netanyahu lied to me.' That's another way of saying, 'I
> didn't get from Netanyahu what I wanted.'[14]

The interview set the tone for the first part of the campaign. Netanyahu believed that his leadership and policies merited a second term.

The perception of being an outsider in the political system helped Netanyahu's case. The type of stranger in a strange land syndrome resonated well with religious Jews, Soviet immigrants and the Sephardim who perceived themselves as being rejected by the traditional veteran elites in Israel.[15] Netanyahu had harboured this sense of alienation in 1996 to help secure the votes of these constituencies.

In political terms, many voters in this group viewed Netanyahu's policies as good ones. According to the Israeli journalist Ari Shavit they viewed Netanyahu as a type of 'national goalkeeper' who was able to say no and who protected Israel's possessions and very survival.[16] In other words, Netanyahu was a product of the deep divisions within Israeli society that were caused by more than simply the debate over policies towards the Arab–Israeli conflict.

The race to win the direct election for Prime Minister was complicated for Netanyahu and Barak, with the initial presence of additional candidates in the ring. The launch of a new Centre Party in January 1999, which contained a group of dissatisfied ex-Likud ministers, and Amnon Lipkin-Shahak, the recently retired Chief of Staff of the IDF, appeared to bring a new start in Israeli centre-ground politics.

The addition of Netanyahu's Minister of Defence, Yitzhak Mordechai, to the party on 23 January 1999, following his dramatic sacking for attacking Netanyahu's policies, appeared to add further credibility to the Centre Party. Soon after, Mordechai was elected as head of the party, largely based on opinion polls that indicated he was slightly more popular than Lipkin-Shahak. From this point on, however, this essentially anti-Netanyahu party started to fall apart. Bickering among its leaders, and difficulties in putting together a meaningful platform, reduced its impact prior to election day.

As winter ended in Israel, Netanyahu's prospects for success at the polls looked no worse than they had been in the previous December. There were, however, worrying signs that Barak and Labour were starting to up their performance in the campaign, and that Barak was making inroads into one of Netanyahu's key constituencies. The momentum was slowly starting to swing Barak's way, after his slow start to the campaign.

PART SIX

Exile

16

Loss

Within 35 minutes after the polls closed in Israel, Benjamin Netanyahu appeared at the Hilton Hotel in Tel Aviv to address his supporters. It was 17 May 1999, and this seemed to be the end of Netanyahu's political career. It was a decisive moment, and one that would both haunt and motivate him in the future. This was a speech that Netanyahu was not accustomed to giving: a concession.

Flanked by Sara, and a tired-looking Ariel Sharon, Netanyahu addressed his supporters, many of whom were in tears. He was direct and to the point. 'The nation decided and we respect that decision, that is the way it has to be in a democracy.' He went on to offer his congratulations to the victor, Ehud Barak. He then shocked his audience by announcing that he was standing down as leader of the Likud with immediate effect. Ariel Sharon was to take over as interim leader until new leadership elections could be arranged.[1]

It was an American-style resignation speech and in a few sentences Netanyahu removed himself from the immediate political future of Israel. The man who had dominated local and international headlines disappeared off into the Tel Aviv night.

Not everybody thought it was the end of Netanyahu. President Clinton sent him a message soon after his resignation speech. 'I appreciate the hard work you did. You're a strong man with a strong historical awareness and we all believe you will be back.' Netanyahu replied, 'Thank you very much but I am taking a long vacation.'[2]

Netanyahu's aides had hoped that the internal Likud polling in the days before the election would be proved wrong. They hoped enough

Israelis were lying to the pollsters and on election day would cast their ballots for Netanyahu and the Likud. It did not happen, and by dawn on 18 May the full extent of the defeat had become apparent.

In the direct election for Prime Minister, Barak secured a near-landslide victory over Netanyahu, winning 56.1 per cent of the vote to Netanyahu's 43.9 per cent. The results of the Knesset elections were equally bad for the Likud, which saw its number of seats drop to only 19, the lowest in living memory. Barak's One Israel list, comprising Labour, David Levy's Gesher and a small religious party, fared only slightly better than the Likud, winning only 26 seats. Barak, as a result, faced the same problems in putting together a governing coalition that Netanyahu had encountered in 1996.

Just over a week after his electoral defeat, Netanyahu appeared to confirm his departure from the political landscape when he announced he was resigning his seat in the Knesset. In a fiery speech to his political base in the Likud Central Committee, Netanyahu hinted for the first time at a future return to politics. Speaking to a passionate audience, who kept interrupting him with chants of 'Long live Bibi, King of Israel', he said:

> The course we charted together will triumph in the end, and we will all witness this victory. With God's help, we shall yet return.

To shouts of 'No' and 'Stay' he informed the crowd:

> This evening I'm announcing my decision to resign my member-
> ship in Parliament. I said that I'm leaving Parliament, but I am
> by no means leaving the battle for the future of the country. I will
> continue to work in my own way to insure this future, and I'll
> continue to serve the national idea as I have over the last 20 years.

What followed was a strangely prophetic health warning to his succes-sor about future negotiations with the Arabs:

> The more we lower the exaggerated expectations of the other side
> and its ability to threaten us, the closer Israel will get to permanent
> peace. They tell us the Arabs won't agree if they don't get everything
> they want. I say the Jews won't agree to demands that they give
> what they can't. And they must not agree.

Now after the elections, Arab expectations are again on the
rise. If Israel complies with their demands, it will soon find itself
dwarfed, shrunken, with its back to the sea. Such a state will be a
constant temptation to threats of aggression and terror.

Israel might find that it enjoys much international sympathy. Its
leaders will receive many compliments, maybe even Nobel Prizes.
But it will not have permanent peace and security, because after a
series of painful withdrawals in the north, and after the establishment of an Arab state in the heart of the country, the Arabs will
come to us and say just one short word: More.

Whoever is unprepared to struggle in negotiations, will find
himself struggling on the battlefield.[3]

Whatever Netanyahu's future intentions, the brutal reality was that
he watched the Likud being taken over by Ariel Sharon, who, at the
same meeting, won a unanimous vote to become the party's temporary
leader. He would eventually be elected its official leader.

In accepting the temporary position, Sharon could not resist having
a dig at Netanyahu. 'It is not enough to have a candidate, bright as he
may be. A candidate needs to have a strong political movement with
him, and we will rebuild it.'[4] And with that, the Sharon era in the Likud
started, and Netanyahu looked to be finally consigned to the dustbin
of history.

Naturally, there was much gloating in the Arab world over Netanyahu's
defeat. His apparently aggressive approach to the Palestinians had made
him public enemy number one. News of his election defeat was greeted
by cheering crowds in Cairo, and in other Arab capitals with the honk-
ing of car horns and shouts of 'bye, bye, fascist'.

Among senior members of the Palestinian Authority there was a more
balanced view. Mahmoud Abbas told Dennis Ross on the balcony of
the American special envoy's hotel room in Jerusalem that he believed
that on a personal level Netanyahu was not as bad as people suggested.
He added, however, he felt that Netanyahu would have been unwilling
to concede much in final status talks, and now the Palestinians would
be negotiating with their natural partners.

The reaction of the Clinton administration to the demise of
Netanyahu was publicly guarded and privately ecstatic. Clinton's
personal election night message to Netanyahu aside, there was a sense

that the Israeli–Palestinian negotiations with Barak at the helm could be accelerated. If the Americans had looked a little more closely at Barak's statements during the campaign, they might have been more concerned.

Just as he advised the newly elected Rabin in 1992, when he was Chief of Staff of the IDF, Barak in 1999 wanted to devote his attentions to the Syrian track of the peace process, and not to the Palestinians. During the election campaign, he made a promise to get the IDF out of Lebanon with or without an agreement with Syria.

Netanyahu thought this little more than an election gimmick, but matched the offer. It is not clear that if he had been elected he would have gone through with such a controversial move – one that did not enjoy the support of large parts of the top ranks in the IDF. Once elected, however, Barak wanted to test the waters with Syria first, to see if he could strike a deal that would include an agreed Israeli withdrawal from the security zone in Lebanon.

Barak's priorities meant that the Americans were forced to place on hold the Palestinian talks that they had hoped to move forward. The Americans' reading of Barak as Rabin II might well have been correct, but Barak had said during the campaign that he envisaged an agreement with the Palestinians on one side of the fence, and 'us' [the Israelis] on the other side of the fence.

In short, he envisaged a separation: a divorce with few points of contact. He also promised to drive a hard bargain in final status talks. So Barak was no Peres, and this was not late 1995, when everything appeared possible, but, rather, mid-1999.

All of these points were not lost on Netanyahu when he looked back over the election and did his own post-game analysis. In the end, Israelis had not so much rejected Netanyahu's policies and management of the peace process, they had rejected the man; his personality and *modus operandi*. Natan Sharansky concurred with this view that the defeat was 'personal not ideological'.[5] On this basis, Netanyahu understood that most Israelis had not moved too far away from his position towards the peace process.

In Israel, different groups offered differing explanations of the reasons for Netanyahu's defeat. There was a general consensus that Netanyahu's actions had been most responsible for losing it rather than Barak's campaign for winning it. A common charge against Netanyahu was that he had alienated most of the key figures in his cabinet.

Several of the Likud ministers who had resigned or been fired left the party and went either to the right of the Likud (in the case of Benni Begin), or to the left of the party, to the newly created Centre Party (Dan Meridor and Yitzhak Mordechai). In other words, Netanyahu managed to alienate both ends of the Likud. The voters took this to mean that this was a personality issue, rather than an ideological one within the Likud.

The management of the coalition was just as problematic, but Netanyahu's style made the problem worse. Barak would struggle in this area, too, with the general consensus emerging that the two separate elections for Prime Minister and the Knesset were creating an impossible coalition problem for prime ministers from both sides of the political spectrum.

In 1999, as Netanyahu handed over power to his old army commander, in the Prime Minister's office in Jerusalem the near impossibility of successfully governing Israel with its relatively new electoral system was not fully comprehended. Netanyahu had been unable to keep his coalition intact for the full four-year term.

The intention of the supporters of the direct election for Prime Minister had had the opposite effect to strengthening the power of the executive. It had failed. At a time when Israeli leaders were being asked to make historic decisions about the future of the state, rainbow ruling coalitions, which the electoral system produced, weakened them politically.

The right in Israel offered a different perspective on the defeat of Netanyahu and the poor showing of the Likud in the Knesset elections. It argued that Netanyahu had abandoned traditional Likud positions that were based on the Revisionist Zionism movement and specifically the writings of Ze'ev Jabotinsky. The agreements that Netanyahu signed over Hebron and the Wye Memorandum were viewed as unacceptable in that they handed over lands to the Palestinians that the right believed were an integral part of Israel.

In this area, Netanyahu's own father, Benzion, led the chorus of disapproval. In the interview that Netanyahu had given to *Time* magazine at the start of the campaign in January 1999, he was asked for his opinions on comments made by his father in an earlier interview. Benzion Netanyahu had purportedly told a journalist that his son would make a better foreign minister than Prime Minister. Benjamin Netanyahu replied, 'The addendum to that that you're not quoting is that he said nobody would be a better Prime Minister. I'll live with that.'[6]

Much of the commentary on Netanyahu's first term in office focused on his relationship with his father. 'Psychobabble', Netanyahu junior termed such analysis. Nevertheless, questions over the influence of Benzion on Benjamin did not go away, even after his father's death in 2012 at the grand old age of 102. Attempting to decipher the mind of Benjamin Netanyahu, people increasingly turned to examining the mind of his father and speculating on the influence he held over political matters.

Israelis were fond of directing foreigners to look at the politics of the father, to help explain his son's record in office. On a certain level, this helps present two important points about Netanyahu that large parts of the Israeli press focused upon: his hawkish outlook towards the Arabs in general, and his alleged reluctance to accept a final deal with the Palestinians that would include the establishment of a Palestinian state.

Despite an apparent reluctance to speak to journalists, whom he believed to be systematically biased towards the left, Benzion Netanyahu added fuel to the fire about his influence on his son. In an interview with the Israeli daily *Maariv* in 2009, he suggested that sometimes he felt he influenced him and sometimes not. In response to a specific question about how much he influenced his son's opinions, he said:

> I have a general idea. Bibi might aim for the same goals as mine, but he keeps to himself the ways to achieve them, because if he expressed them, he would expose his goals.[7]

When the journalist asked if this was what Benzion wanted, he said:

> No, I just believe that it could be so, because he is smart, because he is very careful, because he has his ways to handle himself. I am talking about tactics regarding the revealing of theories that people with different ideology might not accept. That's why he doesn't expose them: because of the reaction from his enemies as well as from the people whose support he seeks. It's an assumption, but it might be so.

So to his father Netanyahu was an ideologue who had strayed from the flock of the fundamentalist Revisionist Zionist ideology only in terms of the tactics he used, in order to mask his true intentions. Benzion was not alone in reaching this conclusion – most of the Israeli media and the Israeli political left shared the same view. This assertion is also supported by a number of veteran foreign observers of Israeli politics.

The common assumption was that Netanyahu's worldview, attitudes towards the Arabs, and the Palestinians in particular, were all shaped by his father's own vision and politics. On top of this, his father was vital to developing Netanyahu's mindset and set of values on Jewish and world history. Natan Sharansky, a minister in Netanyahu's first government, added in an interview with the *New Yorker* in 1998:

> In his day to day activities, it [history] helps Bibi to somehow stay in focus. He gets caught in the daily struggles, but he always has the view of history on his mind.[8]

Added to this was Netanyahu's seeming need to ingratiate himself to his hard-to-please father. Benzion was never a man who showed much emotion. Even when his own son was being sworn in as Prime Minister in 1996, he sat in the public gallery showing no outward sign of delight and pleasure that his son was becoming Israel's leader. Instead, while Netanyahu served as Prime Minister, Benzion passed the time of day by telephoning his son after some of his speeches in order to correct his Hebrew grammar.[9]

17

Father

Over the summer months of 1999, Netanyahu adjusted to life after the political circus that had dominated his time for more than a decade. He reflected on the commonalities of his personal narrative to his father, but, crucially, also the differences in political outlook and culture that made them distinct from one another.

The sum total of these differences was that his father was an ideologue and was not reconciled to any recognition of Arab and Palestinian rights in the conflict. His son was not. What they did share was the sense of being strangers in a strange land: for Netanyahu senior the strange land was the United States, and for Netanyahu junior it was Israel.

Benzion Mileikowsky was born in Warsaw, at a time when Poland was still part of the Russian empire. In 1920, when he was 10, his family left for Palestine. Soon after, Benzion's Lithuanian-born father, Rabbi Nathan Mileikowsky, changed the family name to the Hebrew Netanyahu (God has given).

Like many Jews of his generation in Palestine, Benzion was politically active and toured Europe and North America trying to convince Jews to return to Zion. In contrast to his father, Benzion lived a secular life, and this lifestyle was passed on to his own three children. Despite Benjamin Netanyahu's use of religious imagery in his speeches, and his frequent walks to the Western Wall to pray, he clearly shares his father's secular orientation.[1]

As a student, Benzion majored in medieval history at the Hebrew University in Jerusalem, from where he graduated in 1933. Soon after graduating, he started co-editing Revisionist publications in Palestine.[2] From 1940 to 1948, he was based in New York, and in 1944 married Tsila Segal, from Petach Tivka, who had studied law at Gray's Inn, London, but never practised it.[3]

From the 1950s to the 1970s, the Netanyahus flitted between living in Israel and the United States, with Benzion securing teaching posts in Philadelphia, at the University of Denver, and finally at Cornell University in New York. He retained a degree of anger towards the Israeli universities that he believed were run and staffed by left-wingers. The sense of discontent he felt about, in effect, having to go into exile to secure a position that would allow him to support his family, did not diminish with the passing of time.

Benzion believed that as a Revisionist Zionist he had been discriminated against for political reasons. He made no secret of his political leanings from an early age. He interrupted his academic career in British-controlled Palestine to become chief aide and secretary to Ze'ev Jabotinsky, the leader of the Revisionist Zionists. After Jabotinsky's death in 1940, he continued as an unofficial guardian of his legacy.

Like Jabotinsky, Netanyahu believed in a 'Greater Israel', a Jewish right to settle on both banks of the River Jordan, while maintaining an Iron Wall until the Arabs recognized the Jewish presence in Palestine.

He also believed in a free economy, in contrast to the socialist-dominated one that characterized the early years of the State of Israel. His preference for a free economy was one characteristic that was clearly passed on to his son, and could be seen in Benjamin's business career and his political endorsement of free-market economics.

He opposed the UN General Assembly partition plan of November 1947, for not giving Israel enough land to survive behind viable and secure borders. His attitude towards the Arabs, if anything, hardened over time, leading him to fall out with Jabotinsky's successor as leader of the Revisionist Zionists, Menachem Begin. This led to him becoming something of an outsider, not only in the United States, but also in the Revisionist Zionist movement of which he was a member.[4]

In the same interview with *Maariv*, during which he had openly speculated about his influence on the politics of his son, he outlined why he didn't believe in the existence of the Palestinian people. As he put it:

The Bible finds no worse image than this of the man from the desert. And why? Because he has no respect for any law, because in the desert he can do as he pleases. The tendency towards conflict is in the essence of the Arab. He is an enemy by essence. His personality won't allow him any compromise or agreement. It doesn't matter what kind of resistance he will meet, what price he will pay. His existence is one of perpetual war.

Israel's must be the same. The two states solution doesn't exist. There are no two people here. There is a Jewish people and an Arab population . . . there is no Palestinian people, so you don't create a state for an imaginary nation . . . they only call themselves a people in order to fight the Jews.[5]

When asked about any potential solution, Benzion's outlook was far from rosy:

No solution but force and strong military rule. Any outbreak will bring upon the Arabs enormous suffering. We shouldn't wait for a big mutiny to start, but rather act immediately with great force to prevent them from going on.

From 1949 onwards, Benzion concentrated on his academic career, while earning additional income as editor of the hugely popular *Encyclopedia Hebraica*. He once told a journalist, 'And for that I got the highest salary in Jerusalem.'[6] He and the family moved to the United States in 1956. Effectively, this was an exile for the Netanyahus, but they did keep the family house in Jerusalem and returned to it later in their lives.

Benzion's research focused on another aspect of Jewish history, the origins of the Spanish Inquisition in fifteenth-century Spain. His scholarly work he sees as fitting within the overall framework of Jewish history of being 'a history of holocausts'.[7] His research findings on the causes of the Spanish Inquisition are unsurprisingly dark. He concluded that Jews would not be saved by conversion. Such was the resentment towards them they would still be subjected to exile and mass killing.[8]

While he was a successful scholar in the United States, Benzion felt that he never received the recognition that his work merited. This sense of dissatisfaction was coupled with a desire to seek revenge on the parts of Israel that he felt were controlled by left-wing elites, namely academia and the media – especially television. His son's deep mistrust of large segments of the Israeli media had its origins in his father's contempt for it.

As a result of his father's career move, Benjamin and his two brothers spent much of their formative years in the United States. For the young Benjamin Netanyahu, the United States represented home. He was fully immersed in the culture and educational values of the US. The family retained an air of superiority that came with the rank of their father and were seen as upwardly mobile Jews.

As he grew up, Netanyahu envisaged his future being in the United States. Much as he admired his father, enjoyed conversations and arguments over Jewish history, he showed little interest in following in his father's footsteps to become a historian. Benjamin sensed there were limited opportunities in the field, and that the salary wasn't especially good.

The key to understanding Netanyahu was that while he was to some extent influenced by the politics and outlook of his father, he was more influenced by American political culture that promoted pragmatism over ideology. That is not to say that his father's politics did not leave their mark on him.

For the young Benjamin Netanyahu it was easy to fall into the same type of mindset as his father. During the 1970s, there was no meaningful peace process between the Israelis and Palestinians, in an era that was characterized by violent exchanges between the two sides. In short, there was no peace plan for resolving the conflict, and the PLO had not met the minimal American requirements for joining the diplomatic process: an abandonment of violence and recognition of Israel.

Netanyahu viewed Israel's war in Lebanon, which started in June 1982, as a legitimate attempt by Israel to impose a military solution on the Palestinian issue. Although he did not serve in the war, his strong defence of it in the United States indicated that he subscribed to its aims. The war, with its heavy civilian casualties as the result of Israeli air raids and shelling, did not go down well in America, even in the era of the strong pro-Israel President Ronald Reagan.

Israeli war aims in Lebanon failed on both military and political fronts. Yasser Arafat and the PLO were able, with international help, to be evacuated from Beirut and set up a new headquarters in Tunis, from where it carried on its campaign against Israel. The failure of the Israelis to install an apparent Christian ally into power in Lebanon also came to define the failed military campaign.

Israel's failures in Lebanon, and the damage to the perception of the country in the United States despite the best efforts of Netanyahu and other pro-Israel groups, led to a slow process of transformation in Israel. The key to the change was the increasing awareness, first among senior members of the IDF, and then among the centre-left politicians, that if Israel could not militarily defeat the PLO, it would at some point have to talk to them.[9]

As Netanyahu started out on his diplomatic career at the United Nations, the political ground beneath Israel was slowly shifting. The debate in Israel was mirrored within the institutions of the Palestinian national movement. Doves within the movement argued that the Lebanon War confirmed that its armed struggle against Israel was not working. They called instead for the abandonment of the armed struggle, and its replacement with a political campaign that would see the PLO call for a two-state solution to the conflict. The hawks in the PLO, and the debate between the two groups, dominated the PLO agenda in the subsequent years.

The changed thinking among both key elements in Israel and the PLO took time to be developed into new policies that transformed the desire of both parties – for differing reasons – to seek an accommodation with each other. While this change did not make the extremist politics of Benzion Netanyahu irrelevant to the new political realities, it meant that it would be difficult for his son to follow such policies in the political mainstream in Israel.

In 1999, as people considered the influence of Benzion on the politics of his son and the government he led, many appeared to miss the point that Netanyahu was a centrist politician who understood how to win elections in Israel – and how to lose them. He may very well have sympathized with his father's attitude towards the Arabs, and specifically the Palestinians, but the policies his government adopted towards the peace process did not reflect this.

Benzion's curious interview with *Maariv*, during which he effectively tried to paint his son as 'one of us' – meaning extremist – failed to reflect his son's record in office. The point he argued, that Benjamin Netanyahu was somehow deceiving the world into thinking that he was something that he was not, was particularly damaging to his son, and provided his political enemies with much ammunition with which to attack him.

According to Benzion there was a difference between what his son believed and what he was able to do as Prime Minister. This was a clear criticism of the role of the Americans in pressuring Netanyahu into doing something he didn't want to do: Hebron and Wye being two major examples.

While it would be naïve to ignore the influence of the Clinton administration in leaning on both the Israelis and the Palestinians at key junctures to reach an accommodation, this was not the primary reason that Netanyahu proved willing to put his name to agreements with Arafat.

Benjamin Netanyahu's upbringing and education in the United States made him more an American politician than an Israeli one. His rapid concession of the election to Barak, and the announcement of his resignation from the leadership of the Likud with immediate effect, was typical of the American rather than the Israeli political system. In these respects, along with his deeply held belief in free-market economics, Netanyahu was more American than he was Israeli.

It was true that he adored his father, wanted to please him, sympathized with his ideology and shared his sense of being an outsider, but this was not translated into the practical – more pragmatic – politics needed to run a country like Israel. The death of Yonatan at Entebbe had moved Benjamin up the ladder in importance to his father.

Benjamin's transformation from middle manager to Prime Minister was, in no small part, down to his newly found ambition to carry the family torch, and to right the perceived injustices that had been inflicted upon his father. There is little evidence to suggest that all of this was translated into any desire to try to implement his father's extremist views towards the Arabs.

In retrospect, in political terms Netanyahu's decision to resign so soon from the leadership of the Likud was a mistake. It is doubtful whether a home-grown Israeli political leader would have erred in this manner. Netanyahu should have stayed and fought for the soul of the Likud.

He genuinely believed that his defeat to Barak did not represent a rejection of his policies, but, rather, was the result of the wheeling and

dealing at both cabinet and coalition levels that he was forced to undertake in order to keep an unruly government from collapsing.

By handing over the reins to Ariel Sharon, Netanyahu allowed his
political rival the opportunity to rebuild the Likud and change its orientation, away from Netanyahu, and towards the new leader. It would
take Netanyahu six years to return to the leadership of the party, by
which time it was on the brink of becoming irrelevant to Israeli politics.

By exiting the stage so soon, Netanyahu lost an ability to help shape
the national debate towards the terms of the final agreement with the
Palestinians. He also missed the opportunity to gain from the political
fallout, when the parties failed to agree a deal just over a year later.

Just as the Netanyahus had relocated to America when Israeli
academia failed to take Benzion into its bosom, Benjamin Netanyahu
looked in the same direction after the Israeli public had so convincingly
rejected him as their political leader. The connection with America as a
shelter from the storm, and as an opportunity to earn a pot of gold, was
therefore passed on from father to son.

This connection between the Netanyahus was far more substantive
than the ideological ones that Netanyahu's political foes back in Israel
liked to highlight. Netanyahu looked to use his contacts to help develop
ties between Israeli high-tech companies and the United States. On
top of this, he joined the lucrative speaker circuit in the United States,
where he continued to draw big audiences.

Over the summer months, the wave of optimism that had originally greeted Barak's victory over Netanyahu started to subside among
Israelis. Familiar problems – forging a viable governing coalition, along
with Barak's autocratic *modus operandi* – quickly reminded Israelis that
the removal of Netanyahu was not the end of the story in terms of solving the country's problems.

If Benzion Netanyahu was displeased with his son's efforts as Prime
Minister and the deals he struck with the Palestinians, he must have
been outraged about what materialized in the brief 18 months of the
Barak government and its peacemaking agenda. While the Netanyahus
watched on from the sidelines, Benjamin's old army commander tried
in vain to complete the circle of peacemaking that Yitzhak Rabin and
Shimon Peres had started in 1993.

The first 18 months of the post-Netanyahu era were to prove difficult ones for Barak, the government, the Clinton administration and

the Palestinians. The only people who gained were the extremists on both sides, who, as the political process unravelled, were able to fill the vacuum with their brand of violence and destruction. Although they didn't know it at the time, many Israelis would come to look back over the first Netanyahu era with a sense of nostalgia, for the relative calm that it had brought them in terms of security.

18

Invisible

His swagger and deeply held sense of inner confidence did not desert Netanyahu as he took his break from political life in Israel, which he preferred to think of simply as a sabbatical. Israel's first and longest serving Prime Minister, David Ben-Gurion, had taken a voluntary sabbatical at the start of the 1950s, before returning to lead the nation in the 1956 War.

Netanyahu's own sabbatical was far less of a voluntary one, but the fact that he considered it to be one at all was a clear indication that he saw his exile from political leadership in Israel as temporary and not permanent.

Netanyahu used his temporary political exile to multiply his personal wealth. His speaking activities alone brought him considerable income. *Globes Israel* estimated that he was paid $60,000 per engagement and gave more than 20 speeches a year around the world. This resulted in him making a profit of around NIS 15 million (New Israeli Shekels) from his speaking activities alone to foreign businesses and at wealthy universities.[1]

Netanyahu's earning potential was not restricted to the speaking circuit; he was also much sought after in the consultancy field. *Forbes Israel* outlined his activities during the period he was out of office:

1. Served for two years as a strategic advisor to BATM Advanced Communications Ltd. He received a salary of several hundred thousand shekels a year, and options, which he subsequently exercised.

2. Electric Fuel (name changed to Arotech Corporation), which he helped broker a deal with Wal-Mart Stores.
3. Earned $150,000 for holding approximately 15 meetings with wealthy people, including the billionaires Idan Ofer and Poju Zabludowicz on behalf of Electric Fuels. *Globes* claimed he received $2.5 million in salary and stock options from these two companies.
4. Senior strategic advisor to Net2Wireless Communications, which he took up in November 2001.[2]

In 2013, *Forbes Israel* described Netanyahu as Israel's sixth richest politician. The magazine estimated his fortune at around NIS 41 million. The magazine argued that Netanyahu had made the vast majority of his personal wealth in the period from 1999 and 2001.[3]

In the United States it was perfectly normal for former leaders to make a post-office earning in this manner, but in Israel it raised more than a few eyebrows. Past prime ministers of the country had quietly retired and written their memoirs, and made extensive use of the small office in Tel Aviv that the state provided to all ex-leaders. None had tried to accumulate a private fortune in the manner that Netanyahu had done.

Netanyahu also courted controversy, when it transpired that he held an offshore bank account with the Royal Bank of Scotland in Jersey, reputed to be one of the best tax havens in the world. Netanyahu did not break any laws, but it created the impression of trying to avoid full tax exposure on his enhanced income. Though the holding of an offshore account was not illegal, the Israeli tax authorities discouraged the practice.[4]

When details of the account became public 15 years later, it was cited by Netanyahu's political enemies as evidence of his lack of Zionist Israeli credentials. The Labour MK Shelly Yachimovich, who was a fierce critic of Netanyahu's financial affairs, issued a strong statement against him:

I suggest that Netanyahu run in the next election for the leadership of the island of Jersey, where he also deposited his money in order to not pay taxes to the state . . . Depositing Netanyahu's funds in a tax haven is the opposite of Zionism, of the love of the state and concern for its citizens. It's simply hutzpah. A vast chasm separates Netanyahu's norms and lifestyle and the public he purportedly represents.[5]

Despite question marks over the depositing of his additional earnings in Jersey, few argued that Netanyahu was anything other than a huge success on the lecture circuit and as a business consultant. He commanded such substantial fees because wealthy individuals and institutions remained interested in what he had to say. The Israeli electorate had rejected him, but his appeal to the international market, particularly in North America, was undiminished.

In the business sector, Netanyahu's finely tuned political sound bites were replaced by a series of highly articulate pitches for the companies he was representing. During these pitches, he was careful to place his talk in the context of Israel's developing economic relations with the outside world. This gave his salesman act a touch of gravitas, and reminded his audience that his political aspirations were far from over.

> The American technology industry has recognized Israel as one of the foremost regions of the world developing next generation, telecommunications technologies. The result has been an unprecedented level of technology transfer between the United States and Israel.
>
> The development of US–Israeli business relationships has resulted in unprecedented, dynamic technology idea and capital transfer between our nations. The dreams of globalization, of learning between cultures, and of peace, cooperation and trust are being realized through the businesses of science and communications resulting from technology.
>
> . . . I believe Israel's BATM, a star of the London Exchange, and its North American subsidiary Telco Systems, have the vision and the resources to be the Grand Slam of the Desert, the company that reshapes the way Israeli technology companies are considered in the global marketplace . . . BATM's technology is world class.[6]

The impression from this pitch, and others he made, was of a man who was capable of developing a successful and highly lucrative career at the top end of business management. The crossover between his political and business networks was very revealing.

As well as making his fortune, Netanyahu was preparing the groundwork for the raising of support for future political campaigns. In this respect, despite his electoral loss to Barak, he remained the favoured politician of the super-wealthy Jewish businessmen based inside and outside Israel.

While Netanyahu made his fortune, political events in Israel developed in an altogether predictable manner. Having taken longer than expected to put together his rainbow coalition, which resembled Netanyahu's, Barak was forced to devote a lot of time and energy to keeping it in place. His preference was to move forward on the Syrian track of the peace process prior to final status talks with the Palestinians. Barak, however, had leftover business from Netanyahu's Wye Memorandum to conclude.

Initial signs on the Palestinian front, however, appeared more optimistic than during the Netanyahu era. On 4 September 1999, Barak and Arafat signed a second Wye Accord at Sharm el-Sheikh with Secretary of State Albright, President Mubarak and King Abdullah also signing as witnesses. The agreement was seen as kick-starting the peace process that had been frozen since December the previous year.

The cabinet ratified the agreement on 5 September by 21 votes to 2, and on 8 September the Knesset approved it by 54 votes to 23. As a result, on 9 September Israel released 199 of 350 Palestinian prisoners within the framework of the Wye II Accords, and on 10 September Israel transferred 7 per cent of the West Bank land from Area C to Area B (Palestinian civil control and joint Israeli–Palestinian security control). All of this helped allow the framework agreement on final status talks to get underway on 8 November.

This, however, was as good as it got. As Netanyahu suspected, talks with the Palestinians would soon unravel even if he were no longer at the helm of the Israeli government. Barak and Arafat failed to come to an understanding over the next Israeli redeployment from the West Bank, after Arafat had refused to sign the map of the proposed redeployment. After seven rounds of talks on the framework agreement for final status talks before the end of the year, little progress was reported in resolving the differences between the parties on any of the core issues.

As Netanyahu persumed, Barak instead had been devoting a great deal of time to the preliminary negotiations with the Syrians. He was essentially making the same offer to Damascus that Netanyahu was reported to have made in the autumn of 1998.

On 13 December 1999, amidst a sense of growing optimism about the Syrian talks, Barak told the cabinet that an agreement was potentially only a few weeks away. He later informed the Knesset that Israel would pay a heavy territorial price for the peace, before he survived a vote of confidence on the issue of a potential withdrawal from the disputed Golan Heights.

Netanyahu, like the rest of Israel, watched Barak's manoeuvrings with the Syrians with considerable interest. The deal that Barak formally offered, while similar in nature to the one Netanyahu put forward, was on this occasion being presented by a government that appeared to be politically stable.

In the end, the direct negotiations that took place in Shepherdstown, near Washington, from 3 to 10 January failed to produce a deal. There were a number of reasons for the failure: notably lack of agreement over the borders of the Golan Heights with the Syrians demanding that Israel withdraw to the 4 June 1967 lines.

Both the Israelis and the Syrians had hoped to secure large-scale aid packages from the United States for signing an agreement. The Israeli–Egyptian peace agreement had been accompanied with such aid. Barak wanted as much as $30 billion to modernize the IDF, and the Syrians also wanted a large amount of military aid.

While the President appeared willing to meet the asking price, Congress made it clear that it would not do so, and was reluctant to offer Syria any aid package. The prospects of a peace deal receded and the talks were not reopened.

The failure of the Syrian negotiations in January 2000 was the start of a devastatingly bad year for Barak and the immediate prospects of Arab–Israeli peace. By the end of the year, Netanyahu would be on the prowl, making plans for a potential political comeback – and Barak's time in office would come to a premature end. Almost everything that could go wrong for Barak, and his peacemaking efforts, did so during the course of a year, which coincided with the last full year of the Clinton administration.

Arguably, the only real positive for the government came when Barak was able to carry out his election pledge to withdraw the IDF from southern Lebanon. He did so, however, without any agreement with the Syrians, which greatly complicated the security arrangement, and did not bode well for the prospects of peace along Israel's border with Lebanon.

The withdrawal of the IDF started on 21 May 2000 and was completed three days later on 24 May. There had been fears that Hezbollah fighters would target the IDF as they withdrew, but the operation passed largely without incident, and the IDF was successfully relocated on the Israeli side of the border fence. While Barak was lauded by the international community for his actions in ending Israel's effective occupation of southern Lebanon, the operation had taken place against the advice of many senior officers in the IDF.

In retrospect, it was a temporary fix for Israel's Lebanon problem, and there would be a major war with Hezbollah six years later. Netanyahu, having made a similar pledge during the same campaign, was in little position to be critical of Barak's moves, but there was deep concern that the withdrawal would set a dangerous precedent that could be used by the Palestinians in the West Bank and the Gaza Strip.

This precedent centred upon the concept gleaned from Lebanon that if you made life difficult enough for the IDF – as Hezbollah clearly had with its guerrilla-style campaign – the IDF would pack its bags and depart the lands it had occupied. Later in the year, several Palestinian leaders admitted to absorbing this point, as they planned and orchestrated their own campaign against the IDF in the areas of the West Bank and Gaza Strip that Israel still controlled.

Unwittingly, Israel had created an impression that it would not stand and fight for territories outside its international borders. For many Israelis this would prove to be a tragic mistake for the country, and it would contribute to the premature ending of Barak's premiership.

On the Palestinian front, Netanyahu's sober warning that the implementation of additional interim stages would prove difficult was borne out as Barak and Arafat, despite extensive negotiations, found it difficult to find common ground. Both leaders, weakened by internal events, looked to try to consolidate their domestic positions, often at the expense of the peace process.

With his coalition starting to crumble, Barak gambled on a one-off summit to try to resolve all the outstanding issues in the peace process, and to essentially negotiate everything in one go. He looked to the Camp David Accords between Israel and Egypt as his precedent.

It was a risky strategy, and initially the Americans were not keen to agree to it. With President Clinton due to leave office in under a year, and with few viable alternatives, the President agreed to host the summit at Camp David.

Arafat was less than happy to attend, arguing with some justification that his position was too weak domestically for him to be able to make the major concessions that the summit would demand of both sides. Clinton, however, convinced him that this might be his last chance to try to finish the peace process with a Labour-led government in Israel. The Americans had watched the process of the near-collapse of the Barak government with concern.

Confirmation that Barak's government had reached the end of the road came on the eve of the Camp David Summit, when, on 9 July 2000, the NRP, Shas and Yisrael Ba'aliyah quit the government. In addition, his Minister of Foreign Affairs, David Levy, said that he would not attend the summit, and he formally resigned on 2 August. Barak pressed on with the summit in the hope of reaching a deal that he would present to the Knesset, and the people, via a new election or a referendum.

The summit was a spectacular failure, ending on 25 July without agreement. President Clinton made it clear to the outside world that he blamed Arafat for this, and went on Israeli television to praise Barak's courage for the offers he made to the Palestinians at the summit. Since the summit, various versions as to what went on have been released, which suggest a more complex narrative than the one outlined by Clinton at its conclusion when he blamed Arafat.[7]

The fallout was difficult for both sides to control. In Israel, while Barak struggled, Netanyahu reminded everybody that his predictions were right. The Israeli left blamed the eventual collapse of the peace process with the Palestinians on the Netanyahu era, which had created the conditions for failure. The Israeli centre and right argued that it was questionable if Arafat wanted peace in the first place.

What shocked many Israelis the most, however, was the extent of the concessions that Barak offered to the Palestinians. Netanyahu, like Peres and Rabin before him, had done little to prepare the nation as to how a potential final status agreement would look. The biggest surprise was Barak's offer on Jerusalem, to effectively divide the city.

Netanyahu watched all of this unfold from the sidelines. He foresaw an opportunity for a major political comeback. Public opinion in

Israel after the failed summit started to shift back towards Netanyahu's perception of the peace process. Despite Barak's attempts to reposition his premiership at the end of the summit into a more centrist location on the political spectrum, he looked finished as a leader.

The biggest obstacle to a Netanyahu comeback would not come from the incumbent Prime Minister, but, rather, from Ariel Sharon, who had taken Netanyahu's seat at the helm of the Likud following the 1999 elections.

The one stumbling block that was placed in the way of a return to active politics for Netanyahu was removed on 27 September 2000. The Attorney General, Elyakim Rubinstein, announced that he had found insufficient evidence to try Benjamin and Sara Netanyahu on charges of stealing gifts considered to be state property, as well as taking bribes from a contractor.[8] The removal of potential charges was seen as the final piece of the jigsaw that would allow Netanyahu, recently returned from the United States, to run for Prime Minister.

Opinion polls taken in Israel on 27 September put Netanyahu and Barak neck and neck for Prime Minister, but with Netanyahu outscoring Sharon and the rest of the potential candidates from the right. The kingmakers of Netanyahu's previous electoral victory in 1996 were already lined up behind him.

'I hope Netanyahu will now be a candidate for Prime Minister. If Barak runs against Netanyahu in elections, Shas will 100% call on our voters to support Netanyahu and I think all the religious parties will do the same,' said Shlomo Benizri, the leader of Shas.[9] With the religious parties once again lining up behind him, Netanyahu was rapidly transformed from outsider to potential alternative Prime Minister.

The re-emergence of Netanyahu on the political scene was neither a fluke nor a coincidence. In between making his private fortune, Netanyahu had been careful to stay in touch with the key players in Israeli politics, especially the religious parties. He remained unconvinced that Israelis were ready to elect the ultra-hawkish Sharon as Prime Minister, and, as a result, he saw an opportunity to try to reassert his control over the right and centre-right in Israel.

The sudden reappearance of Netanyahu out of nowhere was quite odd. It reflected the deep sense of pessimism that characterized Israeli society following the collapse of the Camp David Summit. The former Prime Minister offered no new policies and no real admission of the failings of his first administration. Israeli society was moving towards Netanyahu's political positions, and not the other way round. Indeed, Netanyahu made it clear that while they might be cosmetic changes to reflect the political realities of the day, he would be offering much of the same in terms of policy and style.

For Barak, a Netanyahu political comeback was potentially terminal for his chances. The Prime Minister understood that by exiting the stage so quickly following the 1999 election Netanyahu was not – in the eyes of the electorate – implicated in the political mess that had occurred since his departure.

There was also a deeper understanding that some of the problems that occurred between 1996 and 1999 might not have wholly been Netanyahu's fault. Barak's difficulties in keeping his coalition together mirrored those of Netanyahu. Blame for the relatively poor performance of Netanyahu and Barak was to some extent being redirected at the flaws in the electoral system that allowed Israelis to directly elect their Prime Minister.

For Sharon, a Netanyahu comeback was arguably a bigger problem than it was for Barak. It was within this context that, on 28 September 2000, Sharon tried to reassert his authority over the right-wing in Israel. He decided to visit the Temple Mount and was accompanied by heavy Israeli security. The visit was seen as provocative by Palestinians and as making an Israeli claim to the holy sites in Jerusalem.

Violence erupted almost immediately with Palestinians throwing rocks at Sharon. The Israeli security forces responded with rubber bullets and tear gas. As a result, violent clashes between Palestinians and the IDF broke out in the West Bank and Gaza Strip, and spread the next day to a number of Israeli cities. Israeli Arabs were heavily involved in the protests and 13 were killed in the clashes. Sharon's visit had led to the outbreak of the Second *Intifada*.

The *Intifada* of 2000 did not resemble the first one in 1987: this was more like a mini-war between the Israelis and Palestinians. As a result of the escalating violence, Barak was given little option but to suspend the peace process with the Palestinians, which he formally did on 22 October 2000.

In political terms, the outbreak of the *Intifada* had dire consequences for Barak, whose support, according to opinion polls, collapsed. The final nail in the coffin for his premiership conceivably came on 29

October, when talks about the establishment of a national emergency government with Ariel Sharon broke down.

Netanyahu was arguably the biggest political winner from the outbreak of the violence. Despite still not formally committing himself to making a return to politics, opinion polls in Israel indicated that he would win a landslide victory if elections were held in the autumn of 2000. In times of violence and threat to national security, the Israeli electorate tends to swing towards the right in the short term, and this was the case as shown in the polls taken after the outbreak of the Second *Intifada*.

For Netanyahu, the biggest obstacle to regaining the premiership, which he had lost so convincingly only 18 months earlier, was Ariel Sharon. The new leader of the Likud had tried to rebuild the party, filling key positions with his own supporters. There were other figures in the party who wanted to run for Prime Minister as well, including Silvan Shalom, who were opposed to standing aside for a potential Netanyahu run for the premiership.

As the violence on the ground worsened, Netanyahu's popularity continued to rise. It was clear that he was more popular among the electorate than he was in the party organs of the Likud under Sharon. He was faced with a critical choice: whether to return to active politics or continue with his successful career as a speaker and a consultant to high-tech companies.

As he considered his options, it was clear that Israel wanted him back in the political fray, but if he were to return he wanted to do so on his own terms. Achieving these terms would not prove to be as easy as he had initially envisaged. The direction of his future career was still far from decided. In the meantime, both Barak and Sharon in their own ways continued to manoeuvre themselves in order to try to prevent the return of Benjamin Netanyahu.

19

False Start

In the wake of the continued violence, a lack of parliamentary support and pressure from within his own party, Ehud Barak announced his intention to resign as Prime Minister on 9 December 2000, and called for a direct election for the Prime Minister to be held within the two months as stated under Israeli electoral law. There was more than met the eye to Barak's resignation, which amounted to an attempt to prevent Benjamin Netanyahu being able to run in the election.

In normal circumstances, direct elections for the Prime Minister and for the Knesset would take place at the same time. There was a clause in Israeli electoral law that allowed for elections to be held separately. Barak's resignation was seen as allowing for an election for Prime Minister without dissolving the Knesset and holding elections for it at the same time.

Problematically for Netanyahu, basic law specified in such circumstances that only members of the Knesset would be eligible to run in an election for Prime Minister. As he had resigned his Knesset seat following his defeat at the polls in 1996, as things stood Netanyahu would not have been able to put his name forward to run in the election.

In the Israeli media Barak's decision to resign was widely seen as a brazen attempt to keep Netanyahu out of the race. As ever, Israeli politicians had one eye on the weekly opinion polls published on television and in the print media that showed support for Netanyahu continuing to grow.

Barak's claim that he was attempting to get a new mandate to help subdue the violence and, if possible, seek a final status deal with the

Palestinians appeared to fool nobody. A campaign to support a change in the electoral law was launched, whereby the new law would not limit the candidates to only existing members of the Knesset. The legislation became known as 'Bibi's Bill', a reference to the man whom the authors of the bill wanted in the race.

Under political pressure to correct the impression that he had tried to prevent Netanyahu from running, Barak announced that he would support the bill that would amend the electoral law. In truth, given the political momentum that the bill had generated, he was faced with few viable alternatives other than to offer his belated support for the bill.

Barak's change of heart appeared to clear the way for Netanyahu to return to active politics. There was speculation as to whether he would challenge Sharon in the Likud, or whether he would simply adopt a more direct route and allow his name to go on the ballot paper for Prime Minister as a type of candidate for national emergency. In the end, Netanyahu never had to make this potentially difficult decision.

What worried him more than Sharon was the fragmented nature of the Knesset in which the increasing power of the smaller and religious parties had made governing very difficult. Netanyahu's predictions that Barak, despite his handsome election victory, would find it just as difficult to govern as he had, had proved to be accurate.

As he considered his options, Netanyahu told his close advisors that he didn't want to experience a rerun of his first premiership, during which he had spent much time managing endless coalition crises. Noting that the same opinion polls that were showing strong support for Netanyahu were also indicating that the parties of the right would make major gains if Knesset elections were held as well, Netanyahu decided to go for broke.

In a show of staggering confidence, he announced that unless the Knesset was dissolved and new elections held for the parliament at the same time as the direct election for Prime Minister, he would withdraw his proposed candidature for Prime Minister. In retrospect, his effective ultimatum appears strange. Clearly overplaying his hand, he had failed to closely analyse the political map of Israel. Had he taken the time to undertake a proper investigation, he would have seen just why the Knesset was not going to dissolve itself.

It was a bad call from a man who prided himself on being the king of the murky wheeling and dealing that defines much of the politics of the Knesset. Once again, the key to Netanyahu's plans lay with Shas and the ultra-orthodox. He received assurances from Shas that it would support him in the Prime Minister's race if he ran against Barak. The opinion polls, however, indicated that if Knesset elections were held Shas would lose a number of seats.

The mistake made by Netanyahu was the assumption that Shas would be willing to pay the price to get him elected as Prime Minister, for his ability to form a narrow based right-wing and religious party coalition. Shas, however, was not willing to pay this price. Instead, its leadership made it clear that it would not support any bill calling for the dissolution of the Knesset.

The result was that the Knesset did eventually pass 'Bibi's Bill' but did not vote to dissolve itself. Netanyahu, as a result, was out of the race seemingly as quickly as he had entered it. His withdrawal opened the way for Sharon to run as the undisputed champion of the right in Israel. It proved to be a costly decision for Netanyahu as he once again disappeared off the political radar in Israel, and Sharon moved to strengthen his control over the Likud and the right in Israel in general.

The concept of self-sacrifice for the good of Netanyahu was a constant factor in his politics. The Likud had essentially been sacrificed in 1996 to help him persuade his two right-wing rivals for Prime Minister, Levy and Eitan, to withdraw from the race. In 2000, he was asking members of the Knesset to give up their seats so that he could potentially have a more favourable parliament that would make it easier for him to govern.

Once bitten and twice shy, Israeli politicians – especially religious ones – were not going to fall on their swords for the good of Netanyahu. In wanting to return on solely his own terms, Netanyahu illustrated that he had lost none of his sense of self-importance and arrogance. The difference in 2000 was that Israelis, who were deeply shocked by the outbreak of the Second *Intifada*, and its intensity, did not seem to mind these personality traits as much as they had done less than two years earlier.

Netanyahu's deep sense of fatalism led him to believe, even after his failure to return in 2000, that it would not be long before the country turned to him once more. Put simply, he still expected to be Prime Minister in the near future, and did not think that either Barak or Sharon would be able to bring quiet to the country and reduce the aspirations of the Palestinians.

As Netanyahu faded once more into the background, the political life of Israel rapidly moved on and focused on the Prime Minister's elections, which were scheduled to take place on 6 February 2001. With the shadow of elections hanging over him, Barak made one last effort to secure an overall final agreement with Arafat. The timing of this effort was critical, as President Clinton was due to leave office on 20 January 2001 to be succeeded by George W. Bush.

With this date in mind talks on final status were resumed on 11 January, but there appeared little prospect of reaching any agreement before Clinton's departure. The President-elect had made it clear during the campaign that he believed the Clinton administration had become over-involved in trying to resolve the Israeli–Palestinian conflict. Bush assured voters that he would not make the same mistake, and that resolving the conflict would not be top of his foreign policy priorities.

When the deadline of Clinton leaving office was reached and passed, the next and final one that occupied the mind of the Israeli and Palestinian negotiators was the Israeli election date of 6 February. If the polls were to be believed, Sharon was set to win a handsome victory over Barak. The only way back for Barak appeared to be a last-minute peace deal with the Palestinians in which he would subsequently make the election a referendum on ratifying the deal.

With this in mind, the formal talks started in Taba, Egypt, on 21 January. Arafat, perhaps belatedly realizing the seriousness of the situation, had instigated the talks. Shlomo Ben-Ami, Israel's Minister of Foreign Affairs, described the talks as the last chance for a generation to agree a comprehensive peace deal with the Palestinians. The agenda for the talks was highly ambitious. Building on the few areas of agreement that had been reached the previous summer at the Camp David Summit, the negotiators tried to bridge the gap on the outstanding issues.

After nearly a week of talks, the negotiations ended without a comprehensive agreement. In statements issued to the press, the parties said that progress had been made, but that they wouldn't be able to reach an agreement before the 6 February Israeli elections. This was a severe blow for Barak and for the rest of the Israeli left. It would prove to be the last chance for the Israeli centre-left and the PLO to secure a deal on their own terms.

The medium- to long-term consequence of the failure at Taba was that the Israeli centre-right would dominate Israeli politics for the next decade and a half. He couldn't have known it at the time, but Ehud Barak would turn out to be the last leader of the Labour Party in Israel who would go on to become Prime Minister. Prior to Barak, every leader of the party from Ben-Gurion to Peres had also served at some juncture as Prime Minister. From this point, successive Israeli governments would be led by a Prime Minister from the centre-right.

As expected, Barak lost the direct election for Prime Minister on 6 February, but by a bigger margin than commentators and the polls had predicted. Ariel Sharon won by a landslide, winning by 62.39 per cent to Barak's 37.61 per cent of the votes cast. The voter turnout was only 62.3 per cent, which was the lowest for any national election in Israeli history.[1] The turnout was put down partly to the boycott of the elections by Israeli Arabs in protest over their treatment during the *Intifada*.

Among Palestinians, the outside world and the Israeli left, and even parts of the Israeli right, there was a great deal of concern about the election of a man who likened himself to a political bulldozer. This was to have been Netanyahu's election: his comeback and the re-election of a known factor. Sharon's election pushed Israel and the Palestinians into new, dangerous and uncharted waters.

Taking a page out of Netanyahu's book, Sharon had indicated during the campaign that he would try to reset the clock back to zero in the negotiations. He would not honour the 'generous concessions' made by Barak at Camp David. The Palestinians responded angrily on election night. The chief Palestinian negotiator, Saeb Erekat, said on CNN:

> If he [Sharon] comes to us and he wants to take us to eat the apple from the beginning, to go back to the zero point, I'm afraid that we will not have a peace process anymore. I'm afraid that I would say, 'God help the Palestinians and Israelis,' because to have a meaningful peace process means that we will continue where we left off.[2]

In public, Yasser Arafat took a more pragmatic line and reacted to Sharon's victory with caution. He urged the continuance of a peace partnership with a Sharon government 'not only on the Palestinian track [but] the Lebanese track and the Syrian track so that we can have a new Middle East'.[3] In private, Arafat feared the worst, and recounted his talks with Sharon at Wye during the negotiations that led to the Wye Memorandum in 1998.

Among many non-Israelis who were veterans of the negotiations, either as participants in the talks or as commentators, there was a sneaking suspicion that Sharon would eventually try to impose a solution on the Israeli–Palestinian conflict. Naturally, such a solution would focus on Israeli security, and not on the interests of the Palestinians.

It might be an overstatement to suggest that Sharon's election made non-Israelis look back on the Netanyahu era with rose-tinted spectacles. It did not. There was arguably, however, a quietly understood admission that Netanyahu would have been more likely to conclude a deal of sorts with the Palestinians than Sharon appeared willing to do in 2001.

Even among Netanyahu's harshest critics there was a sense that he at least wanted to be seen to be doing the right thing. Mahmoud Abbas admitted this at the meeting he had with Dennis Ross on the special envoy's hotel balcony, following Netanyahu's election defeat in 1999. For Palestinians, Sharon remained a very different kettle of fish.

Memories are long in the Middle East. For the Palestinians, Sharon was still, in their eyes, the evil architect of the 1982 Lebanon War, and his alleged connection with the massacres at Sabra and Shatila refugee camps in Beirut made him a figure of hate among Palestinians. Warmonger, murderer, fascist, and other epithets were attached to Sharon by the Palestinians. His election in Israel was seen as opening a dangerous phase in Israeli–Palestinian relations.

The election victory of Sharon damaged the chances of Netanyahu returning to the premiership. Sharon was a forcible and highly effective political manager, who set about strengthening his control over the Likud party organs at the expense of Netanyahu. In putting together his first cabinet, Netanyahu was a notable absentee as the former Prime Minister continued his activities in the private sector.

Netanyahu watched on as people started to compare Sharon with President Charles de Gaulle, the former French strongman who made peace with the Algerian National Liberation Front. The arrival in the White House of President George W. Bush in the month prior to Sharon's election victory helped pave the way into Washington for the new Prime Minister. Sharon and Bush knew each other from Bush's earlier visit to Israel, when he had gone on one of Sharon's famous 'bus and sandwich' propaganda tours of the West Bank.

With the ongoing Palestinian *Intifada*, including a wave of suicide bombings in Israeli cities and towns, the security hawk Sharon appeared to have a lock on the premiership. His election victory had catapulted him from second-tier politician to the top of the tree. If Netanyahu wanted to return to politics he would have to do so accepting the leadership of the Likud and the country by Sharon.

Although Netanyahu rarely publicly acknowledged any specific mistakes he made, there remains a sense that he underestimated Sharon's electability, or perhaps overestimated the common sense of the Israeli electorate. Whatever the cause of the miscalculation, the idea that Netanyahu could simply return from the United States and pick up from where he had left off from his first premiership was a little ambitious.

On a deeper level, there was a connection between Israel being in trouble and the electorate turning towards Netanyahu. Many of those Israelis who were calling for him to return to office in late 2000 were the very same voters who had him kicked out of the same office a year and a half earlier. Netanyahu's personality had not changed, nor had he offered a Nixon-style apology for the mistakes he had made during his first term in office. Netanyahu did not come back to the people: the people came back to him.

To some extent this would set an important precedent for the rest of his career. Whenever Israel looked to be under threat, be it from the Palestinians, the Iraqis or, in recent times, the Iranians, the majority of Israeli voters look to Netanyahu as the 'goalkeeper of the state'. The overplaying of his hand during the autumn of 2000, however, was a serious error that postponed his return to the premiership for nearly nine years.

Elections in Israel would by then be very different. Soon after the Sharon government took office, the direct elections for Prime Minister were scrapped. At the next election, the leader of the largest party that won the Knesset election would be invited by the President to form the next government. As the next Knesset elections were scheduled for 2003, this would mean that Sharon would seek re-election after only two years in office.

The abolition of the direct election for Prime Minister, which Netanyahu had robustly supported against the Likud whip, was a sensible move. It had encouraged a fragmentation of the Knesset, instability, coalition management problems and political inertia.

The implications of its abolition for Netanyahu were that if he wished to run for Prime Minister once again he would have to do so as the leader of the Likud. There was little prospect of somebody from a smaller party or splinter group achieving enough seats to be asked by the President to form a government.

In short, Netanyahu would have to come home and work within a largely Sharon-controlled Likud, if he were to stand a chance of achieving his ambition of leading Israel once more. It would prove to be a long and winding road, but Netanyahu, through largely unforeseen circumstances, would reach its end, almost as the last man standing.

Netanyahu thought that Israel was waiting for him to lead, but, in reality, before returning to the premiership he needed to remind Israelis of his talents in the diplomatic arena and in reforming Israel's economy. In doing this, he would agree to return to public service, forgoing his lucrative private sector activities. He would also come to accept the leadership of Sharon and serve in his government.

It was as if Netanyahu was being asked to do the political apprenticeship he had not taken prior to his first stint as Prime Minister. Chalking up political achievements, and rising to the top of the political pile for reasons other than being the most likely candidate to win an election, were his aims. All the time, however, he continued to build his team, develop his strength in the Likud and, most importantly, maintain ties with potential wealthy donors. In private, he was waiting for the opportunity to lead once again.

Netanyahu understood that Israeli politics had not been completely Americanized, in so much as defeated candidates were not written off entirely, and many returned. He consoled himself with Shimon Peres's record: he had failed to establish a government after the 1977, 1981, 1984 and 1988 elections. Played four: lost four.

In 2007, however, Peres won the election to become President of Israel. Two years later, he would have to make one of his most difficult decisions as President and it concerned his old political foe Benjamin Netanyahu.

President Peres held the political fate of Netanyahu in his hands. He had to make a choice that could make or break the career of the man who had defeated him in the 1996 election. Netanyahu's prospects remained in the hands of someone he had accused of appeasing terrorism and of planning to divide Jerusalem. It proved to be a long and nervous wait for Netanyahu, while President Peres carefully considered his options before making his important decision.

PART SEVEN

Return

20

Invitation

On 20 February 2009, Benjamin Netanyahu sat next to Shimon Peres in the presidential residence in Jerusalem. He looked slightly nervous. He was focused on trying his best not to smirk, or look smug, or triumphant. He understood why he had been invited to the residence, and waited to hear the President utter the words that he had longed to hear for a decade.

After the banks of cameras and reporters fell quiet, Peres came straight to the point.

> The Basic Law: The Government obliges me to bestow the task of forming the government on one of the Knesset members within seven days of my receiving the official election results.
>
> At the conclusion of the consultations, delegates representing 65 incoming Knesset members – a majority of the Knesset – recommended that I task MK Benjamin Netanyahu with forming the next government.
>
> Therefore, in accordance with the authority vested in me by the Basic Law: The Government, I have decided to bestow the task of forming the next government on MK Benjamin Netanyahu, while noting that a majority of the delegations expressed their wish that the government formed will be a broad government, and requesting that this desire be taken into account in the forming of the government.
>
> MK Benjamin Netanyahu has expressed to me his willingness to take this task upon himself.

I hope that the process will be completed quickly. The people of Israel need governmental and political stability so that we will be able to cope with the challenges standing before us.[1]

Netanyahu's appointment was made despite the fact that the party he led had not emerged from the Knesset elections, held ten days earlier on 10 February, as the largest party. This aside, the election represented a triumph for Netanyahu, who rejuvenated the fortunes of the party and had more than doubled the number of seats it had won in the previous election.

The meeting represented a hugely decisive moment in the career of Benjamin Netanyahu. During the days that had followed the election, the media had been full of speculation as to which party leader Peres would nominate for Prime Minister.

The centre-left argued they had the largest party and would be able to put together a coalition. Tzipi Livni, the leader of the largest party in the Knesset, argued that she should be offered the first chance to form the government from her fellow party member, President Peres.

The reality of the electoral maths slowly dawned on Peres, as he carefully studied the results, and concluded that the centre-left would not be as able to form a government. Peres understood that Netanyahu, as head of the right-wing block, clearly enjoyed a majority at coalition level. Faced with little choice, Peres had summoned Netanyahu to his residence to give him the good news.

The meeting was awkward and stiff: a reminder of their political rivalry from the 1996 elections in which Netanyahu had defeated Peres in Israel's first direct election for Prime Minister. Peres, who had assumed the Presidency in July 2007, had hoped for a centre-left victory in Israel's elections.

Such a victory, Peres hoped, would have reinvigorated the peace process with the Palestinians. Netanyahu, he sensed, would defer it, avoiding concluding any agreement with the Palestinians.

Peres wished Netanyahu success, but feared the worst. The two parted in the knowledge that they would have to find ways of working together over the subsequent four years on the peace process and a range of other issues. Both men appeared statesman-like as they shuffled around one more time for the cameras.

The Israeli centre-left would take some time to forgive Peres for designating Netanyahu as Prime Minister, but Peres hoped that there was still a prospect of establishing a government of national unity that would include the parties of the centre-left. There wasn't.

As Netanyahu departed the residence, he addressed the press as the Prime Minister designate. After just over a decade away, he was returning to the Prime Minister's office to lead Israel for a second time. He promised to put together a governing coalition as soon as possible. In reality, he had already put much of the coalition in place, and had been endorsed by key parties that would come to join his government.

His invitation to form a government came exactly one month after Barack Obama had been inaugurated as President of the United States on 20 January 2009. The two new leaders were seen as being at opposite ends of the political spectrum.

After Netanyahu became Prime Minister designate, the *New York Times* recalled a story that Netanyahu was fond of telling about his first meeting with Barack Obama, which had taken place in Jerusalem in the summer of 2008. At the time, Obama was the Democratic nominee for President and was visiting Israel as part of his campaign for the presidency.

As they moved to the side of the room, Obama said:

> You and I have a lot in common. I started on the left and moved to the centre. You started on the right and moved to the centre. We are both pragmatists who like to get things done.[2]

Whatever the merits of this assessment, the Obama–Netanyahu relationship became central to not only Israel–US ties since, but to the Middle East peace process. When Netanyahu told the story in 2009, he did so with much delight and viewed Obama's comments as a type of endorsement. It was also a reminder that, while much of Israel and the outside world viewed Netanyahu as hawkish, he considered himself to be a pragmatist.[3]

On 31 March 2009, Netanyahu presented his government to the Knesset. The foreign policy section of his speech set out one of the clearest articulations of his beliefs and mindset. The address was vintage Netanyahu, linking the present difficulties to the past and the future.

For President Obama, the speech served as a wake-up call as to the potential difficulties that lay ahead. For all the apparent mutual warm feelings during their first encounter in Jerusalem, the content of the speech outlined a divergent path in terms of the priorities of Netanyahu and Obama.

Netanyahu started off the speech with his usual phoney reticence about being chosen to form the government. 'It is not with the elation of the victorious that I stand before you today, but rather with a feeling of heavy responsibility,' he said. He then moved on to express his regret that he was not standing before the Knesset as leader of a national unity government. Here his sentiments were more genuine, but his finely tuned political antenna told him that this had been a non-starter.

Having done with the political small talk, he moved on to the substantive section on security and the peace process. Here his message was direct, sobering and angry. He first set out the problems:

> The security crisis we are facing originates from the rise and spread of radical Islam in our region and in other parts of the world. The greatest threat to humanity, and to the State of Israel, stems from the possibility that a radical regime will be armed with nuclear weapons or that nuclear weapons will find a home in a radical regime.

Netanyahu then moved to the specific threat and the issue that would dominate US–Israeli relations for the rest of the era of Obama and Netanyahu. In delivering his words, which he knew would be translated into English for the international press, he made sure that his intonation and stress transmitted the right tone of anger that built to a crescendo, before he reminded the Knesset that Israel could take care of itself in this dangerous world. As he put it:

> It is a mark of disgrace for humanity that several decades after the Holocaust the world's response to the calls by Iran's leader to destroy the State of Israel is weak, there is no firm condemnation and decisive measures – almost as if dismissed as routine.
>
>   However, the Jewish people have learnt their lesson. We cannot afford to take lightly megalomaniac tyrants who threaten to annihilate us. Contrary to the terrible trauma we experienced during the last century when we stood helpless and stateless: today we are not defenceless. We have a state, and we know how to defend it.[4]

He then turned his attention to Hezbollah and Hamas and delivered the standard Israeli line:

> Terrorists from radical Islam now threaten us from both the north and the south. We are determined to curb terrorism from all directions and fight against it with all our might.[5]

It was in the Palestinian negotiations that Netanyahu tried to offer something of a new policy. His focus on economic development was viewed by his political foes as a means of delaying having to offer major political concessions. It was seen in the White House as another worrying development and as confirmation that Israel had moved to the right.

Netanyahu made his case to the Knesset:

> My Government will act vis-à-vis the Palestinian Authority to achieve peace on three parallel tracks: economic, security and political. We strive to assist with the accelerated development of the Palestinian economy and in developing its economic ties with Israel.
>
> We will support a Palestinian security mechanism that will fight terror, and we will conduct on-going peace negotiations with the PA, with the aim of reaching a final status arrangement. We have no desire to control another people; we have no wish to rule over the Palestinians.
>
> In the final status arrangement, the Palestinians will have all the authority needed to govern themselves, except those that threaten the existence and security of the State of Israel. This track – combining the economic, security and political – is the right way to achieve peace.
>
> All previous attempts to make shortcuts have achieved the opposite outcome and resulted in increased terror and greater bloodshed. We choose a realistic path, positive in approach and with a genuine desire to bring an end to the conflict between our neighbours and us.[6]

The final paragraph was arguably the most revealing, in that Netanyahu was telling the world that he did not expect there to be a final status deal with the Palestinians in the immediate future. Indeed, he was saying that any attempt to try to reach a comprehensive settlement with the Palestinians could make matters worse as, he claimed, it had in the past.

In academic language this reeked of Netanyahu opting for a strategy of conflict management over conflict resolution. This choice also did not bode well for US–Israeli relations, as the Obama administration was still locked into trying to resolve the Israeli–Palestinian conflict and not to manage it.

Netanyahu concluded his presentation of the government with a reminder to the Knesset, and the rest of the world, of his brother Yonatan, and the importance of the Netanyahu family narrative in the character of the new Prime Minister.

> Citizens of Israel, I asked myself how best to express the depth of my feelings at this event, on the eve of Passover 2009. I chose to read an excerpt from one of the final letters written by my late brother, Yoni, approximately one year before he fell during the operation to rescue the hostages in Entebbe:
>
> 'Tomorrow is Passover,' wrote Yoni. 'I always saw it as our most wonderful holiday; it is an age-old holiday celebrating freedom. As I sail backwards on the wings of history, I travel through long years of suffering, of oppression, of slaughter, of ghettos, of ostracism, of humiliation; many years that, from an historic perspective, do not contain one ray of light; but that is not the case because of the fact that the core remained, hope existed, the idea of freedom continued to burn through the fulfilment of the tradition of the ancient holiday.
>
> This, in my opinion, is a testament to the eternalness of the aspiration for freedom in Israel, the continuity of the idea of freedom. The Passover holiday,' he wrote, 'awakens in me an emotional affinity, also because of the Seder which, like it does for all of us, reminds me of forgotten moments from our personal pasts, my past. I clearly remember the Seder we held in Talpiot, Jerusalem when I was six.
>
> Among the participants were a number of elders like Rabbi Binyamin and Professor Klausner, and my father was also there. There was a large table and there was light. I find myself in my past, but I do not only mean my own personal past, but also the way I see myself as an inseparable link in the chain of our existence and independence in Israel.'[7]

The impression that Netanyahu wanted to convey in his address was of a determined, pragmatic leader, who was more at ease with himself

and his personal history than he had been during his first term as Prime
Minister. A one-line summary of the speech would read simply: this
time, things will be different.

In a nod to the other important member of his family, his historian
father, Benzion, the new Prime Minister included a selective history of
the Jewish people:

> The State of Israel was established during its most difficult hour, an
> hour during which the words of the Declaration of Independence
> echoed in our ears: 'The Land of Israel was the birthplace of the
> Jewish people. Here their spiritual, religious and political identity
> was shaped. Here they first attained statehood, created cultural
> values of national and universal significance and gave to the world
> the eternal Book of Books.
>
> After being forcibly exiled from their land, the people kept faith
> with it throughout their Dispersion and never ceased to pray and
> hope for their return to its land and for the restoration in it of their
> political freedom.'
>
> There is no more wondrous a journey in history than that of the
> Jewish people. There is no struggle more just than its struggle to
> return to its homeland and build a life here as a free and sovereign
> nation. There is no question mark, not about the right, not about
> the justice and not about the existence of the people of Israel and its
> country. There is no question mark, and we will not allow anyone
> or any country to raise a question mark over our existence.
>
> The 20th century proved that the future of the Jewish people is
> dependent on the future of the State of Israel, and therefore it is our
> duty to do all that is necessary to ensure the security, strength and
> prosperity of our country.[8]

All of this seemed to confirm Natan Sharansky's point, that Netanyahu
was fond of attempting to put the present day into a historic context.
Throughout his speech he was trying to reassure Israelis that he understood where they came from, who they were and where he was going
to lead them in the future. He wasn't totally successful in reassuring all
Israelis, but it was a better effort than anything from his first premiership.

On the political front, he had stated his position on Iran and the
Palestinians, in the belief that he was articulating the views of most

mainstream Israeli voters on the two issues that defined the era and Israel's relations with the Obama administration. This was not the speech of an ideologue, but, rather, a pragmatist, who believed that Israel was facing an unprecedented threat to its existence.

With its dramatic tones, emotive language and focus on economic improvement for the Palestinians, it was a speech that might have been given by the late Moshe Dayan, from the Labour Party. Netanyahu looked and sounded more statesmanlike, but the potential divisions with President Obama reminded everyone of his difficult relationship with President Clinton.

Netanyahu believed that he could convince President Obama, and the world, of the merits of his positions towards Iran and the Palestinians. In his eyes, Israel had turned to him in its hour of need. The onset of the global financial crisis, and the continued threats posed by Hezbollah and Hamas to Israel, appeared greater than ever. On top of this, the Iranian nuclear programme presented a new challenge to Israel's military hegemony in the Middle East, and potentially to the very existence of the state.

During the presentation of his government to the Knesset, Netanyahu had been careful not to adopt a 'told you so' message. Instead, he portrayed himself as a Churchill-style leader, who would guide the country through the real and perceived dangers that Israel faced. His credentials, as both a successful manager of Israel's economy and guardian of the country's diplomatic position with the outside world, were important reasons in his political return.

The mistakes he made during the 2001 election campaign had consigned him to a position of having to accept the leadership of his rival, Ariel Sharon of the Likud and of Israel. It looked as if Netanyahu had missed his opportunity to lead Israel for a second time, as Sharon continually strengthened his leadership of the centre-right in Israel. Internationally, Sharon rapidly went from pariah figure to international statesman, who was warmly welcomed in the White House, Downing Street and the Élysée Palace.

To his credit, Netanyahu had not sulked on the political sidelines from 2001 until his return to the premiership in 2009. Rather, he had joined the Sharon government and worked to rehabilitate himself as a minister and political heavyweight in Israel.

At the same time he never abandoned the ambition to lead Israel again, or the belief that the country would one day turn to him for

INVITATION   223

leadership. In the meantime, he concentrated his energies on trying to
resolve, or manage, the difficult issues that were brought before him as
a minister.

His speech to the Knesset, on 31 March 2009, marked the end of
a long road of political redemption for Netanyahu that had started in
2002. But his rise back to power had proven to be full of obstacles and
false starts. In the end, he had been able to position himself as the politician that Israelis turned to when they felt most fearful, in both their
present day lives and about their future prospects.

Back in November 2002, this triumphant return appeared a long
way off, when the Prime Minister, Ariel Sharon had – a little reluctantly – asked Netanyahu to serve in his new government as Minister of
Foreign Affairs. The month of November 2002, however, would come
to be one that Netanyahu would want to forget.

Two months prior to his appointment as Minister of Foreign Affairs,
the king of the politics of fear returned to the international stage in
Washington as a 'private citizen' to offer the Americans key advice,
which would have a far reaching impact for the United States and the
whole of the Middle East.

21

November

On 12 September 2002, Benjamin Netanyahu appeared before the House Committee on Government Reform to testify about Saddam Hussein and his alleged nuclear and weapons of mass destruction programme. Since 9/11, Netanyahu had increasingly appeared in the media, as a talking head with expertise in combating international terrorism. His tough, uncompromising stand made him a popular guest on mainstream television news shows, despite the fact that he was no longer officially active in politics.

His testimony to the committee, in which he called for military action against Iraq, was a forerunner to his speech on the Iranian nuclear programme to the United Nations ten years later. Indeed, the two texts that Netanyahu delivered in 2002 and 2012 were remarkably similar, with Iraq replaced by Iran in the subject line. His diplomatic advisor, Ron Dermer, who was sitting behind Netanyahu when he appeared before the House Committee in 2002, wrote Netanyahu's UN speech in 2012.[1]

In his evidence in 2002, Netanyahu made a strong case for action against Saddam Hussein. It is important to recall exactly what warnings he gave to the committee. Speaking slowly and employing his trademark pauses for dramatic effect, he said:

Last year, a few days after September 11, I was given the privilege of appearing before this committee to discuss the issue of terrorism.

But had I been given the opportunity to speak to you before September 11, I would have offered similar suggestions about how the war on terrorism should be fought and how it can be won. I would have pointed out that the key to defeating terrorism lies in deterring and destroying those regimes that harbour, aid and abet terror.

I would have argued that to root out terror, the entire terror network, consisting of half a dozen terror regimes and some two-dozen terrorist organizations, would have to be brought down. Most important, I would have warned that the greatest danger facing our world is the ominous possibility that any part of this terror network would acquire nuclear weapons.

Yet even had I presented my views in the most coherent and persuasive fashion, I have no doubt that some of you, perhaps many of you, would have regarded them as exaggerated, even alarmist. But then came September 11, turning fiction into fact and the unimaginable into the real.

That single day of horror alerted most Americans to the grave dangers that are now facing our world. Those Americans understand that had Al Qaeda possessed an atomic device last September, the city of New York would not exist today. They realize that we could all have spent yesterday grieving not for thousands of dead, but for millions.

But for others around the world, the power of imagination is apparently not so acute. It appears that these people will have to once again see the unimaginable materialize in front of their eyes before they are willing to do what must be done. For how else can one explain opposition to President Bush's plan to dismantle Saddam Hussein's regime?

I do not mean to suggest that there are not legitimate questions about a potential operation against Iraq. Indeed, there are. But the question of whether removing Saddam's regime is itself legitimate is not one of them. Equally immaterial is the argument that America cannot oust Saddam without prior approval of the international community.

This is a ruler who is rapidly expanding his arsenal of biological and chemical weapons. This is a dictator who has used these weapons of mass destruction against his subjects and his neighbours. And this is a tyrant who is feverishly trying to acquire nuclear weapons.

The Wye Plantation Summit in the United States, 19 October 1998. Netanyahu, Clinton, Arafat and their staff. OHAYON AVI

Signing of the Wye Agreement at the White House on 23 October 1998. Right to Left: Benjamin Netanyahu, Bill Clinton, King Hussein of Jordan, Yasser Arafat. OHAYON AVI

With US Secretary of State Hillary Clinton on 31 October 2009.

Prime Minister Benjamin Netanyahu with US President Barack Obama, during his visit to Washington to start direct negotiations between Israel and the Palestinian National Authority, 10 September 2010.

With Minister of Defense Ehud Barak, 14 November 2012, during a visit to the northern border with Syria. KOBI GIDEON

At the funeral of his father, Benzion, with Sara and his sons, Avner and Yair.
OHAYON AVI

US President Barack Obama on a visit to Jerusalem. Exchanging words with Prime Minister Netanyahu during a ceremonial dinner, 21 March 2013.
MARK NEYMAN

With US Secretary of State
John Kerry on the roof of the
State Department in Washington,
30 September 2013.
KOBI GIDEON

Benjamin Netanyahu sits
with IDF orphans inside a
'Yasur' helicopter during a
pilot graduation course at
the Hatzerim Air Base, 27
June 2013. AMOS BEN GERSHOM

Portrait of the Netanyahu
family taken during an official
visit to Japan, on 14 May 2014.
KOBI GIDEON

Prime Minister Benjamin Netanyahu during a meeting with the heads of the Israeli security organisations in Tel Aviv, 14 June 2014, following the kidnapping of three Israeli teenagers in the West Bank. KOBI GIDEON

In his office in Tel Aviv preparing for a television interview with ABC News (USA), 23 November 2014. HAIM ZACH

During his visit to the US to deliver a speech to a Joint Session of Congress, Benjamin Netanyahu speaks at the AIPAC Conference, 2 March 2015. AMOS BEN GERSHOM

Prime Minister Benjamin Netanyahu visits Masada, 8 July 2013. KOBI GIDEON

My country understood the dangers posed by a nuclear-armed Saddam two decades ago, well before September 11. In 1981, Prime Minister Menachem Begin dispatched the Israeli Air Force on a predawn raid that destroyed the Iraqi nuclear reactor at Osirak.

Though at the time all the world's governments, even our closest friend, condemned Israel, history has rendered a far kinder judgment on that act of unquestionable foresight and courage.

History's judgment should inform our own judgment today. Did Israel launch that preemptive strike because Saddam had committed a specific act of terror against us? Did we coordinate our actions with the international community? Did we condition that operation on the approval of the United Nations?

No, Israel acted because we understood that a nuclear-armed Saddam would place our very survival at risk. Today, the United States must destroy that same regime because a nuclear-armed Saddam will place the security of our entire world at risk.

Make no mistake about it. Once Saddam has nuclear weapons, the terror network will have nuclear weapons. And once the terror network has nuclear weapons, it is only a matter of time before those weapons will be used.

Two decades ago it was possible to thwart Saddam's nuclear ambitions by bombing a single installation. Today nothing less than dismantling his regime will do. For Saddam's nuclear program has changed. He no longer needs one large reactor to produce the deadly material necessary for atomic bombs.

He can produce it in centrifuges the size of washing machines that can be hidden throughout the country – and Iraq is a very big country. Even free and unfettered inspections will not uncover these portable manufacturing sites of mass death.

Knowing this, I ask all those who oppose the President's plan – do you believe that action can be taken against Saddam only after he builds nuclear bombs and uses them? Do these critics believe that a clear connection between Saddam and September 11 must be established before we have a right to prevent the next September 11?[2]

The United States got the message. Six months after Netanyahu's testimony, coalition forces invaded Iraq in March 2003, rapidly overthrowing the regime of Saddam Hussein. The occupation of Iraq that followed was much less successful for the United States, whose forces found no major evidence of nuclear, biological, chemical weapons or weapons development programmes.

Within the Democratic Party in the United States there was a feeling that the 'private citizen' Netanyahu had helped press President Bush and his administration into going to war against Iraq. The full implications of this were not fully felt until Netanyahu tried to assert pressure on President Obama to take action against Iran over its nuclear programme.

Back in 2002, Netanyahu's high media profile in the United States did not go unnoticed in Israel. Netanyahu effectively announced that he was returning to politics and that he would be challenging the Prime Minister, Ariel Sharon, for the leadership of the Likud in the party leadership primary, scheduled to take place before the next Knesset elections.

Netanyahu believed that Sharon had not fulfilled his election promise from 2001, to end the violence against Israelis. Indeed, as Netanyahu reminded everyone, the violence had actually worsened since 2001. While he welcomed the military operations Sharon had launched against the Palestinians, he did not think that they were strong enough and called for firmer measures to be taken.

He also differed from Sharon on the 'Arafat Question'. Netanyahu called for the Palestinian leader to be expelled, and argued that the Hebron Agreement that he had signed with Arafat was null and void due to the actions of the Palestinians. Sharon did not support the exile of Arafat as a viable strategy, but did agree that he was no longer a partner for peace with Israel.

In trying to wrestle the leadership of the Likud away from Sharon and in preparation for the next Knesset elections, Netanyahu attacked Sharon positions. The veteran hawk had shifted his candidature towards the political centre of Israeli politics. In response, Netanyahu shifted his position towards the right.

The Likud primary was particularly important, as the party was well ahead in opinion polls, and it was therefore widely accepted that the winner of the Netanyahu–Sharon contest would be the next Prime Minister. Sharon's centrist strategy was an indication that he already had one eye on the post-election coalition-forming process, which he hoped would produce a new national unity government.

One month before the Likud leadership primary was due to take place the Labour Party had left the existing national unity government. Officially, Labour quit over funding of Jewish settlements in the West Bank and Gaza, which it claimed was at the expense of benefits to the low-income workers, pensioners and single-parent families in Israel.[3] In reality, the party wanted to use the months before the Knesset elections to try to distance itself from the Likud in the hope of picking up more votes.

The exit of the Labour Party meant that two key ministerial posts needed to be filled by Sharon: foreign affairs and defence. On 1 November, after a meeting between Sharon and Netanyahu at the Prime Minister's farm in the Negev, Netanyahu agreed in principle to join the government as Minister of Foreign Affairs. The details of the deal were finalized in the subsequent days.

Netanyahu had demanded changes to Sharon's economic plans, which he felt did not stimulate growth. He argued that the biggest threat to Israel was the economic recession and this needed to be addressed by a radical overhaul of the economy. He also called for Sharon to adopt the harder approach to quelling the Palestinian violence that he advocated.

In the end, Sharon largely persuaded Netanyahu to join the government under the basis of its existing guidelines. These had been agreed between Sharon and the Labour Party prior to his taking office in March 2001. For Sharon, having his Likud leadership rival in the government was seen as a good move in the belief that it would restrict Netanyahu's ability to criticize him in the leadership campaign.

It was indeed a strange situation, as the two men started their respective campaigns. In Netanyahu's first major interview after being sworn in as Minister of Foreign Affairs, he spent most of the interview outlining his differences with Sharon and explaining why he, and not Sharon, was the best man to lead the country. During the course of the interview with the politically sympathetic *Jerusalem Post* reporter Caroline Glick, the new Minister of Foreign Affairs went on the offensive.

In response to the question, 'Do you think you were a successful Prime Minister?', a defiant Netanyahu reminded Glick:

Yes and I think the public thought I was successful, because in retrospect, a year and a half after I was defeated I was going to be re-elected by the greatest majority in Israeli history. All the polls were placing me at 70%. And the reason that was the case is because people looked in retrospect at the three years that I served and saw the virtual absence of terror and the economic liberalization moves that I made, and concluded rightly that those were years of security and prosperity.[4]

The most interesting part of the interview came when he was asked to respond to claims by Sharon's advisors that his appointment as Minister of Foreign Affairs was aimed at stopping him from criticizing the government, as you couldn't be a minister in the government and attack it.

In short, it was a means of preventing Netanyahu from attacking Sharon and his record in government. At the same time, as Glick outlined, it did not prevent Sharon's aides from attacking Netanyahu. Sharon's son, Omri, was briefing the press that Netanyahu did not get along with people.

In response, Netanyahu continued to indicate that the country was in a worse state in 2002 than when he left office in 1999. He talked specifically about the economy as a key area of difference between himself and the Prime Minister. As he put it:

I am running because the country is in dire straits and we have to get it out. That doesn't mean that I personally attack the Prime Minister. But you have to be blind . . . I spoke about my economic views and I have been critical of the government's economic poli-cies. But I don't want to concentrate on the malaise. I want to concentrate on solutions. Mine will be a government of solutions.[5]

Netanyahu's strategy of trying to outflank Sharon from the right was not without dangers. It is worth remembering again that Israeli national elections were won from the centre and not from the flanks. It appeared that Netanyahu had in mind a repetition of his 1996 election strategy, in which he started on the right with the intention of unifying this block, before shifting to a more centrist approach for the direct election for Prime Minister.

Given Sharon's careful cultivation of the centre ground of Israeli politics since 2001, it would have been problematic for Netanyahu to have challenged him from the centre. There was a certain irony about all of this. During the latter stages of the Netanyahu government, it was Netanyahu who, as Prime Minister, adopted more centrist orientation, while his Minister of Foreign Affairs, Ariel Sharon, pursued a more right-wing agenda towards the peace process. In 2002, the roles were reversed, with the outlooks of both candidates changing.

The campaign for the Likud leadership was characterized by restraint from both candidates from using public personal attacks against one another, but behind the scenes there were accusations similar to Omri Sharon's attack on Netanyahu's personality. For his part, Netanyahu's team focused their brief for the press on questions over Sharon's alleged lack of understanding of macro-economic policy.

There was good reason for both candidates to exercise restraint during the short campaign: in November 2002 Israel was engaged in a mini-war with the Palestinians. A brief recall of the events during the month illustrates the problems caused by near-total collapse of the peace process with the Palestinians.

9 November 2002
The IDF killed the head of Islamic Jihad in Jenin, Iyad Sawalha, whom Israelis held responsible for two suicide bombings in 2002.

10 November 2002
A Palestinian gunman fired on a kibbutz near the West Bank, resulting in the deaths of five Israelis, including a mother and her two young sons.

12 November 2002
The IDF raided the West Bank town of Tulkarem and laid siege to Nablus. A two-year-old Palestinian child was shot dead.

15 November 2002
Palestinian gunmen killed 12 Israelis after opening fire on a group of settlers making a pilgrimage to a holy site in Hebron.

18 November 2002
A 23-year-old Israeli Arab, Tawfiq Fukra, allegedly attempted to hijack an El Al flight to Istanbul. No one was hurt.

19 November 2002
Five Palestinians were killed as the IDF raided the West Bank town of Tulkarem, aiming to capture Tarek Zaghal, one of the leaders of the al-Aqsa Brigades.

21 November 2002
A Palestinian suicide bomber killed 11 Israelis, many of them children, on a crowded Jerusalem bus.

22 November 2002
A British United Nations official and an 11-year-old Palestinian boy died after the IDF raided a Palestinian refugee camp in Jenin.

28 November 2002
Nine Kenyans along with three Israelis died in a suicide bomb attack on an Israeli-owned hotel near Mombasa, Kenya. At the same time, terrorists also attempted to shoot down an Israeli passenger jet taking off from Mombasa.

Three Palestinians opened fire on Likud party offices in Beit Shean, during the party's leadership election. Six Israelis died in the attack along with the three attackers.[6]

Polling took place in the primary election on 28 November 2002, but was overshadowed by the attacks in Kenya and on the Likud offices in Beit Shean. Sharon won the race easily, and left little room for Netanyahu to accept the result as anything other than a crushing defeat.

An exhausted and disappointed Netanyahu conceded defeat after the first exit polls were announced. He had made the classic mistake of fighting the wrong campaign at the wrong time on the wrong issues. All that was left for him to do was to offer his congratulations to Sharon. He addressed his supporters:

We must unite around our party's values and around the man who was chosen to lead our party, Ariel Sharon. I am confident that you as well as I will work to guarantee that the next government will have the power to overcome the terror and return the peace and calm into our lives.[7]

The major trap that Netanyahu had fallen into was to blame Sharon for the poor state of the Israeli economy when most Israelis blamed the Palestinians for the near-collapse of the economy. Netanyahu's tough rhetoric on security did not look practical given the continued involvement of the United States in the peace process. Essentially he looked out of touch with the political realities of the day. The violence that characterized the month of November did not lead to any significant increase in support for Netanyahu, and may have actually strengthened Sharon's standing in the Likud.

The roots of Sharon's success, and Netanyahu's defeat, also lay in Sharon signing up new members to the Likud who would vote for him. This was exactly what Netanyahu had done a decade earlier, but in 2002 he was outmanoeuvred by the veteran politician on this score.

The support that Sharon enjoyed in the Likud, and in the wider country, meant that, at best, Netanyahu had to content himself with being number two in the party. Despite a joint appearance at the Likud HQ after the contest was over, the two men did not trust each other. In private, Sharon planned to clip Netanyahu's wings, but decided to wait until after the Knesset elections to act.

On his part, Netanyahu spent the campaign for the Knesset elections acting as a loyal foot soldier to Sharon, towing the government's line and arguing that there was no alternative to a Likud-led government. In addition, from his desk in the ministry of foreign affairs, he tried to put the best possible spin on Israel's political and military policies towards the Palestinians.

In the foreign ministry, Netanyahu was in his element. Maybe his father would be proved right: perhaps his son would turn out to be a better Minister of Foreign Affairs than Prime Minister.

Addressing the EU Ambassadors conference on 17 December 2002, he again made the connection between the Palestinian and Iraqi situations. He argued that, in practice, there could be no progress in political talks with the Palestinians without far-reaching changes in the PA leadership, and that the expected American offensive in Iraq might facilitate such changes.[8]

Israel went to the polls on 28 January 2003 in elections for the Sixteenth Knesset. As the direct election for Prime Minister had been dropped, voters cast only one ballot with the leader of the largest party, widely presumed to be the Likud, being asked to form a governing coalition.

The campaign had been one of the dullest in living memory. Sharon had tried to reassure centrist voters that he had a peace plan that would be unveiled after he had restored calm to the country. Few believed him, but with the opposition Labour Party in disarray, he wasn't really pressed into offering much detail on his plan.

The result of the election was a triumph for Sharon, with the Likud winning twice as many seats as the second party. The Likud doubled its number of seats from the 1999 election, and, with a total of 38 seats, it once again became the dominant force in Israeli politics. Prior to the elections, despite Sharon being directly elected as Prime Minister, the Likud had not won the Knesset elections of 1999 and the Labour Party had been the largest party.

The post-election period must have irritated Netanyahu as Sharon put together a right-wing coalition along with the religious parties (minus Shas). Sharon was effectively able to put together exactly the same coalition that Netanyahu had planned if he had been elected as the leader of the Likud. In reality, Sharon did not have many options when the Labour Party rejected joining a government of national unity.

At the time, Sharon appeared to dominate Israeli politics and was able to control the centre ground as well as the right-wing of the country. He also paid a great deal of attention to US–Israeli relations: he was the most frequent foreign visitor to the White House.

Sharon was deeply worried that his new coalition would cause concern in Washington that he was turning his back on finding any political solution to the Palestinian peace process. He still hoped to bring the Labour Party into the coalition at a later date – if and when the party leadership changed and was more agreeable to the idea.

In order to try to curry favour with President Bush, by showing his so-called good intentions to the peace process, Sharon offered Washington a sacrificial head.

22

Finance

Benjamin Netanyahu was dismissed as Minister of Foreign Affairs in a phone call from Ariel Sharon, who offered him the ministry of finance in its place. Netanyahu had previously indicated that the foreign ministry was the only portfolio he was interested in holding. The terse and brief phone call ended with a stunned Netanyahu rejecting Sharon's offer.[1]

The dismissal of Netanyahu from the ministry of foreign affairs was a shrewd tactic by Sharon that in one bold move solved many of his problems. It reassured Washington of his good intentions by getting rid of the minister who, during the Likud leadership campaign, had adopted an extremely hawkish line towards the Palestinians. It also ensured that Sharon alone would be responsible for conducting relations with the Bush administration. Netanyahu's replacement, Silvan Shalom, was considered to be much less problematic for Sharon.

Sharon also fully understood that the ministry of finance had proved to be something of a graveyard for politicians with leadership ambitions. Ministers of finance were forced to make difficult economic choices that always carried political ramifications, most of them negative.

This usually meant that the minister offended a particular sector by not giving it a big enough slice of the economic cake. Given the perilous state of the Israeli economy in 2003, it was likely that the minister would have to offend quite a considerable number of key constituencies from which he might one day need support in a leadership challenge.

Part of Sharon's thinking was a hangover from the Likud leadership election campaign in November of the previous year, during which

Netanyahu had taunted him that he knew little about economics. Netanyahu's assertion during the campaign that the cause of Israel's economic ills was not the fault of the Palestinians, but, rather, the government's policies, had also irked Sharon and his advisors.

'You think you can do better? Go and fix it then.' Sharon didn't utter these words to Netanyahu, but his proposal to appoint him to the ministry of finance implied exactly that thinking. Sharon also understood that if Netanyahu took the job it would keep him in the cabinet, while at the same time stopping him criticizing the government's economic policies and Sharon's policies on peace and security. He also believed that Netanyahu would be tempted by the offer.

Sharon's thinking was spot on. As Netanyahu considered his options, he looked back over what had been a very mixed return to Israeli politics since 2000. Despite his renewed popularity, he had overplayed his hand in 2000, and had failed to dislodge Sharon as leader of the Likud in November 2002. There weren't many political options left to him, as the all-powerful Sharon prepared to present his new government to the Knesset.

The option of remaining outside the government and becoming its chief critic from the right-wing was highly risky for a politician like Netanyahu, who still believed that he would one day return to the premiership. In the spring of 2003, Israel found itself in a virtual state of emergency with the Palestinian peace process on hold and the near-collapse of the economy the most serious issues requiring urgent attention.

What most tempted Netanyahu about Sharon's offer was his deeply held belief that he was the only man capable of introducing the necessary liberalization of the economy, specifically the privatization of key sectors of it and reduction in Israel's extensive welfare provision.[2] Put simply, Netanyahu wanted to introduce 'Thatcherite' and 'Reaganite' economic reforms in Israel.

When he spoke with Sharon for a second time, Netanyahu indicated that he was interested in the offer, but demanded total control over economic policy and a free hand to impose the economic reforms, both of which, he argued, were essential in turning the economy around. Sharon agreed to his demands, and so when he presented his new government to the Knesset on 27 February 2003, Netanyahu was a member of the cabinet.

Despite having apparently handed over control of the economy to Netanyahu, during the course of his address to the Knesset on the presentation of his government Sharon reminded his new Minister of Finance of the importance of the economy to his premiership. Specifically, he stuck to his position that it had been the Palestinians and the global recession that were the root causes of the problems:

> My new government's primary mission will be to confront the economic situation, in an attempt to maintain market stability and return to the path of growth and prosperity.
>
> I believe that the members of the new government share a common denominator – in recognizing the importance of this confrontation and in their outlook of the economic path that should be followed.
>
> The economic situation, which has, in the past few years, been affected by the situation of the global economy and the terrorist campaign against us, requires us to make difficult and painful decisions. We will all have to mobilize for this effort. Each one will be required to make concessions and compromises.
>
> I am confident that with the proper cooperation of all of us – the Government, the Histadrut, the employers and employees – we can end the economic recession and return to the path of growth.
>
> It will not be easy. But this government was not elected to make easy decisions.[3]

It was intended to serve as a gentle reminder to Netanyahu as to who was the senior of the two. Sharon's comments did, however, provide an an early warning to Netanyahu of the vested interests in the economic status quo that he would have to take on if his reforms were to be fully implemented.

In historical terms, Netanyahu's tenure as Minister of Finance was relatively short, lasting two and a half years, but his impact was significant as he implemented a series of reforms to the Israeli economy. In many ways these reforms completed the work of Shimon Peres from the mid-1980s. Peres had introduced a programme of economic reforms in response to the hyperinflation that dogged the Israeli economy at the time.

Prior to Netanyahu's arrival in the ministry, the Israeli economy was characterized by a large and inefficient state sector, groups with a strong vested interest in maintaining the economic status quo, as well as high levels of public debt and inflation. Israel's welfare state placed an unsustainable burden on the economy.

Netanyahu, as a result, argued that Israel's economy was in dire need of significant reform, and that the previous government had failed to implement the necessary reforms for fear of offending strong political interest groups. He outlined his views in an interview during a visit to the United States with the Israeli newspaper *Haaretz*. He argued:

> Everything we are doing now has already been done over the past 20 years in other countries that have surged forward, from New Zealand to Chile . . . In the past, Israel was a 'bad' country for business – with its Histadrut, taxes, welfare – and things could not go on this way. On the other hand, we have the advantage of being a technological country, and if we combine this with a pro-business climate, our economy will also surge forward. That is the message I want to send in Washington – look at us, see the changes.[4]

In 2003, there was an additional factor, to which Sharon alluded but about which Netanyahu was much more sceptical: the damage inflicted upon the Israeli economy by the ongoing violence with the Palestinians. Much of the success story of the economy during the era of the Oslo Accords came from foreign investment in the economy, especially Israel's famed high-tech sector. A lot of this investment turned out to be highly mobile.

When the Second *Intifada* broke out at the end of September 2000, and the intensity of its violence increased, foreign investors simply pulled their capital out of the country. Laptops were closed and key personnel relocated to Asia or other hubs across the globe. Without realizing it, the Palestinians had discovered an effective weapon against Israel, namely damage to its economy.

Netanyahu accepted the premise that the Second *Intifada* had hurt the economy, but he argued that the deeper causes of the malaise were to be found in the structural problems inherent in the economy almost since the creation of the state in 1948. He put together a radical plan of action of reforms and methods for dealing with those groups that tried to thwart the implementation of his reforms.

He was fond of telling an old story from his army days. The public sector had become a fat man resting on a thin man's back, he said. If the Israeli economy was to be successful, it would have to reverse these roles. The private sector would need to become the fat man, something that would only happen with tax cuts and a reduction in public spending.[5]

There were four main components to Netanyahu's reform plans: the privatization of key public companies, deregulation and tax breaks to benefit the private sector, wage reform and a shrinking of the welfare state.[6] These all constituted ambitious targets, and Netanyahu staked his political reputation on achieving all his goals. Unlike previous occasions, when there was a sizeable gap between his rhetoric and his action, this time he was deadly serious about implementing his ideas.

By and large, from his perspective, he was successful, although the social costs of the reforms were heavily criticized by his political opponents. In terms of privatization, he oversaw the controversial sale of the national airline El Al and a government-owned bank, the Discount Bank, the third largest in Israel.

He saw the private sector as being able to run these companies much more efficiently than the state. He also partly privatized the national telephone company, Bezeq. He was also successful in bringing competition into the energy sector, and encouraged new private ventures in this previously closed sector of the economy.

In the spirit of true 'Thatcherite' reform, Netanyahu cut taxes to help stimulate the economy. Like Margaret Thatcher, Netanyahu was a firm believer in putting money into people's pockets and letting them choose how best to spend it, rather than giving it to the state to allocate in services. This policy proved to be very popular with Israel's middle classes, but naturally was less popular with lower-income groups.

As *Forbes* magazine noted, the highest rate of individual taxation was reduced from 64 to 44 per cent, and corporate tax was reduced from 36 to 18 per cent. Controversially, government spending was capped for three years. The pension ages were raised for both men and women.[7]

In trying to attract greater foreign investment into the country Netanyahu liberalized the bond markets to encourage the inward flow of foreign capital. He also liberalized currency exchange laws. Netanyahu viewed high levels of foreign investment as vital to the health of the country. He wanted to make investment as easy as possible.

In terms of the trade unions, Netanyahu once again took a leaf out of Margaret Thatcher's book. He moved to essentially take on the unions in an attempt to weaken their power to resist the changes he wished to implement. He privatized the pensions of workers, and removed the right to strike unless the union's members had approved the industrial action in a ballot. In addition, he introduced legislation to make it easier to fire employees.

He saved his greatest wrath for what he saw as the militant trade union practices in the Histadrut, one of the last bastions of the Labour Zionist economy. He understood that the Histadrut appeared to have the power to shut down the country whenever its leaders felt like it. The frustration and lack of patience was clear for all to see. He argued:

> This has to be changed by law. Otherwise, this isn't a state. It's madness. A group of gangsters and hypocrites is oppressing workers everywhere, preventing a recovery program that would save the workers, shutting down the economy and sending factories fleeing, causing the most strikes in the world, while the entire rest of the world is streamlining and competing, and there's a free flow of products and goods. We can't continue this way.
>
> The industrialists agree with me, but aren't standing with me. Essentially, I'm fighting a one-man battle for the country's future. That's how I feel.[8]

He then argued that there were no alternatives to economic reform, and that the leaders of the Histadrut were living in fantasy land. He understood that arguably his most decisive conflict would be with the Histadrut, part of whose leadership led the campaign to block his reforms. He went on:

> What does the Histadrut want exactly to happen here, do they think someone will let us live like this? We'll just get trampled over by billions of Chinese and billions of Indians . . .
>
> Who could come to a country of high taxes, insane bureaucracy and swollen unions? Who would come to such a country? What are they thinking in the Histadrut, that they'll send us back to Clerksville? Histadrutstan? Welfare-handout-land? We simply don't have an existence if we do not make these necessary changes.[9]

In terms of the welfare state, he followed the Thatcher model by making it harder to get unemployment benefits, and by offering incentives to work for the individual and to the companies to hire them. He especially wanted to encourage greater employment levels among the Israeli Arabs and the ultra-orthodox. These two sectors were previously viewed as having poor levels of employment, and were costly to the state.

The results of the reforms started to be felt almost immediately. Typical economic indicators such as Gross Domestic Product rose by an average of 5 per cent a year from 2003 onwards. By 2006, exports of Israeli goods and services had more than doubled, and public debt was reduced to more sustainable levels. The unemployment rate was around 11 per cent when Netanyahu took over the ministry in 2003, but fell to around 6 per cent by 2008.

Crucially, taxes went from 35.6 per cent of GDP in 2000 to 30.5 per cent in 2015. By 2007, the reforms that Netanyahu introduced during his time in the ministry meant that Israel was able to balance the state budget.[10] Netanyahu still credits these reforms for making Israel's recent high-tech boom possible.

The reforms had not been without their critics, many of whom were in the Likud. The party had traditionally been associated with protecting the interests of lower-income groups in Israeli society, and had developed strong ties with Israelis of Sephardic origin, many of whom fell within this group.

Critics focused on the charge that Netanyahu's reforms had increased social inequality in Israel. In layman's terms the rich got richer, and the poor became poorer under Netanyahu. This was certainly true, and the widening income gap between the high- and low-income workers would come back to haunt him later in his political career.

Even after he left the ministry, Netanyahu continued to keep a close eye on the reforms and lobbied for additional ones. After his return to power in 2009, he was careful to appoint ministers of finance who would continue the reforms he believed still to be needed in the economy. Indeed, Netanyahu's first choice for the ministry would be Benjamin Netanyahu himself, and he remains reluctant to entrust the ministry to traditional *Likudniks* who favour a more redistributive economy.

Naturally, those who look at the American influence on Netanyahu focus on the political aspects of this impact. In economic policy, Netanyahu was equally, if not more, influenced by right of centre

American economics such as Reaganomics, and economic theories like the 'Laffer Curve', put forward by American economists. In this respect, Netanyahu did not appear to belong in the Likud.

This disconnect between Netanyahu and the Likud on socio-economic issues appears all the more remarkable given the strength of feeling within the party that it represents the disaffected in Israeli society, and not the fat cats. Despite shifts in Israeli politics, the Likud has never been the traditional party of the middle class or the wealthy – the very groups that saw the greatest advancement as a result of Netanyahu's package of economic reforms.

Ariel Sharon was no fool. He had appointed Netanyahu in the knowledge that if he did implement the economic reforms, he would lose many friends in the party. For once, Netanyahu portrayed himself as putting the good of the country above and beyond his own narrow-based political interests. While it was clear that he hoped to attract new party members to the Likud from the middle classes and the high-income groups, the party remained very much in the pocket of Sharon and his supporters.

Throughout his career, Netanyahu has attracted headlines for his apparent hawkish approach to the peace process, but in terms of impact his economic reforms have been as important in shaping the development of the state as his policies towards peace and security. It would be an exaggeration to suggest that Netanyahu was a one-man band (as he suggested to *Haaretz*), but among the political elite he had few peers who felt strong enough to take on the powerful economic cartels and other vested interest groups in the country.

In drawing inspiration from the United States for his economic policies, as well as Margaret Thatcher, Netanyahu once more illustrated that he was not a conventional Israeli politician in the traditional sense of the word. His outlook and orientation were more international and globalist. He was very much a man out of sync with much of the political elite in Israel, which focused more heavily on domestic and regional issues.

For Netanyahu, with the onset of greater globalization and linkage between economic markets, it was a case of adapt or die. His reforms were, at times, not wholly perfect, and some were only partially implemented during his two and a half years as Minister of Finance. Without the reforms, however, Israel would have been poorly prepared to try to weather the storm of the global recession that hit the world's economies towards the end of the decade.

The programme of reforms would not be fully implemented due to political developments in the peace process, which eventually brought Netanyahu's time at the ministry of finance to an end. Successors continued the reforms, albeit at a much slower pace. In some ways Netanyahu, without knowing it, in August 2005 timed his departure from the ministry well. The global economic crisis was just around the corner, and that storm was left to his successors to weather.

23

Separation

The saga of Netanyahu versus Sharon was never going to end well for the Likud and for the country. The catalyst for their eventual split was the Israeli disengagement from Gaza, which Sharon brought to the cabinet for approval on 7 August 2005. The unilateral withdrawal from Gaza represented an admission that the peace process with the Palestinians was not going to lead to any meaningful negotiations in the immediate future.

The Prime Minister argued that evacuating the 21 Israeli settlements in Gaza, in which some 8,500 Jewish settlers lived behind fortified fences, surrounded by 1.3 million Arabs, would improve Israel's security. Others were more sceptical, arguing that the Palestinians would see an Israeli withdrawal as a sign of weakness. There was also concern about the impact on an already fractured Israeli society.

The effects of the withdrawal on Israeli politics were difficult to predict, with commentators talking of a potential realignment of the parties to reflect the political changes. Much of the analysis from talking heads on television, and from columnists in the newspapers, focused on the Sharon versus Netanyahu rivalry, and what each would do in the period following the withdrawal.

Prior to the cabinet meeting, Netanyahu, who appeared so focused and determined in the arena on economic reforms, dithered over the question of the pull-out from Gaza. In the interview with *Haaretz* in October 2004, extensively on his programme of economic reforms, he was asked at the conclusion whether or not he would be supporting

Sharon's plans for Israel to withdraw from Gaza. His reply appeared to indicate an affirmative with a proviso:

> I will support the disengagement, according to the stages agreed in government. After the first stage, if there is a catastrophe, Sharon will stop it, not me. If there's no catastrophe, we'll advance to stage two, and then three, and four. The public wants to leave Gaza. Gaza is gone. The question is whether we go with it – in other words, will the county be set ablaze with internal strife. Therefore, we need a referendum in order to reach a wide consensus.[1]

The proviso of a referendum was a big call. Israel had never had one and with elections due, at the latest by the end of 2006, it appeared a bit superfluous to ask for a referendum on the withdrawal, which enjoyed widespread support among the Israeli public.

Within the Likud, however, it was a different story completely. In 2004, the party had voted overwhelmingly against the pull-out in a non-binding party referendum.[2] In short, while Sharon enjoyed support among the majority of the wider Israeli public, in the Likud he was going against the party line. To some extent this had started to translate into the popularity stakes between Sharon and Netanyahu. Roughly speaking Netanyahu was becoming more popular than Sharon in the Likud, while Sharon was much more popular than Netanyahu nationally.

For much of the summer of 2005 Netanyahu had prevaricated on the issue of whether he would support the withdrawal or not. Prior to the final vote, Netanyahu had voted in favour of the withdrawal in two cabinet votes on the issue, and two votes in the Knesset on the same issue. At the same time, he had risked the wrath of Sharon by backing calls in the Knesset to delay the evacuation and supporting a referendum on the issue.[3]

During the 18 months between Sharon's declaration of his intention to withdraw from Gaza and the final vote in the cabinet, Netanyahu had steadfastly refused to resign from the government, despite pleas from groups opposing the withdrawal. With his voting record, and his refusal to resign, the indications were that he would support the withdrawal in the final vote on it in the cabinet. There remained, however, a degree of mystery and intrigue as to whether he would be willing to support the Prime Minister.

Nobody, especially Sharon, fully understood Netanyahu's carefully planned intentions for the cabinet meeting of 7 August 2005. During the course of the meeting he informed Sharon and the rest of the cabinet who were in the room that he was resigning from the government. He handed over his letter of resignation, which read more like the opening salvo in an as yet unannounced contest for the leadership of the Likud. Netanyahu wrote in his letter:

> We have reached the moment of truth today . . . There is a way to achieve peace and security, but a unilateral withdrawal under fire and with nothing in return is certainly not the way.[4]

He then went outside and spoke to the assembled press, and told them that the withdrawal from Gaza would create 'a base for terror'. He added, 'this is happening against all the warnings. I can do nothing about this from the inside, so I'll leave.' With his letter and short statement, Netanyahu had at that moment prompted a seismic shift in Israeli politics.

Supporters of Sharon and his disengagement plans were quick to turn on Netanyahu, accusing him of resigning simply in order to challenge Sharon. Even many of Netanyahu's supporters were surprised by the timing of his departure, given the ample opportunity he had to resign in one of the earlier votes on the withdrawal.

David Makovsky, one of Israel's most astute political commentators, argued that the polls indicated that the timing of Netanyahu's challenge was motived by his ambitions to replace Sharon, and in this context his timing was spot on. Three days after his resignation a poll published by *Haaretz* of members of the Likud found that 47 per cent of party members supported Netanyahu to 33 per cent for Sharon. Nationally, however, Sharon and his withdrawal remained popular.[5]

A poll published on 12 August by a rival Israeli newspaper, *Yedioth Ahronoth*, indicated that the Israeli public found Sharon more credible than Netanyahu by 40 per cent to 20 per cent, and that 58 per cent supported the policy of withdrawing from Gaza.[6] In short, the polls appeared to confirm that Sharon was more popular among the wider public than in the Likud. This important distinction was not lost on the Prime Minister as he and his team of advisors planned their next moves.

Netanyahu's critics in the media argued that he had stayed in the government long enough to ensure that the withdrawal was carried out, and by quitting he could claim that he had opposed the plan if it went wrong (as it did from an Israeli perspective). Key members of the cabinet rounded on him focusing their attacks on his flip-flopping (changing his position) on the issue. 'You cannot dither in the wind every morning anew and say my opinion's changed and now it's different,' said the Minister of Defence, Shaul Mofaz.[7]

Naturally, Sharon offered his own rebuke to Netanyahu. 'He is someone who runs from responsibility,'[8] Sharon told the media. He saved his biggest salvo until Netanyahu announced on 30 August 2005 that he would be challenging Sharon for the leadership of the Likud.

Upon hearing the news, Sharon launched a carefully articulated personal attack against his challenger that was aimed at Netanyahu's alleged Achilles heel. Sharon said the challenge had not been unexpected and then went on to add:

Netanyahu is pressured easily, gets into a panic, and loses his senses. To run a country like Israel a leader needs to have reason and judgment and nerves of steel, two traits he does not have.[9]

Sharon repeated what many critics had said about Netanyahu's character, especially the part about panicking too easily. It was a politically motivated attack, the type of which Sharon and Netanyahu had tried to avoid during their previous leadership campaign. It was also a sign of things to come as Sharon considered his future in the Likud.

Netanyahu's defence about the timing of his resignation from the cabinet, and decision to once again seek the leadership of the Likud, was not without merit. Caroline Glick in the *Jerusalem Post* put the case for the defence of Netanyahu. In a spirited article she wrote what was essentially a riposte to Sharon's character attack on Netanyahu:

Netanyahu's willingness to risk his political career rather than share ministerial responsibility for a policy that will wreak strategic disaster on Israel shows a strength of character and a moral backbone that are rare in politics generally and in Israeli politics specifically.

While his detractors were quick to claim that the decision was belated, the fact of the matter is that by holding out in the government for the past year, Netanyahu demonstrated extraordinary responsibility. By remaining in the government he was able to enact the most important economic reforms Israel has ever undergone.

... The economic reforms Netanyahu has enacted as finance minister will empower the people to take control of their financial future in a way that was impossible before he entered office. And this will do much to change the way Israelis think of themselves and the government, to the benefit of both.[10]

The argument that Netanyahu hung on in the government to implement his package of economic reforms gained credibility when Sharon appointed the ex-Mayor of Jerusalem, Ehud Olmert, as Netanyahu's replacement as Minister of Finance.

Ehud Olmert did not pursue with the same rigour additional economic reforms. Instead, it was more of a case of normal service being resumed, with the Sharon-led government returning to the old ways of maintaining the economic status quo.

Netanyahu's resignation and challenge to Sharon's leadership of the Likud led, in part, to Sharon taking a leaf out of his rival's book and announcing his own resignation as leader and a member of the Likud on 21 November 2005. At the same time, he dissolved the Knesset and prepared to form a new party, which was eventually named Kadima (Forward) three days later in 24 November.

Sharon tried to make light of the change, claiming that the idea had only come to him one night recently. This was not the case. His key advisors had been working on the plans since the summer months in the realization that he would find it difficult to continue his policy of disengagement in the West Bank. On this issue the opposition in the Likud would have proved even greater than that over the Gaza withdrawal.

The establishment of Kadima and the desertion of several Likud ministers and MKs to the new party threatened to end the Likud's position as the dominant party in Israeli politics. The party had been in power either as head of a narrow-based coalition, or as part of a national unity government since 1977 (with the exception of the four years of the Rabin–Peres era from 1992 to 1996 and the 18 months of the government led by Ehud Barak from 1999 to 2001).

Netanyahu responded to the new situation as best he could, but many of those who remained in the Likud were in a state of shock about the events that had taken place. Sharon and Kadima confirmed their centrist political orientation by attracting several former Labour Party politicians to their ranks, including the former Prime Minister Shimon Peres.

Those who joined Kadima from the ranks of the Likud were a curious mixture of Sharon followers, opportunists and political misfits. Like most political splits there was no clean ideological break. At least one of the leading figures who joined was regarded as coming from the right-wing of the Likud. The apparent rationale for many policies that crossed over was career opportunism and the hope that they would be offered a leading job in Sharon's post-election cabinet.

Netanyahu's immediate priorities were to stem the flow of desertions to Kadima and to establish his authority over the Likud in time for the leadership primary in the middle of December. Neither task was particularly easy to achieve. Netanyahu soon discovered the two challenges were interrelated with candidates for the leadership of the Likud withdrawing from the race and joining Kadima, including the Minister of Defence, Shaul Mofaz.

The minister had seen his low poll rating in the Likud leadership contest, as well as the Likud's lowly standing in the Knesset race, and chosen to cross sides in order to try to keep his job in a Sharon-led government after the Knesset elections. This was pure political opportunism, but it left Netanyahu with the fear that any of the candidates he looked like beating in the Likud leadership race could simply leave the party and seek a senior position in Kadima.

Israeli politics experienced something of a second shockwave when, on 18 December, Ariel Sharon suffered a stroke. This was followed on 4 January 2006 by another yet more serious stroke that this time incapacitated the Prime Minister. Given the centrality of Sharon to Kadima, there were concerns that the party's support, which polls put as giving them around 40 seats in the Knesset, would decline. Ehud Olmert succeeded Sharon as acting Prime Minister, and was elected by Kadima on 16 January to lead the party in the Knesset elections.

In leaving the Likud, Sharon had removed the potential for Netanyahu to succeed him as Prime Minister. Instead, Netanyahu won the Likud leadership primary, held on 19 December 2005, beating

Silvan Shalom. Netanyahu won handsomely, securing 44.4 per cent of the vote to Shalom's credible 33 per cent with the far-right candidate, Moshe Feiglin, taking just over 12 per cent of the vote. In a damning indictment of the state of the Likud at the time, only 40 per cent of party members bothered to cast their ballots in the primary.

So Netanyahu was back at the helm of the party, five and a half years after he had resigned the leadership. The trouble was that there wasn't much of a party left to lead. To make matters worse for him, many of the politicians and activists who had remained in the Likud were angry with Netanyahu over his economic reforms, which they argued had caused the most pain in traditional Likud constituencies.

Most worrying for the new leader were the opinion polls, which, despite a brief spike following Netanyahu's victory in the primary election, consistently indicated that the Likud was likely to win no more than 14 or 15 seats in the Knesset elections. At the same time as trying to improve the poll ratings, Netanyahu moved to deepen his control over the party just as he had done following his victory in the 1993 leadership election.

In terms of positioning strategies for the party, Netanyahu argued that Kadima had seized the centre ground so the Likud would have to occupy its traditional right-wing position. The Likud list of candidates for the Knesset included the majority of senior figures in the party who had opposed Sharon's disengagement plans. There were problems in the lack of candidates that would be able to connect with voters who had suffered as a result of Netanyahu's economic reforms.[11]

At the end of January 2006, Netanyahu's and the Likud's prospects in the election appeared to get a boost when Hamas won the Palestinian Legislative Elections. For Netanyahu, this was confirmation that the withdrawal from Gaza had been wrong and that there should be no implementation of disengagement in the West Bank.

Both Netanyahu and the Likud expected to receive a boost in the polls from the Hamas victory in the Palestinian elections, but it never materialized. Polls published after Hamas' victory indicated little change in the levels of support for the Likud. The polls also suggested that Netanyahu's personal popularity rating was lower than that of either Olmert, of the Kadima Party – or the leader of the Labour Party, Amir Peretz.

There were a number of reasons for his poor showing, ranging from the social costs of the economic reforms, his flip-flopping voting record on the withdrawal from Gaza and public sympathy for his rival, Ariel Sharon, who remained on a life-support machine in hospital.

Any hope that the telegenic candidate Netanyahu could persuade Olmert to take part in an election debate was soon lost, as Kadima made it clear that this wasn't going to materialize. Ahead in the polls, Olmert had everything to lose in a debate with Netanyahu, so declined on the basis that he was too busy running the country. In the absence of any debate to get over his message, Netanyahu tried a television spot to offer some sympathy to those lower-income groups that had been badly affected by his economic reforms.

Even in doing this Netanyahu was forced to tread carefully. He accepted that his reforms had caused real hardships, but argued that he had inherited a complete mess of an economy from his predecessor as Minister of Finance. The trouble with this was his predecessor was his number two in the Likud, Silvan Shalom. While it might appear sensible politics to trash an inter-party rival, the man who might challenge your leadership once again, there were fears that Shalom might join the exodus to Kadima.

The elections took place on 28 March 2006, and Netanyahu tried his best to lower the already low expectations for the Likud at the polls. In the end the Likud finished in joint third place with Shas (and secured that place by the narrowest of margins over Avigdor Lieberman's party, Yisrael Beiteinu). The Likud lost 26 seats and ended up with only 12 seats in the Knesset.

As expected, Kadima won the election, but with a lower number of seats than at one time they had looked like they were going to win. With 29 seats to the Labour Party's 19, Kadima were clearly in a strong place to form the government. Netanyahu's one-time rival from the Likud would serve as Prime Minister and implement the peace and security policies that Ariel Sharon had supported so strongly.

Clearly, no amount of political spin could paint the results as anything other than a spectacular rejection of Netanyahu and the Likud by the electorate. Netanyahu tried his utmost to make the best possible case, by suggesting that the party would return to its once dominant position in Israeli politics. Few people believed him. Netanyahu's defiant words sounded empty and hollow. Addressing the party faithful he said:

Likud was dealt a body blow . . . Sharon left Likud absolutely fragmented and smashed to smithereens. Israelis ultimately will realize
that our path to achieve security and peace is the right path. We will
come back to better days.[12]

He outlined why he thought the party had done so badly in the polls.
As he put it:

I spoke with generations of Likud voters and I heard the anger and
the frustration over the economic measures that we were compelled
to take in order to save the Israeli economy. I intend to continue
along the path we have only just begun in order to ensure this
movement is rehabilitated and takes its rightful place in the nation's
leadership.[13]

This was Netanyahu's way of saying 'no surrender' and no deviat-
ing from the economic path he had laid out as Minister of Finance.
Arguably, one of the most intriguing aspects of Netanyahu the politician was his strong ideological commitment to economics versus his
more pragmatic approaches towards peace and security.

The problem for Netanyahu and the Likud was that those members
of the public who embraced his economic reforms, the middle class and
high-income earners, largely rejected his approach to the peace process
as too out of step with the political mainstream.

In geographic terms, the party lost support in its traditional strongholds, like the development towns with their lower-income inhabitants.
In many of these areas, Avigdor Lieberman's Yisrael Beiteinu overtook
the Likud. Lieberman, who in the past had managed Netanyahu's office,
was emerging as one of the main rivals to Netanyahu's leadership of the
right in Israel.[14]

As the new Knesset session opened with the presentation of the new
government by Ehud Olmert, Benjamin Netanyahu found himself in
a strange and unwanted position as leader of the opposition in Israel.
But were it not for Sharon leaving the Likud, the chances were that it
would have been Netanyahu giving the speech of presentation of his
government. The political gods had conspired against Netanyahu, but
he still believed that his policies on peace and security as well as the
socio-economic ones remained correct.

From 2006 to 2009, Netanyahu worked tirelessly to rehabilitate himself and the Likud in Israeli politics. At the centre of his struggle was the building of a new identity for the Likud that distinguished it from Olmert and Kadima. He also strengthened his control over the party, shown by his re-election as party leader on 14 August 2007, when he won 73 per cent of the votes cast.

As leader of the opposition, his most crucial decision came in 2008 after Ehud Olmert had been forced to resign amid multiple allegations of corruption. Tzipi Livni replaced Olmert as leader of the Kadima, and Prime Minister designate. Livni was considered to be dovish on the peace process, and supported making major concessions. Extrovert, engaging and chic, Livni was popular in European capitals and in America. Her critics in Israel argued that she lacked the killer instinct to become Prime Minister.

That was one charge that was never laid at Netanyahu's door. Reminding the Knesset of his ruthless streak, Netanyahu refused to join her coalition when she was tasked by President Peres to form a new government. Netanyahu didn't stop there; he spent hours lobbying Shas and other parties not to join her coalition either. In the end, Livni was forced to give up and the Knesset was dissolved with the date of the election set for 10 February 2009.

There were risks to Netanyahu's strategy of forcing the country into early elections. The opinion polls pointed to the Likud making major gains from the previous elections, but a large part of the electorate remained undecided as to which party they would support in the election.

In the end, Netanyahu's gamble paid off, but only just. The rewards for him, however, were significant. In returning to power, as the king of all comebacks, Netanyahu surveyed the new political landscape in Israel with a sense that he had fulfilled his destiny to lead Israel for a second time. His rivals for power had fallen by the wayside, one by one, for different reasons.

Ariel Sharon remained in a coma, dying in January 2014. Sharon's successor, Ehud Olmert, would become the first Prime Minister in Israel's history to be convicted of corruption. His successor, Tzipi Livni, while still a highly popular figure outside Israel, would see her power base reduced and would eventually team up with the Labour Party in the 2015 elections.

From 2009 onwards, the key competition to Netanyahu came in the form of Avigdor Lieberman, but, while an important figure, he was never able to match Netanyahu's Machiavellian political skills. The second coming of Netanyahu was to prove very different from his first stint as Prime Minister. In Israel, he effectively became more like 'King Netanyahu', such was his hegemony in the country.

Having re-established his control over Israel, he shifted from shaping Israel to trying to shape the Middle East region. At the centre of this attempt was his deeply held will that Israel must do everything possible to stop Iran from developing its nuclear programme. This policy would come to dominate Israeli politics, and its relations with the Obama administration.

By 2015, however, Netanyahu's grip over power in Israel looked to be loosening, and his ability to convince the United States of the merits of the cornerstone of his foreign policy over the Iranian nuclear programme was close to failure.

PART EIGHT

King

24

The Speech

On 3 March 2015, Benjamin Netanyahu became only the second foreigner to have addressed a joint session of Congress three times, the other being Winston Churchill. The context of the speech was as important as the words he spoke during his 40 minutes at the podium. It was a decisive moment in Netanyahu's career both in the context of his domestic political position and for the cornerstone of his foreign policy objectives – namely, stopping Iran's nuclear programme.

Netanyahu went to Washington in the midst of an Israeli election campaign that he was struggling to dominate. Opinion polls in Israel pointed to a narrow victory for the Zionist Union (the Israeli Labour Party, led by Isaac Herzog, and Hatnuah, led by Tzipi Livni) in elections that were scheduled to take place two weeks later on 17 March.

As he stood to make his speech, wearing his favoured blue tie, the Likud was polling in the low-twenty seats mark, versus mid-twenty seats for the Zionist Union.[1] For the first time in a long while, Netanyahu looked like he might lose an election in Israel.

The timing and motives for his visit to the United States were highly controversial. As well as taking place at the tail end of an election campaign back home, the visit occurred as the United States looked to finalize a deal with Iran that would bring to an end its nuclear programme. President Obama had not invited Netanyahu to Washington, and he did not meet with him during his stay. Instead, Republican Party members of Congress who were opposed to the potential deal with Iran had issued the invitation.

Netanyahu had hesitated a little before accepting it. Given the seriousness of the issue and its centrality to his foreign policy objectives, he was not overtly concerned that the invitation had not originated from the White House. What worried him more was whether the visit and speech would be seen back in Israel as political opportunism and electioneering, as an attempt at bucking the trend of his unfavourable poll ratings in the last weeks of the election campaign.

The opportunity to address Congress, along with all the coverage his visit would attract, was too much to resist. Netanyahu calculated that the risk of causing offence to a lame-duck President was outweighed by the opportunity to try to influence Congress before it considered the final deal, if one were to be agreed with Iran. In Netanyahu's eyes, there was no contradiction in the purpose of his speech between influencing a vital public debate and public relations consideration. The two remained indelibly linked.

As the date of the speech approached he was, however, slightly taken aback by the level of controversy that it attracted in both Israel and the United States and among Jews and non-Jews. All of this, along with the barely concealed displeasure of the leader of the free world, was carefully taken into account as the speech was drafted and softened a little around the edges. The intention was to make it sound less like what it really represented: a challenge to the foreign policy of the United States, being presented by a foreigner, in the cradle of American democracy.

The speech was in truth not one of Netanyahu's best: the middle section got a little lost in technical detail, and parts of it were too steeped in fear-mongering language and questionable historical join-the-dots lines. Most problematic was that it went into great detail in identifying the crux of the problem, but offered only scant and poorly articulated alternatives to the deal that the Obama administration was said to be close to agreeing with Iran.

Netanyahu had spoken on the subject of Iran in better speeches than the one he gave to Congress on 3 March. It suffered from trying to cater to too broad an audience. It was at various points intended for President Obama, Congress, Americans, Iranians, and Israelis watching back home. Multiple-audience speeches are never easy to write, and the key message sometimes gets lost in the fog of talking across to different groups.

The imagery of the speech was also not as clearly articulated as it should have been. Seemingly, Netanyahu was trying to sell himself as Winston Churchill attacking the appeasement of Hitler during the 1930s. Without saying it directly, President Obama was seen as a modern-day Neville Chamberlain – nice guy, but someone who didn't understand the pursuit of evil.

The speech was stamped with Netanyahu's organizational traits and nods to history. Its resemblance in tone and content to his address 'as a private citizen' to the House Committee in 2002 revealed a worrying lack of progression in his mindset and also the perceived set of threats facing Israel, and the West in general.

After the usual pleasantries, Netanyahu started by addressing the charge made by his political opponents in Israel and within large parts of the Democratic Party in America (around 50 of whom boycotted the speech) of the political nature of his presence before Congress.

> I know that my speech has been the subject of much controversy. I deeply regret that some perceive my being here as political. That was never my intention.[2]

As usual, he paused for effect and emphasis. He wanted his audience to absorb his good intentions in coming to Washington. He then moved on to try to defuse the row with President Obama over his speech by paying the President a lengthy tribute:

> We appreciate all that President Obama has done for Israel. Now, some of that is widely known. Like strengthening security cooperation and intelligence sharing, opposing anti-Israel resolutions at the U.N.
>
> Some of what the President has done for Israel is less well-known . . . And some of what the President has done for Israel might never be known, because it touches on some of the most sensitive and strategic issues that arise between an American President and an Israeli Prime Minister. But I know it, and I will always be grateful to President Obama for that support.[3]

His wordy tribute to the President was meant to transmit the meaning that good friends can disagree over things, but this does not diminish the value of the friendship.

Netanyahu turned next to his favourite subject of Jewish history. Just as he had when he presented his government to the Knesset upon his return to power in 2009, he offered a history lesson to the lawmakers. His aim was to link the past to the present and to the future by using a selective narrative that indicated a successful thwarting of an attack against the Jewish people. As he put it:

> We're an ancient people. In our nearly 4,000 years of history, many have tried repeatedly to destroy the Jewish people. Tomorrow night, on the Jewish holiday of Purim, we'll read the Book of Esther. We'll read of a powerful Persian viceroy named Haman, who plotted to destroy the Jewish people some 2,500 years ago. But a courageous Jewish woman, Queen Esther, exposed the plot and gave for the Jewish people the right to defend themselves against their enemies. The plot was foiled. Our people were saved.
>
> Today the Jewish people face another attempt by yet another Persian potentate to destroy us. Iran's Supreme Leader Ayatollah Khamenei spews the oldest hatred, the oldest hatred of anti-Semitism with the newest technology. He tweets that Israel must be annihilated. You know, in Iran, there isn't exactly free Internet. But he tweets in English that Israel must be destroyed.
>
> For those who believe that Iran threatens the Jewish state, but not the Jewish people, listen to Hassan Nasrallah, the leader of Hezbollah, Iran's chief terrorist proxy. He said: 'If all the Jews gather in Israel, it will save us the trouble of chasing them down around the world.'[4]

From there Netanyahu broadened out the issue of the Iranian nuclear programme into one that was bigger than simply a problem for the Jews. In doing this, he also introduced the imagery of the Second World War and sought to remind people in an indirect manner about the Holocaust:

> But Iran's regime is not merely a Jewish problem, any more than the Nazi regime was merely a Jewish problem. The 6 million Jews murdered by the Nazis were but a fraction of the 60 million people killed in World War II. So, too, Iran's regime poses a grave threat, not only to Israel, but also the peace of the entire world. To understand just how dangerous Iran would be with nuclear weapons, we must fully understand the nature of the regime.[5]

He then moved on to offering a short history of modern Iran, which naturally focused on developments from 1979 onwards. In doing so he brought in the historic threat to American interests and lives caused by the Iranian Revolution.

The people of Iran are very talented people. They're heirs to one of the world's great civilizations. But in 1979, they were hijacked by religious zealots – religious zealots who imposed on them immediately a dark and brutal dictatorship. That year, the zealots drafted a constitution, a new one for Iran. It directed the revolutionary guards not only to protect Iran's borders, but also to fulfill the ideological mission of jihad. The regime's founder, Ayatollah Khamenei, exhorted his followers to 'export the revolution throughout the world.'

Iran's founding document pledges death, tyranny, and the pursuit of jihad. And as states are collapsing across the Middle East, Iran is charging into the void to do just that. Iran's goons in Gaza, its lackeys in Lebanon, its revolutionary guards on the Golan Heights are clutching Israel with three tentacles of terror. Backed by Iran, Assad is slaughtering Syrians.

Backed by Iran, Shiite militias are rampaging through Iraq. Backed by Iran, Houthis are seizing control of Yemen, threatening the strategic straits at the mouth of the Red Sea. Along with the Straits of Hormuz, that would give Iran a second choke-point on the world's oil supply.

Iran took dozens of Americans hostage in Tehran, murdered hundreds of American soldiers, Marines, in Beirut, and was responsible for killing and maiming thousands of American service men and women in Iraq and Afghanistan.

Beyond the Middle East, Iran attacks America and its allies through its global terror network. It blew up the Jewish community center and the Israeli Embassy in Buenos Aires. It helped Al Qaida bomb U.S. embassies in Africa. It even attempted to assassinate the Saudi Ambassador, right here in Washington, D.C.

In the Middle East, Iran now dominates four Arab capitals, Baghdad, Damascus, Beirut and Sanaa. And if Iran's aggression is left unchecked, more will surely follow. So, at a time when many hope that Iran will join the community of nations, Iran is busy gobbling up the nations. We must all stand together to stop Iran's march of conquest, subjugation and terror.

Now, two years ago, we were told to give President Rouhani and Foreign Minister Zarif a chance to bring change and moderation to Iran. Some change! Some moderation! Rouhani's government hangs gays, persecutes Christians, jails journalists and executes even more prisoners than before.

Iran's regime is as radical as ever, its cries of 'Death to America,' that same America that it calls the 'Great Satan,' as loud as ever. Now, this shouldn't be surprising, because the ideology of Iran's revolutionary regime is deeply rooted in militant Islam, and that's why this regime will always be an enemy of America.[6]

The question of a potential rethink of Iran as part of the new strategies that the United States and Europe were considering in their conflict with the Islamic State was then attacked by Netanyahu, who was essentially saying that Iran remained a much greater strategic threat to Western interests than the poorly armed ISIS. He pleaded with Congress not to be fooled into shifting policy towards Iran due to ISIS:

Don't be fooled. The battle between Iran and ISIS doesn't turn Iran into a friend of America. Iran and ISIS are competing for the crown of militant Islam. One calls itself the Islamic Republic. The other calls itself the Islamic State. Both want to impose a militant Islamic empire first on the region and then on the entire world. They just disagree among themselves who will be the ruler of that empire.

In this deadly game of thrones, there's no place for America or for Israel, no peace for Christians, Jews or Muslims who don't share the Islamist medieval creed, no rights for women, no freedom for anyone. So when it comes to Iran and ISIS, the enemy of your enemy is your enemy.

The difference is that ISIS is armed with butcher knives, captured weapons and YouTube, whereas Iran could soon be armed with intercontinental ballistic missiles and nuclear bombs. We must always remember – I'll say it one more time – the greatest danger facing our world is the marriage of militant Islam with nuclear weapons. To defeat ISIS and let Iran get nuclear weapons would be to win the battle, but lose the war. We can't let that happen.[7]

After this came the specific attack on the proposed nuclear deal. This was a harder area to execute as the exact details of a deal were not known. The general framework of a deal had been widely published and this provided Netanyahu with his ammunition to make his case for rejecting it. He said:

> But that, my friends, is exactly what could happen, if the deal now being negotiated is accepted by Iran. That deal will not prevent Iran from developing nuclear weapons. It would all but guarantee that Iran gets those weapons, lots of them.
>
> So you see, my friends, this deal has two major concessions: one, leaving Iran with a vast nuclear program and two, lifting the restrictions on that program in about a decade. That's why this deal is so bad. It doesn't block Iran's path to the bomb; it paves Iran's path to the bomb. So why would anyone make this deal? Because they hope that Iran will change for the better in the coming years, or they believe that the alternative to this deal is worse?
>
> Ladies and gentlemen, I've come here today to tell you we don't have to bet the security of the world on the hope that Iran will change for the better. We don't have to gamble with our future and with our children's future.

In case his audience hadn't got the message, Netanyahu then returned to using the precedent of the Holocaust in a direct manner implying that he as Prime Minister of Israel would not allow something similar to happen. Reminding Congress of another invited guest who was in the audience, he went on:

> With us today is Holocaust survivor and Nobel Prize winner Elie Wiesel. Elie, your life and work inspires to give meaning to the words, 'Never Again.' And I wish I could promise you, Elie, that the lessons of history have been learned. I can only urge the leaders of the world not to repeat the mistakes of the past. Not to sacrifice the future for the present; not to ignore aggression in the hopes of gaining an illusory peace.
>
> But I can guarantee you this; the days when the Jewish people remained passive in the face of genocidal enemies, those days are over. We are no longer scattered among the nations, powerless to

defend ourselves. We restored our sovereignty in our ancient home. And the soldiers who defend our home have boundless courage. For the first time in 100 generations, we, the Jewish people, can defend ourselves.

He wrapped up his speech with a stark reminder that Israel would take action on its own if it were forced to, but preferred to work with the United States to resolve the crisis.

> This is why as Prime Minister of Israel, I can promise you one more thing: Even if Israel has to stand alone, Israel will stand. But I know that Israel does not stand alone. I know that America stands with Israel. I know that you stand with Israel. You stand with Israel because you know that the story of Israel is not only the story of the Jewish people but of the human spirit that refuses again and again to succumb to history's horrors.[8]

As the standing ovation and the applause came to an end, and Netanyahu left Congress after what was arguably the biggest speech of his life, the verdicts and reviews began to roll in. Like it or loathe it, the speech was vintage Netanyahu and encompassed all the facets of his character, his appeal and his problems.

The speech scored well in execution. Madeleine Albrights's comments from 1998, that she had to pinch herself to remember that Netanyahu wasn't American, seemed appropriate. Few foreigners could have delivered the speech speaking American – both in terms of language and style of delivery. In this sense, the delivery was reminiscent of President Clinton (Netanyahu had closely studied his oratory during the 1992 American presidential campaign).

Drawing on history was a mechanism that Netanyahu employed to try to give some gravitas and sense of perspective to his message. Comparing the Israeli/Jewish historical narrative to that of the United States was again a smart ploy. Netanyahu liked to talk of mutual and shared interests between Israel and the United States that had been in place for decades. All of this was preaching to the already converted in Congress.

Where the speech became more problematic was in its abject failure to offer any concrete alternative proposals to the deal being negotiated with the Iranians, short of using the war option. This failure was representative of the biggest flaw in 'Netanyahuism', the absence of positive counter-proposals.

Netanyahu had become the master politician for defining and articulating the politics of fear. Put simply, he understood the root causes of problems, but had no idea how best to fix them. His speech to Congress, as a result, left many people who watched it with the feeling they had after eating a fast-food meal. Nice while you ate it, probably was not good for you and you soon forgot about it.

President Obama's response to the speech was cleverly scripted along these lines. His advisors told the President to make it clear that he had been too busy attending to affairs of state to watch the speech on television, but had read a transcript of it. The President was primed for reporters with a seemingly off-the-cuff statement when he appeared at the White House later the same day.

In his comments the President repeatedly focused on the point that Netanyahu offered nothing new in the speech or any alternative proposals. His words read like an attack not only on Netanyahu's Iranian policy, but on his entire political philosophy. As the President told reporters:

I did have a chance to take a look at the transcript. And as far as I can tell, there was nothing new. The Prime Minister I think appropriately pointed out that the bond between the United States and Israel is unbreakable, and on that point, I thoroughly agree.

He also pointed out that Iran has been a dangerous regime and continues to engage in activities that are contrary to the interest of the United States, to Israel, and to the region. And on that we agree.

He also pointed out the fact that Iran has repeatedly threatened Israel and engaged in the most venomous of anti-Semitic statements, and no one can dispute that.

But on the core issue, which is how do we prevent Iran from obtaining a nuclear weapon which would make it far more dangerous and would give it scope for even greater action in the region.

The Prime Minister didn't offer any viable alternatives. So let's be clear about what exactly the central concern should be, both for the United States and for Israel. I've said since and before I became president that one of my primary goals in foreign policy would be preventing Iran from getting nuclear weapons, and with the help of Congress and our international partners, we constructed an extraordinarily effective sanctions regime that pressured Iran to come to the table to negotiate in a serious fashion.

They have now been negotiating over the last year, and during that period, Iran has, in fact, frozen its program, rolled back some of its most dangerous highly enriched uranium and subjected itself to the kinds of verification and inspections that we had not previously seen. Keep in mind that when we shaped that interim deal, Prime Minister Netanyahu made almost the precise same speech about how dangerous that deal was going to be. And yet, over a year later, even Israeli intelligence officers and in some cases members of the Israeli government have to acknowledge that, in fact, it has kept Iran from further pursuing its nuclear program.

Now, the deal that we are trying to negotiate that is not yet completed would cut off the different pathways for Iran to advance its nuclear capabilities. It would roll back some elements of its program. It would ensure that it did not have what we call a breakout capacity that was shorter than a year's time. And it would subject Iran to the most vigorous inspections and verification regimes that have ever been put in place.

The alternative that the Prime Minister offers is no deal, in which case Iran will immediately begin once again pursuing its nuclear program, accelerate its nuclear program, without us having any insight into what they're doing. And without constraint.

And his essential argument is if we just double down on sanctions, Iran won't want to do that. Well, we have evidence from the past decade that sanctions are not sufficient to prevent Iran from pursuing its nuclear ambitions. And if, in fact, it does not have some sense that sanctions will not be removed, it will not have an interest in avoiding the path that it's currently on.

So the bottom line is this. We don't yet have a deal. It may be that Iran cannot say yes to a good deal. I have repeatedly said that I would rather have no deal than a bad deal. But if we're successful in negotiating, then, in fact, this will be the best deal possible to prevent Iran from obtaining a nuclear weapon. Nothing else comes close. Sanctions won't do it. Even military action would not be as successful as the deal that we have put forward.

And I think it is very important not to be distracted by the nature of the Iranian regimes' ambitions when it comes to territory or terrorism. All issues which we share a concern with Israel about and are working consistently with Israel on. Because we know that if, in fact, they obtained a nuclear weapon, all those problems would be worse.

So we're staying focused on the central issue here. How do we prevent Iran from getting a nuclear weapon? The path that we proposed, if successful, by far is the best way to do that. That's demonstrable.

And Prime Minister Netanyahu has not offered any kind of viable alternative that would achieve the same verifiable mechanisms to prevent Iran from getting a nuclear weapon.

So I would urge the members of Congress who were there to continue to express their strong support for Israel's security, to continue to express their strong interest in providing the assistance Israel needs to repel attacks.

I think it's important for members of Congress on a bipartisan basis to be unified in pushing back against terrorism in the region and the destabilizing efforts that Iran may have engaged with, with our partners. Those are all things on which this administration and Israel agree.

But when it comes to this nuclear deal, let's wait until there's absolutely a deal on the table that Iran has agreed to, at which point everyone can evaluate it. We don't have to speculate. And what I can guarantee is that if it's a deal I've signed off on, I will be able to prove that it is the best way for us to prevent Iran from getting a nuclear weapon. And for us to pass up on that potential opportunity would be a grave mistake. It's not one that I intend to make, and I will take that case to every member of Congress once we actually have a deal.[9]

Obama delivered his message in a stern, serious and unsmiling manner. His tone was that of a teacher ticking off a student for submitting a piece of work that lacked any originality. Just as Netanyahu had hoped that Mitt Romney would defeat Obama in the 2012 Presidential election, so Obama hoped that Herzog and Livni would unseat Netanyahu in Israel's elections, two weeks after the speech. President Obama was hoping for a fresh start with a new Prime Minister in Israel with a more sympathetic position towards a potential deal with Iran.

Netanyahu arrived back in Israel to a mixed reception, and with an election campaign that was threatening to inflict a second electoral defeat upon him. The reception of his speech did little to alter the political balance in the country. Polling data, taken in the days following its delivery to Congress, indicated that the Likud had received no significant political bump from it in terms of any major increase in support for the party.[10]

The speech also had a limited impact on Congress. It pleased those members of Congress who opposed the deal, but did little to convince supporters of the President, or, crucially, those who were undecided.

Great speeches, such as Winston Churchill's wartime addresses in 1940 and 1941, were beautifully written and delivered with clarity and passion, but most important of all impacted upon policies and events. Netanyahu's speech to Congress was delivered in a clear, and at times, passionate manner, but lacked any impact on events.

The debate over how best to deal with the threat of the Iranian nuclear programme had come a long way since Netanyahu and Obama had assumed office in 2009. From Netanyahu's perspective, Iran had dominated his foreign policy since coming to power, as well as being an important factor in the formation of his governments.

Defeat at the hands of President Obama over Iran was compensated for by the other key decisive split in US–Israeli relations during the Netanyahu–Obama era, the thorny question of the Palestinian peace process. In this area, Netanyahu was far more successful in resisting pressure from the Obama administration to yield major concessions to the Palestinians.

Both in terms of strategies and tactics, Netanyahu outmanoeuvred Obama on the Palestinian front far more easily than he had been able to do with President Clinton during his first time as Prime Minister between 1996 and 1999. Neither Netanyahu nor Obama formally acknowledged the linkage of the Iranian and Palestinian issues in detail. There were, however, instances when Netanyahu used Israeli restraint on a potential military strike against Iran as a means for buying some relief from the Americans to take the pressure off Israel on the Palestinian front.

The Netanyahu–Obama dance around the Israeli–Palestinian peace process had started in earnest with two speeches in June 2009, one given by Obama in Cairo and the other by Netanyahu in Ramat Gan, Israel. Question marks about Netanyahu's remarks, and follow-up actions, would dominate the peace process in the subsequent years from 2009 onwards. There was a great deal of speculation as to the extent that Netanyahu had undergone a genuine political transformation.

25

Challenge

Benjamin Netanyahu was far too seasoned a politician to think that the political honeymoon that followed his return to power in 2009 would last long. In light of Kadima's reluctance to join a government of national unity, the key component in the coalition became the Labour Party and its leader, Ehud Barak.

Barak had returned to public office and to the leadership of the Labour Party on 12 June 2007. In contrast to Netanyahu, during his comeback campaign Barak had acknowledged the mistakes and problems that had characterized his brief time as Prime Minister. Six days after regaining the Labour Party leadership, Barak had been appointed Minister of Defence in the Olmert-led administration.

In the 2009 elections, the Labour Party was beaten into fourth place and won only 13 seats. Barak and the party argued that, in light of their poor performance, they would go into opposition and work to rehabilitate the party with the electorate. Netanyahu wanted Barak in the government as his Minister of Defence in order to help deal with the Iranian threat. Barak, as a result, was able to convince his party and, albeit a little reluctantly, it joined the coalition.

The Netanyahu–Barak axis became the central focus of Israeli politics for the next four years with both men working closely on the three threats of Iran, Hezbollah and Hamas. Barak was a perfect political fit for Netanyahu. He was widely regarded in Israel as having an excellent strategic military mind, an area in which Netanyahu was not strong. More to the point, he agreed with Netanyahu that the military option towards the Iranian nuclear threat needed to be fully explored and potentially activated.

On the political front, despite his victory over Netanyahu in the 1999 direct election for Prime Minister, Barak in 2009 was a much weaker rival to Netanyahu's leadership of the country. With his limited popularity among the electorate, and with ongoing threats to his leadership of the Labour Party, it was unlikely that Barak was going to once again challenge for the number one position in the government.

On top of this, Netanyahu, at the time, liked Barak on a personal level, and on a professional level trusted his judgement. The appointment of Barak also meant that Netanyahu did not have to give the number two portfolio in the government to a *Likudnik*, who might use the position to mount a challenge to his leadership of the party and the country. Together Netanyahu and Barak devised and implemented Israel's security policies, including those directed towards the Palestinians.

President Obama recalled the dramatic offers that Barak had made to the Palestinians in 2000 at Camp David, and in 2001 in Taba, and hoped that the presence of Barak in the Netanyahu government would pull the Prime Minister towards the political centre in Israel. By 2009, Barak had largely disowned these concessions, but he was still thought to be open to making major concessions to the Palestinians in any final status negotiations.

The presence of Shimon Peres in the presidency also appeared to be a hopeful sign to the Americans. Put simply, the Americans felt that Peres could also help guide Netanyahu towards the political centre ground. Although the position of President in Israel is a largely ceremonial one, Peres was seen as a leader who would be willing to make his own views on the peace process heard to the Prime Minister.

In giving Netanyahu the task of forming the government after the 2009 election, Peres had made it clear that he wanted a centrist/unity government, which would actively pursue the peace process with the Palestinians. The Obama administration also sought Peres's views on the domestic political lie of the land in Israel, and to clarify the direction in which Netanyahu was taking the country.

Like a cagey boxer in the ring, Netanyahu didn't want to make the first move in the uncharted waters of the Obama era. He received the customary invitation for an Israeli Prime Minister to meet with the President at the White House on 19 May 2009.

During the course of the meeting, Obama focused his attention on Israel and Palestine, arguing that continued Jewish settlement in the

West Bank was unacceptable. He wanted Netanyahu to commit his government to the two-state solution, but the Prime Minister resisted making any such declaration in Washington.

For Netanyahu the meeting with Obama was all about Iran and making the case for action against it sooner rather than later. The two differing priorities of the President of the United States and the Prime Minister of Israel did not bode well for US–Israeli relations for the subsequent years. Obama talked of hope, Netanyahu of fear. It wasn't just their agendas that weren't coordinated; their outlooks on the world came from opposite ends of the spectrum.

Netanyahu was pragmatic enough to understand that the main result of the meeting with President Obama was that the status quo of doing little on the Palestinian peace process was not acceptable to the President. It was widely known that Obama aimed to launch a major charm offensive on the Muslim world, in order to try to repair some of the damage caused by his predecessor's policies in the Middle East.

The President threw down the gauntlet to Netanyahu during his important speech on 4 June 2009 at Cairo University. The speech was intended to reconnect the United States with the Muslim world, but it was his comments on Israel and Palestine that drew the greatest attention. He offered his harshest words for Israel and expressed sympathy for the plight of the Palestinians. This was not the normal attitude of an American President.[1]

The speech set out Obama's policy towards the Israeli–Palestinian conflict in the clearest manner possible, at the centre of which was the two-state solution. Netanyahu listened to the speech intently, as it was broadcast live across the globe. The section on the Israeli–Palestinian conflict made for sober listening. In front of a wildly enthusiastic crowd, Obama said:

> America's strong bonds with Israel are well known. This bond is unbreakable. It is based upon cultural and historical ties, and the recognition that the aspiration for a Jewish homeland is rooted in a tragic history that cannot be denied.[2]

The President then went on to address the problem of Holocaust denial and to warn the Arabs that this was not acceptable.

Around the world, the Jewish people were persecuted for centuries, and anti-Semitism in Europe culminated in an unprecedented Holocaust. Tomorrow, I will visit Buchenwald, which was part of a network of camps where Jews were enslaved, tortured, shot and gassed to death by the Third Reich. Six million Jews were killed – more than the entire Jewish population of Israel today.

Denying that fact is baseless, ignorant, and hateful. Threatening Israel with destruction – or repeating vile stereotypes about Jews – is deeply wrong, and only serves to evoke in the minds of Israelis this most painful of memories while preventing the peace that the people of this region deserve.[3]

He turned his attention to the Palestinians and here he departed from the norm by outlining his empathy for their plight and suffering. He offered more than this, however, by categorically supporting the creation of an independent Palestinian state. He said:

On the other hand, it is also undeniable that the Palestinian people – Muslims and Christians – have suffered in pursuit of a homeland. For more than sixty years they have endured the pain of dislocation. Many wait in refugee camps in the West Bank, Gaza, and neighbouring lands for a life of peace and security that they have never been able to lead.

They endure the daily humiliations – large and small – that come with occupation. So let there be no doubt: the situation for the Palestinian people is intolerable. America will not turn our backs on the legitimate Palestinian aspiration for dignity, opportunity, and a state of their own.[4]

The President focused on what he expected from the Palestinians and the Israelis. He reminded both sides of what they needed to do:

For peace to come, it is time for them – and all of us – to live up to our responsibilities. Palestinians must abandon violence. Resistance through violence and killing is wrong and does not succeed.

. . . Now is the time for Palestinians to focus on what they can build. The Palestinian Authority must develop its capacity to govern, with institutions that serve the needs of its people. Hamas does have support among some Palestinians, but they also have responsibilities.

To play a role in fulfilling Palestinian aspirations, and to unify the Palestinian people, Hamas must put an end to violence, recognize past agreements, and recognize Israel's right to exist.

At the same time, Israelis must acknowledge that just as Israel's right to exist cannot be denied, neither can Palestine's. The United States does not accept the legitimacy of continued Israeli settlements. This construction violates previous agreements and undermines efforts to achieve peace. It is time for these settlements to stop.

Israel must also live up to its obligations to ensure that Palestinians can live, and work, and develop their society. And just as it devastates Palestinian families, the continuing humanitarian crisis in Gaza does not serve Israel's security; neither does the continuing lack of opportunity in the West Bank. Progress in the daily lives of the Palestinian people must be part of a road to peace, and Israel must take concrete steps to enable such progress.[5]

The key section for Netanyahu was the issue of the Jewish settlements and Obama's effective demand that he freeze any new settlement building. Netanyahu fully understood that such a move would not play well with his right-wing constituency.

In the final part of the section on the Israeli–Palestinian conflict, Obama challenged the wider Arab world to help support a potential Palestinian state and to recognize Israel. The final sentence was a direct challenge to Netanyahu to come out publicly in support of the two-state solution.

Finally, the Arab States must recognize that the Arab Peace Initiative was an important beginning, but not the end of their responsibilities. The Arab–Israeli conflict should no longer be used to distract the people of Arab nations from other problems. Instead, it must be a cause for action to help the Palestinian people develop the institutions that will sustain their state; to recognize Israel's legitimacy; and to choose progress over a self-defeating focus on the past.

America will align our policies with those who pursue peace, and say in public what we say in private to Israelis and Palestinians and Arabs. We cannot impose peace. But privately, many Muslims recognize that Israel will not go away. Likewise, many Israelis recognize the need for a Palestinian state. It is time for us to act on what everyone knows to be true.[6]

The speech was a triumph for Obama and remains, arguably, one of the finest of his first term in office. It was well received in its target market, the Muslim world, and in particular among many Palestinians who saw it as evidence of the emergence of a more critical approach towards Israel emanating from Washington.

Netanyahu viewed it as a challenge, but in his pragmatic way started carefully to prepare his response to President Obama. One thing that impressed Netanyahu about Obama's speech was its sense of drama and history. He wanted his response to reflect a similar approach and for any concessions that he was going to offer to be given the maximum publicity across the globe.

He chose to present his ideas at Bar-Ilan University, and to use an address there to make his response. His press team carefully trailed that the Prime Minister would be issuing a crucial announcement. President Peres and the head of the opposition were consulted in an apparent attempt to show a degree of national unity on the policy announcement.

Netanyahu presented his ideas on 14 June 2009 to the Begin–Sadat Center for Strategic Studies at Bar-Ilan University. Predictably, the order of the subjects in Netanyahu's speech was the opposite of Obama's, reflecting their different political agendas.

Starting with Iran, Netanyahu talked about the nuclear programme as the greatest threat facing Israel. He then moved on to the challenges for Israelis caused by the global economic crisis. This was followed by a call for Arab states to help foster a stable regional peace.

Only then did he turn to the subject most people were waiting to hear about: the resolution of the conflict with the Palestinians. After his preamble about the impact of the conflict on people's lives, including a reference to the loss of his own brother, he came to his main point – he was accepting the two-state solution to the conflict. As he put it:

I turn to you, our Palestinian neighbours, led by the Palestinian Authority, and I say: 'Let's begin negotiations immediately without preconditions.'

In my vision of peace, in this small land of ours, two peoples live freely, side-by-side, in amity and mutual respect. Each will have its own flag, its own national anthem, its own government. Neither will threaten the security or survival of the other. These two realities – our connection to the land of Israel, and the Palestinian population living within it – have created deep divisions in Israeli society. But the truth is that we have much more that unites us than divides us.

I have come tonight to give expression to that unity, and to the principles of peace and security on which there is broad agreement within Israeli society. These are the principles that guide our policy. This policy must take into account the international situation that has recently developed. We must recognize this reality and at the same time stand firmly on those principles essential for Israel.[7]

Next came his preconditions for accepting a Palestinian state. There were essentially two issues that needed to be addressed. He went on:

I have already stressed the first principle – recognition. Palestinians must clearly and unambiguously recognize Israel as the state of the Jewish people.

The second principle is: demilitarisation. The territory under Palestinian control must be demilitarized with ironclad security provisions for Israel. Without these two conditions, there is a real danger that an armed Palestinian state would emerge that would become another terrorist base against the Jewish state, such as the one in Gaza. We don't want Kassam rockets on Petach Tikva, Grad rockets on Tel Aviv, or missiles on Ben-Gurion airport. We want peace.

In order to achieve peace, we must ensure that Palestinians will not be able to import missiles into their territory, to field an army, to close their airspace to us, or to make pacts with the likes of Hezbollah and Iran. On this point as well, there is wide consensus within Israel. It is impossible to expect us to agree in advance to the principle of a Palestinian state without assurances that this state will be demilitarised. On a matter so critical to the existence of Israel, we must first have our security needs addressed.

Therefore, today we ask our friends in the international community, led by the United States, for what is critical to the security of

Israel: Clear commitments that in a future peace agreement, the territory controlled by the Palestinians will be demilitarised: namely, without an army, without control of its airspace, and with effective security measures to prevent weapons smuggling into the territory – real monitoring, and not what occurs in Gaza today.

And obviously, the Palestinians will not be able to forge military pacts. Without this, sooner or later, these territories will become another *Hamastan*, and that we cannot accept.

I told President Obama when I was in Washington that if we could agree on the substance, then the terminology would not pose a problem. And here is the substance that I now state clearly:

If we receive this guarantee regarding demilitarization and Israel's security needs, and if the Palestinians recognize Israel as the state of the Jewish people, then we will be ready in a future peace agreement to reach a solution where a demilitarized Palestinian state exists alongside the Jewish state.[8]

Finally, he outlined his vision for a resolution of the rest of the issues and with it a reference to the thorny issue of Jewish settlements:

Regarding the remaining important issues that will be discussed as part of the final settlement, my positions are known: Israel needs defensible borders, and Jerusalem must remain the united capital of Israel with continued religious freedom for all faiths. The territorial question will be discussed as part of the final peace agreement. In the meantime, we have no intention of building new settlements or of expropriating additional land for existing settlements.

But there is a need to enable the residents to live normal lives, to allow mothers and fathers to raise their children like families elsewhere. The settlers are neither the enemies of the people nor the enemies of peace. Rather, they are an integral part of our people, a principled, pioneering and Zionist public.

Unity among us is essential and will help us achieve reconcilia-tion with our neighbours. That reconciliation must already begin by altering existing realities. I believe that a strong Palestinian economy will strengthen peace.

If the Palestinians turn toward peace – in fighting terror, in strengthening governance and the rule of law, in educating their

children for peace and in stopping incitement against Israel – we
will do our part in making every effort to facilitate freedom of
movement and access, and to enable them to develop their economy. All of this will help us advance a peace treaty between us.[9]

The contents of the speech were heavily criticized by the Palestinian
Authority. Saeb Erekat, the Palestinian negotiator, wrote in response:

> Benjamin Netanyahu spoke about negotiations, but left us with
> nothing to negotiate as he systematically took nearly every permanent
> status issue off the table. Nor did he accept a Palestinian state. Instead,
> he announced a series of conditions and qualifications that render a
> viable, independent and sovereign Palestinian state impossible.[10]

Reaction from the White House, however, was much more favourable.
Officials in the Obama administration saw Netanyahu as having caved
in to American pressure over the question of the two-state solution.
Officials glossed over the important point that Netanyahu had rejected
Obama's demands for a complete freeze on Israeli settlements in the
West Bank.[11]

In Israel, the speech was viewed as a careful and balanced one.
President Peres went further with the hyperbole. Addressing the press
after Netanyahu's speech he said, 'True and courageous. It constituted
an opening toward direct negotiations for both a regional peace and a
bilateral peace between Israel and the Palestinians.'[12]

For Netanyahu personally, the statement represented a major shift
and a pragmatic acceptance of political realities in Israel and in the
Obama-led United States. He had been careful not to be seen to have
given the Americans everything that President Obama had demanded
in his speech in Cairo. There were important domestic reasons for holding back on some issues.

Being seen as not having surrendered entirely to the Americans was
a political necessity for Netanyahu in selling the two-state solution
to his right-wing constituency. Many on the right-wing in Israel still
considered the acceptance of the establishment of a Palestinian state as
collective national suicide by Israel.

Once Netanyahu had given the Americans what they wanted in terms
of accepting the possibility of a Palestinian state they concentrated their

efforts on the other item that Obama had outlined in his Cairo speech, the settlements. On this issue, Netanyahu proved a tougher nut to crack, making it clear in meetings with both Secretary of State Hillary Clinton and President Obama that he would not agree to a permanent freeze on settlement construction. There were also major differences on whether or not building in Jerusalem would be included in any potential agreement.

Eventually a compromise agreement was reached, which allowed both Netanyahu and Obama to portray it as creating a meaningful opportunity to try to restart the negotiations with the Palestinians. On 25 November 2009, Netanyahu announced a halt to all new residential construction in the West Bank for a period of ten months. The agreement covered only the West Bank, not Jerusalem, and did not include public infrastructure projects such as schools and community centres.

Netanyahu managed to get the proposals passed by the Israeli Security Cabinet and made it clear to the Americans that this was as much as he was willing to concede on the settlement issue. Speaking to the assembled press, Netanyahu did his utmost to spin the agreement as best he could:

> I hope that this decision will help launch meaningful negotiations to reach a historic peace agreement that would finally end the conflict between Israel and the Palestinians.
> . . . We have been told by many of our friends that once Israel takes the first meaningful steps toward peace, the Palestinians and Arab states would respond.
> . . . Now is the time to begin negotiations, now is the time to move forward towards peace. Israel today has taken a far-reaching step toward peace, it is time for the Palestinians to do the same.[13]

He talked of the agreement being 'a far-reaching and painful' decision, a veiled warning to the Americans not to press him for more. Almost as soon as Netanyahu announced the moratorium, commentators speculated that it was aimed more at making peace with the Obama administration than with the Palestinians. This, by and large, was an accurate assessment.[14]

The Palestinians rejected the moratorium on settlement building in the West Bank as not going nearly far enough. They argued that the

American failure to shift Netanyahu into accepting a permanent settlement freeze, including Jerusalem, was a bad precedent as to how far Obama would be able to pressure Netanyahu in any final status talks.

Netanyahu's move did not break the impasse, which was characterized as being talks about potential negotiations, with the American mediators becoming ever more frustrated by both sides. By essentially keeping the Americans onside, Netanyahu was able to buy himself some more time without having to enter into meaningful negotiations that would require him to make historic compromises.

The Netanyahu–Obama relationship was initially characterized by Obama's demands, which Netanyahu, a little reluctantly and partially, met. Netanyahu, however, was in for the long haul and part of his strategy was based on watching Obama's wave of goodwill and optimism recede. In the meantime, with the help of a divided and at times politically self-destructive Palestinian leadership, he planned to sit tight and try to move the agenda back towards the Iranian nuclear programme.

In the meantime, he worked to ensure that the political impasse with the Palestinians did not damage Israel's international standing and looked towards developing Israeli economic ties with markets in China and Asia. The absence of any orchestrated Palestinian violence helped create the impression to Israelis that the status quo under Netanyahu of no peace and no war was sustainable in the short- to medium-term.

Events in the Arab world, starting in December 2010, would add further motives for Netanyahu to move cautiously in the area of peacemaking. All of this would strengthen his control over Israeli politics and help him emerge as the dominant figure in the subsequent years.

26

Relationships

The onset of the Arab Spring, from 18 December 2010 onwards, became the catalyst for the deteriorating relationship between Netanyahu and the Obama administration. The fallout from the events surrounding it helped entrench Netanyahu's control over power in Israel. At first, it appeared that the Arab Spring might help push the Middle East forward, but in the short-term it pushed it backward. [1]

As Netanyahu told the Knesset nearly a year later on 31 October 2011:

> The Arab street has awoken; old regimes have toppled, others are swaying and new ones are rising. No one can guarantee how good or how stable these new regimes will be, nor their attitude towards Israel. Unfortunately, this attitude, which left much to be desired to begin with, is not expected to get any better in some, or most, of the new regimes, not in the foreseeable future.
>
> These new regimes depend on the masses, the raging masses, of which many of the people have been systematically poisoned with anti-Semitic and anti-Zionist propaganda. This incitement began even before the State of Israel was established, and continues at full steam today.
>
> . . . If the positions of the religious extreme do not become more moderate, I doubt that any of the high hopes that blossomed in the Arab Spring will come true. It is possible that these hopes will only be fulfilled a generation from now, after this wave subsides, when progress will be given a chance to lead the Arab world down a new path.

If I had to summarize what will happen in our region, I would use two terms: instability and uncertainty.

Regional powers that have control in the Middle East will try to ensure they have greater influence on the new regimes – influence that will not always support us or be of benefit to us, to say the least. One of these regional forces is Iran, which continues its efforts to obtain nuclear weapons.

. . . To cope with the instability and the uncertainty we are faced with, we need two things: strength and responsibility. Strength in all areas: security, economy, society, everywhere; and responsibility in navigating the stormy sea in which we are sailing. We must continue to strengthen Israel in all areas of security so that we can respond to the new challenges and threats we are facing.[2]

The speech was a robust defence of his policy of using the Arab Spring as a rationale not to offer substantial political concessions to the Palestinians or to the wider Arab world. Once again, in times of perceived threat Israeli society took a step towards the right. Netanyahu's coalition, which had been cobbled together after the 2009 elections, had not been expected to survive very long. But with the onset of the Arab Spring it looked as if it would become the first government in recent history to last the full four-year course of the Knesset.

The rapid souring of the Arab Spring, and its takeover by radical elements, appeared to illustrate that the caution Netanyahu had shown towards the peace process had been well founded. His plan for effectively trying to sit out the Arab Spring before making any potential concessions towards the Arabs also resonated well among many Israelis, who were focused on security rather than peace.

Netanyahu's outlook, while increasingly accepted in Israel, was not welcomed in Washington. Earlier in the year, Netanyahu and Obama had experienced 'a clash of visions' over the Israeli–Palestinian conflict and the impact of the Arab Spring. The disagreement resulted in one of the most extraordinary press conferences of the President's first term, which followed Obama's meeting with Netanyahu in the Oval Office on 20 May 2011.

The story had begun on the previous day when President Obama made a keynote speech on the Middle East at the State Department in Washington. The address was intended as an update on his Cairo speech to take into account the dramatic events that were sweeping the Arab world.

The part of the speech that made headlines focused on the President's efforts to break the impasse in the Israeli–Palestinian conflict. The speech was timed to coincide with the arrival of Netanyahu in Washington the next day.

Obama announced a significant shift in American policy in arguing that the pre-Six Day War 1967 borders – with minor land swaps to reflect the large Israeli settlement blocks in the West Bank – would be the foundation for a negotiated agreement between the Israelis and Palestinians. This went well beyond what Netanyahu had in mind for the borders of any state for the Palestinians.

The sensitive nature of the policy change was illustrated by the repeated lobbying by Israeli officials right up to the end for Obama to make changes to his proposed speech. The *New York Times* reported that, while the White House denied making any changes to the text under Israeli pressure, it admitted that Obama did make some last-minute modifications to the address that delayed his appearance by 35 minutes.[3]

The President's words did not make for pleasant reading for Netanyahu:

> The United States believes that negotiations should result in two states, with permanent Palestinian borders with Israel, Jordan, and Egypt, and permanent Israeli borders with Palestine. The borders of Israel and Palestine should be based on the 1967 lines with mutually agreed swaps, so that secure and recognized borders are established for both states. The Palestinian people must have the right to govern themselves, and reach their potential, in a sovereign and contiguous state.[4]

Next came the part that was meant to douse Israeli fears, as the President reminded the world that a Palestinian state would be demilitarized. Needless to say, this part did not please the Palestinians who saw it as an unnecessary prerequisite. As the President said:

> As for security, every state has the right to self-defence, and Israel must be able to defend itself – by itself – against any threat.

Provisions must also be robust enough to prevent a resurgence of terrorism; to stop the infiltration of weapons; and to provide effective border security. The full and phased withdrawal of Israeli military forces should be coordinated with the assumption of Palestinian security responsibility in a sovereign, non-militarized state.[5]

The rest of the speech contained imagery employed by the ex-British Prime Minister Tony Blair when dealing with the Northern Irish peace process. Obama talked of 'looking to the future and not being trapped by the past'. Amidst the brave, somewhat rambling and at times disjointed speech, the comments about the 1967 borders made all the headlines in the American and world press.

Obama's motives for the speech were well spelled out by a former US Ambassador to Israel, Martin Indyk, who said, 'He's [Obama] moving into a crisis-management mode; laying out principles to preserve the two-state solution and to prevent a UN resolution on a Palestinian state.'[6] While Indyk, and other American commentators, highlighted the pro-Israel sentiments in much of the speech, Netanyahu was furious with both the contents and its timing.

By way of a robust response, the Prime Minister issued a statement declaring Obama's ideas were a wholly unacceptable basis for the resolution of the conflict with the Palestinians. In the tersely worded statement Netanyahu said:

Israel believes that for peace to endure between Israelis and Palestinians, the viability of a Palestinian state cannot come at the expense of the viability of the one and only Jewish state. That is why Prime Minister Netanyahu expects to hear a reaffirmation from President Obama of U.S. commitments made to Israel in 2004, which were overwhelmingly supported by both Houses of Congress.

Among other things, those commitments relate to Israel not having to withdraw to the 1967 lines which are both indefensible and which would leave major Israeli population centers in Judea and Samaria beyond those lines. Those commitments also ensure Israel's well being as a Jewish state by making clear that Palestinian refugees will settle in a future Palestinian state rather than in Israel. Without a solution to the Palestinian refugee problem outside the borders of Israel, no territorial concession will bring peace.

Equally, the Palestinians, and not just the United States, must recognize Israel as the nation state of the Jewish people, and any peace agreement with them must end all claims against Israel.[7]

The subtext to this was that Netanyahu was coming to Washington to try to right a wrong. His meeting with the President on 20 May 2011, as a result, became one of potential drama and high stakes diplomacy. The media frenzy that accompanied the build-up to the meeting indicated the scale of the differences between the two leaders in terms of policy and outlook. The meeting did not disappoint those people who were waiting for the drama.

As Netanyahu arrived in Washington, he felt Obama's speech had laid an ambush for him. During the course of his visit, he would be given ample opportunity in media interviews, in speeches to Israeli lobby groups and in a keynote speech to Congress on 24 May 2011 to address his problems with Obama's newly stated position.

The two leaders held their meeting at a later time than had been the custom for their six previous ones. Obama's advisors wanted to make sure that the meeting would be too late for the evening television news in Israel.[8] Both sides described the meeting as difficult, with the two men outlining their different visions of the Arab Spring, their positions on the Israeli–Palestinian conflict and the Iranian nuclear programme.

In most cases, the press conference that followed such meetings was characterized by both leaders talking about their mutual goals, what bound them together as allies and glossing over the differences they had just covered during the private part of the meeting. The leaders usually ended with warm words about continuing to work together to find solutions to the outstanding issues and saying that they would remain in close contact as their two governments moved forward. The White House then released an official photograph of the private part of the meeting to illustrate the warmth of the discussions.

The first part of the press conference that followed went according to the norm, with the President taking just over seven minutes to summarize the meeting in the most positive spin possible. As Obama concluded his comments he said:

So, overall, I thought this was an extremely constructive discussion. And coming out of this discussion, I once again can reaffirm that the extraordinarily close relationship between the United States and Israel is sound and will continue, and that together, hopefully we are going to be able to work to usher in a new period of peace and prosperity in a region that is going to be going through some very profound transformations in the coming weeks, months and years.[9]

Obama was something of a master at the art of turning difficulties into positives. As he handed over to the Prime Minister, he expected Netanyahu, also a master at this art, to do the same and make a similar style address to the press corps. Netanyahu had other plans.

Instead, the Prime Minister issued a strongly worded rebuke to the President for trying to create a peace that was not based on political realities. The unsmiling Netanyahu looked straight at Obama, whose expression was like thunder:

What we all want is a peace that will be genuine, that will hold, that will endure. And I think that the – we both agree that a peace based on illusions will crash eventually on the rocks of Middle Eastern reality, and that the only peace that will endure is one that is based on reality, on unshakeable facts.

I think for there to be peace, the Palestinians will have to accept some basic realities. The first is that while Israel is prepared to make generous compromises for peace, it cannot go back to the 1967 lines – because these lines are indefensible; because they don't take into account certain changes that have taken place on the ground, demographic changes that have taken place over the last 44 years.

Remember that, before 1967, Israel was all of nine miles wide. It was half the width of the Washington Beltway. And these were not the boundaries of peace; they were the boundaries of repeated wars, because the attack on Israel was so attractive.

So we can't go back to those indefensible lines, and we're going to have to have a long-term military presence along the Jordan. I discussed this with the President and I think that we understand that Israel has certain security requirements that will have to come into place in any deal that we make.[10]

For Netanyahu to speak to a President of the United States in his own office in this stern manner was something quite out of the ordinary.

Previous Israeli prime ministers had behaved very differently for the cameras in the White House, smiling nicely and remembering that the United States provided Israel with over $3 billion of aid annually. In this respect, and in many others, Netanyahu did not behave like a traditional Israeli leader.

In reality, it was like watching two prizefighters eye each other up at the weigh-in for a championship fight. It was rare for two political leaders so proficient in the art of communication to so openly go up against one another. The body language of both men was as interesting as the words they spoke. Obama could barely contain his contempt for Netanyahu, and vice versa.

Instead of coming to a close following his rebuke to the President, Netanyahu decided to continue. Sounding strangely like his father he attempted to give Obama a short history of the Jewish people. By this stage, the President's stony expression had turned to an icy glare as he listened to the Prime Minister's words:

> Mr. President, you're the leader of a great people, the American people. And I'm the leader of a much smaller people. It's the ancient nation of Israel. And, you know, we've been around for almost 4,000 years. We've experienced struggle and suffering like no other people. We've gone through expulsions and pogroms and massacres and the murder of millions. But I can say that even at the dearth of – even at the nadir of the valley of death, we never lost hope and we never lost our dream of reestablishing a sovereign state in our ancient homeland, the land of Israel.
>
> And now it falls on my shoulders as the Prime Minister of Israel, at a time of extraordinary instability and uncertainty in the Middle East, to work with you to fashion a peace that will ensure Israel's security and will not jeopardize its survival. I take this responsibility with pride but with great humility, because, as I told you in our conversation, we don't have a lot of margin for error. And because, Mr. President, history will not give the Jewish people another chance.[11]

Rarely in politics have closing words such as those that Netanyahu uttered following his seven minutes in front of the camera meant so little:

So in the coming days and weeks and months, I intend to work
with you to seek a peace that will address our security concerns,
seek a genuine recognition that we wish from our Palestinian neigh-
bors to give a better future for Israel and for the entire region. And
I thank you for the opportunity to exchange our views and to work
together for this common end. Thank you, Mr. President.[12]

The resistance of Netanyahu to accept Obama's position regarding
the 1967 borders meant, in reality, the end of serious attempts by
the Americans to address the Israeli–Palestinian conflict prior to the
American presidential campaign taking over the President's agenda.[13]

During that campaign Netanyahu, once again, did not behave like
a typical Israeli Prime Minister who merely watched and waited for
the outcome from the sidelines. Instead he meddled in the campaign,
making it clear that in his opinion the best outcome for Israel would be
the election to the American presidency of Mitt Romney.

The Obama–Netanyahu relationship, while never personally warm,
had its ups and downs following this most difficult of meetings. The
peak came in September 2011, when Obama helped secure the release
of Israelis who were trapped in their embassy in Cairo, during an
Egyptian protest march. Obama used everything at his disposal to help
free the Israelis. Netanyahu, in turn, went out of his way to pay tribute
to Obama's personal intervention, which he saw as having been vital to
securing the release of the Israelis.

Arguably the deepest trough came on 3 November of the same year
at the G-20 Summit in France, when Obama was overheard on an open
microphone in conversation with President Nicolas Sarkozy. 'I cannot bear
Netanyahu, he's a liar,' Sarkozy told Obama, who was apparently unaware
that the microphones in the meeting room had been left on. 'You're fed up
with him, but I have to deal with him every day,' Obama replied.[14]

Both leaders tried their best to play down the gaffe when it was
broadcast around the world five days later on 8 November. The publication of the comments was met with stony silence from the Prime
Minister's office in Jerusalem. A member of Netanyahu's coalition did
offer a response when prompted by CNN:

It's unpleasant. We would all like to be loved, and all love to have
great relationships with each other. And I'm sure it would be nicer

to know that our Prime Minister is loved. But at the end of the day, what did Machiavelli say? It's more important to be feared than loved.[15]

Being seen as having stood up to President Obama was perceived by many Israelis as a good thing. Despite professing his admiration for Israel and the historical ties between it and America, Obama was never really able to connect with many Israelis. This removed his ability to talk over the Prime Minister and appeal directly to Israelis in the manner that President Clinton succeeded in doing.

Partly for this reason, and also because most Israelis did not concur with Obama's position of an Israeli return to 1967 borders, the President was much less of a danger to Netanyahu's control over the country than was generally perceived. On top of this, Netanyahu believed that Congress ran protection for him against the President and he was careful to cultivate close ties with key members of Congress from both parties.

As a result, Obama found himself facing a leader of a foreign country who was expert at playing American political games and whose power base in Congress was so strong that he could not be dismissed as just any old foreign leader. Netanyahu and Obama were both aware that any major shift towards introducing sanctions against Israel of either an economic or political nature would come up against fierce opposition in Congress.

In many respects, such as fundraising, organization of a campaign, economic policies and on foreign affairs, Netanyahu could have been a stronger candidate for the Republican Party to run against Obama in 2012 than Mitt Romney. He looked like a leader of the Republican Party, spoke like one and enjoyed all the trappings of the good life that seemed to come naturally to so many Republicans.

As the Arab Spring turned increasingly to the Arab or Islamic Winter, Netanyahu's scepticism about Obama's optimism concerning the changes in the Arab world appeared to have been well founded. This point, together with the lack of meaningful peace overtures from the Palestinian Authority in the West Bank and from Hamas in Gaza, reduced the pressure on Netanyahu to offer concessions to restart peace negotiations.

27

Protests

The internal pressure imposed on Netanyahu during 2011 came from a most unexpected source in Israel: the social justice protests that swept across the country during the summer months. The root cause of the protests remains a hot topic of debate.

The Arab Spring and the push for political, social and economic change in the states that bordered Israel were always going to have some spillover effect. The upheavals in the Arab world might well have impacted upon the timing of the protests, but the deeper long-term catalyst for the protests was the economic reforms started by Netanyahu during his tenure as Minister of Finance.

The tent protests that developed into mass demonstrations were sparked by rises in the cost of living, particularly in housing. The widespread use of social media platforms such as Facebook to help organize the protests and disseminate demands was a first in Israel. This also made the protests highly dynamic and heightened the ability of the vast array of organizers to get their message over to the Israeli media and the numerous foreign journalists based in the country.

Netanyahu, and the rest of the government, were caught off-guard and were initially slow to react. In retrospect, nobody should have been surprised by the protests. There had been significant increases in the cost of living for Israel's low-income and middle classes, as well as strong economic dissatisfaction among Israel's youth population and high levels of unemployment in key sectors of society.

Cases of poverty were on the increase, as many Israelis struggled to find work, pay their bills and buy basic consumer goods, priced much higher in Israel than in the United States or Western Europe. Poverty was nothing new in Israel, but the gap between the rich and the poor was widening to levels that far exceeded other Western-style democracies, and this placed strains on social cohesion in the country.

By the summer of 2011, many Israelis had suffered enough and were joining the social protests. While Netanyahu talked of how much better off Israelis were compared to Israel's neighbouring states, it went over the heads of many of the protestors, who were more interested in comparing their standard of living to Americans and Western Europeans.

As the leader of economic liberalization and market reform in Israel, Netanyahu was singled out for harsh criticism by the protestors. The origins for the malaise in the Israeli economy ran much deeper than Netanyahu's economic policy. The old Labour Zionist economy that characterized the first 55 years of the State of Israel until 2003 was inefficient, and its sustainability in the new globalized markets was questionable.

Netanyahu's reforms brought the Israeli economy into line with other Western capitalist ones. Tensions between the pursuit of wealth and Zionism have been an important factor for those in Israel arguing for a more redistributive economy. Netanyahu saw no alternative to economic reform, and for him this was a vital component in securing Israel's future.

The social protests in Israel caused much excitement, led to a new form of much needed political participation in the country and created a new class of young and ambitious leaders, several of whom entered party politics. It challenged Netanyahu to defend his economic philosophy, and to adopt a new, kinder and more human tone in his pronouncements on the economy. At the end of the day, it is debatable whether or not the protests led to any major changes in the micro-economic policies of the government.

Netanyahu raised the issue during his address to the Graduates of the National Security College, on 25 July 2011, five days before the protests snowballed into mass demonstrations across Israel. Netanyahu reminded the audience:

> This is true also with regard to the economy. There are plenty of reasons why we would like to see a developed and dynamic economy, but the most simple, prosaic reason is that we have no other

way of financing our defence – and defence costs a lot of money.
Weapons cost a lot of money, forces cost a lot of money and development costs a lot of money, and it keeps going up and up.

. . . We have tackled the economic problem by doubling our GNP
per capita in comparison with our neighbours. We were more or less
equal, but now we are 10 or 15 times larger than our neighbours. It
is as if our population was 10 or 15 times greater, although we have
a lot of neighbours. We have tackled it also through our economy
of knowledge and our technological economy. I am a great believer
in this, on condition that there is freedom of entrepreneurship. Free
economy is a necessary pre-requisite for a growing economy – a
growing economy that now surpasses European countries in its GNP
per capita – something that did not exist a decade ago.[1]

All this was normal Netanyahu-speak for 'everything is functioning
well'. As the scale of the protests grew, the Prime Minister was told in
no uncertain terms that the status quo was not acceptable. Following
the biggest rallies in Israel's history on 3 September 2011, when around
300,000 Israelis joined the protest, Netanyahu came under severe pressure to be seen to be doing something to satisfy the demonstrators.

Israelis carried banners that said, 'An entire generation wants a future'
and 'The people demand social justice'. Other banners carried slogans
attacking the government and Netanyahu in particular.

The main problem that Netanyahu faced in dealing with the protestors was the wide range of demands they made, ranging from tax cuts
for low-income workers to the expansion of free education and larger
government housing budgets. Netanyahu warned the protestors that he
would not be able to satisfy all of their demands.[2]

Netanyahu was eventually able to weather the political storm as the
protests died down after the government promised to look seriously
into aspects of its economic policies. There was also a feeling that a solution to Israel's economic ills was not so easy to achieve. Nobody really
presented a viable alternative to Netanyahu's free-market economics.

In his opening remarks to the winter session of the Knesset on 31
October 2011, Netanyahu, as well as presenting his thoughts on the
impact of the Arab Spring, devoted a large part of his speech to both a
defence of his economic policies and an acceptance that changes needed
to be made as a result of the social protests of the summer of 2011.

Starting with his traditional approach of summarizing the state of the global economy, Netanyahu was keen to remind Israelis that, unlike the rest of the world which was in economic meltdown as the result of the credit crunch, the Israeli economy, for all the protests, was doing rather better. As he put it:

> Over the last few years, the world economy has been in a crisis which is not over yet. The sea is stormy there too. Major Western countries that did not act responsibly, that did not heed the danger, were occupied with chatter and did not do what was required of them – those countries now find themselves on the verge of bankruptcy. Not only have their credit ratings gone down, but many, many people are unemployed.
>
> So far this economic storm has skipped over Israel. There is no doubt that the responsible way in which Israel has conducted itself over the last decade contributed to that fact.[3]

He then moved on to a defence of the free-market economy. This part of his speech might have been given by Ronald Reagan or Margaret Thatcher, rather than by the Prime Minister of Israel. Looking back through history, it would be hard to find any other Prime Minister who would have included these words in their address – with the possible exception of Shimon Peres during the mid-1980s.

> There is one golden rule that every citizen knows from his own home economy: over time, if you spend more money than you make, you will eventually go bankrupt. The overdraft grows and you collapse. This is true for a family and it is true for a country. There are countries around the world that forgot the rule, and are now paying dearly.
>
> Israel acted differently, responsibly. That is how I acted as Finance Minister, it is how the finance ministers after me acted, and it is how we act today. But you cannot generate the growth that is vital for creating jobs, growth that is vital for resources, for education, health, you cannot generate growth only by responsibly sticking to the budget. In order to make the market grow one must encourage competition. Not cartels, not monopolies, but fair, supervised competition that benefits the consumer.

Competition is not the enemy of the consumer. On the contrary – it is the consumer's greatest friend. It reduces prices, improves service, reduces gaps, and raises the standard of living. Lack of competition in Israel is one of the most severe causes for the increase in the cost of living, and that is why a year ago, Mr. Speaker, not now, not two or three months ago, I established the Committee on Increasing Competitiveness in the Economy. That is why we are advancing the section of the Trajtenberg Committee's recommendations on increasing competition in the market, and for good reason.

Netanyahu had smart political antennae and he understood that his government needed to be seen to do something to alleviate the burden on the lower-income workers and middle classes.

A TV poll taken by Channel 10 in Israel, at the height of the social protests over the summer of 2011, suggested that around 85 per cent of Likud voters supported the protests, as well as 98 per cent of Kadima supporters.[4] As a result, he tried to focus on the concrete measures he had taken and was willing to take. He said:

Yesterday, at the Cabinet Meeting held in Tzfat, we approved the recommendations of the committee dealing with taxation; we cancelled the planned increase on excise tax, a step that benefits every Israeli citizen; we reduced the purchase tax and duty on commodities; we gave extra tax credit points to fathers of children up to the age of three, which will be very helpful for young couples. But these are only the first steps.

I am pleased that all the Members of Knesset want to help, and you will all have the opportunity to do so, as I plan to introduce several bills to the Knesset during this session that will help the citizens – guaranteed. Education for preschoolers will cost less, the burden of taxes will not be so heavy and housing will be more available.

I am aware of the real difficulties which you speak about, Mr. Speaker, and I am committed to solving them, including resolutions that we will pass during this session, and I hope the opposition will help too.

Finally, he reminded Israelis that he would not be abandoning his free-market economic approach and returning to the old Israeli model of a bloated and inefficient public sector.

Members of the Knesset, I promised that I would give you an answer. We are committed to acting with the utmost social sensitivity to change priorities, but I do not accept the claim that the free-market system has collapsed, that we must return to a centralized economy run by clerks, an economy in which the government must be involved in everything and control everything, an economy in which the citizens will have to run around government buildings and beg before the bureaucratic powers. We have been there and we are not going back. That is how to kill an economy, how to destroy it.

Margaret Thatcher once famously stated that the lady was not for turning. In 2011, despite massive protests, Israel discovered that Benjamin Netanyahu was not for turning either. It was a major risk for him to take, given that the lower-income groups continued to be supporters of the Likud and would be required to turn out in force if Netanyahu was to have a chance of being re-elected in the Knesset elections scheduled for 2013.

With increased challenges on his socio-economic policies, continued deep divisions over secular/religious issues and little meaningful progress on the Palestinian front, Netanyahu moved into defensive mode. This was the area in which he felt most comfortable and his decision-making centred upon preparing for potential conflict with Iran and continued ones with Hamas in Gaza and Hezbollah in Lebanon.

It was within this context that, on 25 October 2012, Netanyahu surprised the Israeli political world with the joint announcement that the Likud and Avigdor Lieberman's Yisrael Beiteinu party would run together in the Knesset elections in January 2013. It was a curious move on several different levels, and many people found it hard to understand Netanyahu's motives for pursuing it.

In electoral terms, the alliance didn't make much sense. The announcement tried to justify the move. 'In Israel, the Prime Minister needs a big, cohesive force behind him . . . A clear mandate that will allow me to focus on the main issues, rather than trifles,' Netanyahu told the gathered press. The main issues were judged to be concerns such as Iran's nuclear programme and the socio-economic problems that Israel continued to face.[5] As he put it:

One ticket will strengthen the government, it will strengthen the Prime Minister, and it will strengthen the country. We are asking the public for a mandate to deal with the security threats, at the top of which is stopping Iran from obtaining nuclear weapons, and fighting terrorism. We are asking for a mandate from the public to continue the changes in the economy, in education and in the need to lower the cost of living.[6]

The only trouble with this thinking was that polls taken in the period immediately following the announcement indicated that the alliance would shrink the number of seats that Likud–Yisrael Beiteinu would win as a joint list in the election from what they would achieve if they ran separately. Netanyahu would also have to pay a political price for the alliance by having to surrender places in the Likud list for the election to Yisrael Beiteinu.[7]

For Lieberman, the alliance was all about succession to Netanyahu. He believed that in his secret discussions with Netanyahu (many of which took place without their respective aides present) he had been tapped to become the successor to Netanyahu when the Prime Minister eventually decided to step down. Corruption allegations, which took Lieberman away from politics at the end of 2012 for nearly a year until he was acquitted in November 2013, reduced the possibility of him taking over from Netanyahu.

Naturally, Netanyahu's critics both at home and abroad saw the alliance as proof that the Prime Minister was going 'dark side' by aligning himself with ultra-nationalist figures such as Lieberman. Zehava Gal-On from Meretz articulated a typical attack from the left and told Israeli Army Radio:

> The Prime Minister is essentially signalling that he has chosen
> the extremist, pro-settlement right, that he has chosen to walk in
> place, not to make progress in the diplomatic process [with the
> Palestinians].[8]

Outside Israel, the alliance was met with deep concern, centring upon the belief that the new alliance increased the chances of an Israeli military strike against Iran and reduced the possibility of an agreement with the Palestinians. There was also a feeling that, by standing side by side with Israel's leading xenophobe, Netanyahu had revealed his true right-wing ideologue identity.

In retrospect, the alliance was born out of political necessity. Netanyahu was never an admirer of Lieberman's cheap brand of ultra-nationalistic politics, despite the latter having headed up Netanyahu's office for part of his first period in government. Fundamentally, Netanyahu did not trust Lieberman and vice versa. He considered it better to have him and his supporters on board, where they could be formally roped into Netanyahu's political agenda.

Top of this agenda was the possibility of an attack on Iran, and the political fallout from such an eventuality. While Israeli mainstream politicians were united in their opposition to the nuclear programme in Iran, there were divisions over a unilateral Israeli military attack against Iran. Netanyahu, as a result, wanted to build as strong a basis of support as possible in the eventuality of an attack on Iran by formally strengthening the links between himself and his political allies.

Previously, he had helped his key partner on the Iran issue, Ehud Barak, maintain his position as Minister of Defence even after he had quit the Labour Party. With an attack on Iran on the horizon, there was a feeling that the resulting conflict would be a multi-dimensional one, involving attacks against Israel from Iran, Hezbollah and potentially also Hamas. Netanyahu was building his wartime inner cabinet and he wanted to make sure that he could exercise as much control over its senior members as possible.

The primary risk for Netanyahu getting into bed with Lieberman was that he might alienate his allies in the Republican Party in the United States. The Israeli journalist Ari Shavit argued that, prior to the alliance with Lieberman, Netanyahu could have claimed to be an Israeli Ronald Reagan or Rudy Giuliani, but not after it. Instead he had cosied up to a man who admired the Russian leader, Vladimir Putin.[9]

In Israel, the new alliance was soon put to the test with Operation Pillar of Defense, which began on 14 November 2012 and lasted until a ceasefire came into effect on 21 November. The conflict was both a continuation of the ongoing struggle with Hamas and the prelude to a much bigger war with Hamas in the summer of 2014.

This was Netanyahu's first large-scale clash with Hamas and, in military terms, thanks largely to Israel's defensive missile shield known as the Iron Dome, Israeli population centres were largely spared from being hit by rockets and missiles fired from Gaza. This was the first time, however, that missiles fired from Gaza reached central Israel and was seen as confirmation that Hamas was following a similar strategy to Hezbollah in attacking centres of Israeli population.

During the course of the conflict there was widespread support for the military operations against Hamas and the government's handling of the crisis. Divisions occurred over the ceasefire, which several leaders on the right argued had left Hamas free to carry on with its military rebuilding and had not removed it as a medium- to long-term threat to Israel. Netanyahu, who during the conflict had to navigate a careful path between dealing with international reaction to the operation and achieving Israel's military goals, claimed the operation was a success.

Once Operation Pillar of Defense was completed, Netanyahu turned his attention to the Knesset elections, scheduled for 22 January 2013. Unlike several of Netanyahu's previous campaigns, this time there appeared little doubt about the outcome. Opinion polls conducted in Israel throughout the campaign put the joint Likud and Yisrael Beiteinu list winning an average of 35 seats.

As a result of the perceived lead, Netanyahu fought a largely risk-free campaign that stressed issues related to national security. His main fear was, with the outcome of the election seemingly not in doubt, the Likud supporters would not come out to vote in large enough numbers. Much of the campaign was therefore concentrated on speaking to the Likud base and ensuring that it was organized and motivated to vote.

Critics of the government, and of Netanyahu in particular, focused their efforts on highlighting the Prime Minister's poor relationship with President Obama, who was sworn in to serve his second term in office in the same month as the Israeli election. A number of parties attacked him on socio-economic issues, arguing that his policies were the root cause of the problems, and that he was not capable of listening to the lower-income groups in the country.

On the day of the election, the Likud–Yisrael Beiteinu emerged as the largest list, but with only 31 seats, a loss of 11 seats from their combined totals from the previous Knesset. In second place was Yesh Atid (There Is a Future), led by a former journalist, Yair Lapid, which won 19 seats. This party focused on socio-economic issues and was seen as centrist in nature.

The other development was the arrival on the scene of Habayit Hayehudi (Jewish Home), led by Naftali Bennett, which won 12 seats. Habayit Hayehudi was positioned to the right of the Likud and was seen as a natural bedfellow in a Netanyahu-led coalition. After the usual fraught coalition negotiations, Netanyahu was able to form a government along with Yesh Atid, Habayit Hayehudi and Hatnuah, which gave him a stable-looking coalition with 68 seats.

By the springtime of 2013, with his new government up and running, Netanyahu appeared to have weathered the political storms and was looking to consolidate his grip on power. Stories in the media started to focus on when, and if, Netanyahu would decide to stand down, with the belief being that this would not happen until after the ongoing crisis over the Iranian nuclear programme had been resolved one way or the other. The presumption was that this would not happen in the immediate future, and therefore Netanyahu would try to serve out his full four-year term as Prime Minister.

What lay ahead for Netanyahu, however, were not relatively calm waters, but, rather, a series of challenges that came close to finishing his political career. What Israelis liked about Netanyahu would fade into the background, to be replaced by the reminders of what they didn't like about him. It was a reversal of fortunes, not major political mistakes, that made Netanyahu face the prospect of defeat in 2015. It would require all his political skills, and his famed flip-flopping on policy, to try to ward off defeat.

Needless to say, in Washington, President Obama would watch reports of Netanyahu's apparent demise with much glee. He hoped to finally get an Israeli leader with whom he could do business. Obama wasn't alone in this, as European leaders hoped that the era of Netanyahu rule in Israel was finally drawing to a dramatic close.

PART NINE

Comeback

28

Indeed

On Monday 16 March 2015, Benjamin Netanyahu instigated a decisive moment, which helped save his political career. On the eve of an election that he looked set to lose, he reached out to his political base and appealed to them to unite behind his leadership.

In a last-minute election campaign interview with the NRG website owned by the Casino mogul Sheldon Adelson, with ties to a Jewish settler newspaper, Netanyahu tried one last desperate throw of the dice to attract voters away from the far-right party, Habayit Hayehudi, and other right-wing parties back to the Likud. Polls indicated that Habayit Hayehudi looked like winning 12 seats, largely at the expense of the Likud, which was polling at between 20 and 22 seats.[1]

Netanyahu looked far from comfortable during the interview, as if he wished that it could be broadcast for domestic consumption only. The words he uttered, however, made headlines across the globe. When asked about the potential creation of a Palestinian state he said:

> I think that anyone who moves to establish a Palestinian state today, and evacuate areas, is giving radical Islam an area from which to attack the State of Israel. This is the true reality that has been created in past years. Those that ignore it are burying their heads in the sand. The left does this, buries its head in the sand, time and again.[2]

He was then asked directly by the interviewer whether no Palestinian state would be created under his leadership; the Prime Minister paused and replied: 'Indeed.'

Netanyahu had just appeared to retract his Bar-Ilan speech in which he claimed to have accepted the two-state solution. Neither of the two explanations given for his apparent change of heart cast him in a particularly flattering light. He was either saying anything to get elected, or had just outed himself as a hardline ideologue who would have made his father proud.

It wasn't long before the criticism began to roll in. The Palestinians claimed not to have been surprised by his comments and the Obama administration reiterated its commitment to the two-state solution. The comments were initially muted, as there was a fear that a strong condemnation of Netanyahu's statement might backfire with polling in Israel due to start the following morning.

As the newswires carried details of Netanyahu's comments, and the responses, footage from earlier in the day of the Prime Minister standing next to a construction site at the settlement of Har Homa in East Jerusalem was still being broadcast. Speaking to the press there, Netanyahu had tried to get the same message of fear over to the Israeli electorate.

Netanyahu warned, 'If Tzipi [Livni] and Bougie [Isaac Herzog] form a government, Hamastan B will be established here.' He also went on to launch an attack against the V15 Campaign that had been launched with the financial backing of liberal American Jews. The core objective of the campaign was to get Netanyahu replaced as Prime Minister.

Netanyahu told his audience in a thinly veiled attack on Danny Abraham, who was one of the main financers of the V15 Campaign:

> I said to him – have you ever been in Har Homa? He said no, and that it was a dangerous settlement. I suggested he go there and said he would make it in time, that he wouldn't be late to the meeting. They took him to the car, returned to the office, and rolled on the floor with laughter.
>
> The man was prepared to go to Sinai and couldn't believe that the car stopped after seven minutes and that he had reached his destination. These are the people telling us who needs to be in government, these are the people who think Har Homa is in Sinai.[3]

It was vintage Netanyahu accusing the United States of becoming involved in the campaign through the funding of this group. Netanyahu chose to forget that wealthy Americans had bankrolled several of his election campaigns. The message resonated well with Israelis who were going to vote for one of the right-wing parties. This group of voters feared liberal American conspiracies as having been directed against Netanyahu.

Monday 16 March 2015 had proved to be an extraordinary day for Netanyahu, who appeared finally to have woken up to the fact that he was about to lose an election, and to be removed from power. With much of the outside world waiting to celebrate his demise (along with plenty of Israelis), Netanyahu looked back and wondered where it had all gone wrong since his victory just over two years earlier in January 2013.

Netanyahu had not done much right since his re-election in 2013, but nor had he made any major mistakes. He had spent much of the time trying to convince the world to adopt a more proactive response to the threat of the Iranian nuclear programme. His speech to Congress earlier in the 2015 election campaign had been the culmination of several years of lobbying of foreign states to stand with him and Israel on the issue.

Netanyahu's hawkish position on Iran reflected the opinion of most Israelis, but it was not deemed as important an issue as pressing the domestic socio-economic ones. While Netanyahu talked of a military response to Iran, Israelis were still struggling to pay for their housing and the continued high cost of living. The social protests had died down, but several parties had taken up the protestors and their social agenda from the left and centre-left of the political spectrum.

There appeared to be a glaring ideological gap between Netanyahu and his love of free-market economics, and those Israelis who were more used to the Zionist economy, which included a large public sector, state subsidies and substantial welfare benefits for the workers. Netanyahu's reform or die message sounded good at academic economic conferences, but ordinary Israelis remained unconvinced by what they viewed as trickle-down economics.

While Netanyahu used the correct vocabulary, taking up the importance of social cohesion in the small state still at war with many of its neighbours, he remained unwilling to alter the course of economic direction. Furthermore, it was clear by the end of 2014, when the government failed to pass the state budget, that Netanyahu and the Likud lacked support to pass meaningful socio-economic legislation.

The centre-left led by Isaac Herzog and Tzipi Livni increasingly viewed the socio-economic arena as the soft underbelly of Netanyahu and the Likud. As a result, they tried to focus the political agenda in Israel away from issues such as Iran, towards a repealing of some of the economic reforms that were closely associated with Netanyahu. For his part, Netanyahu attempted to keep Israelis focused on what he saw as the related triple threats of Iran, Hezbollah and Hamas.

The political battle that Netanyahu found himself in was essentially one over the agenda. With little sign that the leadership of the Palestinian Authority would be willing to negotiate, and with Netanyahu seemingly content with the status quo of no peace and no war, there was little debate about the peace process. The talk was of fear, not only from Iran, but also of creeping sanctions against Israel and increased international isolation.

Naturally, Netanyahu was at the centre of all this talk, but none of the opposition politicians offered much in the way of viable alternatives in the Palestinian arena. They pledged to reignite the peace process without explaining exactly what they would do. Phrases like 'rescuing Israel from its international isolation' sounded good to the peace camp in Israel, but made little inroads into Netanyahu's support base.

The difficult relationship between Netanyahu and Obama and its impact on Israel's bi-lateral ties with the United States were also highlighted as reasons for replacing Netanyahu. The general consensus among the opposition in Israel was that Netanyahu and his policies were damaging Israel's place in the world, at a time when other governments were taking a more critical approach to Israel.

While the opposition in Israel talked of the need for change, Netanyahu continued to talk about unity and strength. In his keynote speech at the winter opening session of the Knesset on 27 October 2014, he reasserted his stark worldview and the continued threats to Israel's security. As he put it:

What we need today in the diplomatic campaign is that same decisiveness, that same strength and that same unity. Because here too there are those who wish to dictate terms to us that will endanger our security and our future and will push the peace that we so long for further away.

Because what the Palestinians demand from us is the establishment of a Palestinian state without peace and without security. They
demand a withdrawal to the '67 borders, the entry of refugees and
the division of Jerusalem. And after all these unrealistic demands,
they are not ready to agree to the fundamental condition for peace
between our two peoples – mutual recognition.

While they expect us to recognize their nation-state, they refuse to
recognize our nation-state. They also are not ready to agree to long-
term security arrangements that would allow us to protect our country.[4]

On the question of the Palestinian state, which he so directly rejected
on the eve of the 2015 Knesset election, Netanyahu still held out hope.
His comments indicated that he did not think that there was much
chance of agreeing to its creation in the near future:

I reiterate for my colleagues in the Knesset: I do not want a
bi-national state, but I equally do not want the establishment of
another Iranian proxy that would endanger our very existence. I
said previously and I repeat: A peace agreement is possible when
the following formula is present – a demilitarized Palestinian state
that recognizes the Jewish state. To that end, the Palestinians must
recognize our basic need for a nation-state of our own. They need to
accept mutual recognition and genuine security.

Experience has shown us that if we relinquish these demands and
follow the 'it'll be fine' method, then nothing will be fine. There
is no doubt that we will receive many compliments; we will be
praised, as will I, for two days, two months, perhaps even two years,
but within a short period of time we will pay an unbelievably heavy
price and we will continue to fight for our lives under much worse
circumstances. And therefore we have no choice but to stand firm
and strong against all pressure.[5]

Much of the speech was reserved for Netanyahu's analysis of Israel's war
with Hamas, which had taken place over the summer months. The war
was Netanyahu's first one that had led to a significant number of Israeli
casualties. Previously, Netanyahu had prided himself on the fact that
his strong stance on security and defence had reduced the potential for
major armed conflicts with the Arabs.

Operation Protective Edge, as the Israelis termed their military operation in Gaza, started on 8 July 2014, and proved to have profound implications for Netanyahu's credibility to lead. The origin of the attacks against him came from different parts of the political divide in Israel, and for different reasons.

The main consequence for Netanyahu from the right was the split with Lieberman, who had demanded that Israel reconquer and reoccupy Gaza in order to get rid of Hamas once and for all. Lieberman, and many others on the right in Israel, believed in the need for a military solution to Israel's problems with Hamas. Anything short of this, they argued, was merely postponing the inevitable next round of fighting with the militant Islamic group.

Central to the charge they made against Netanyahu was that his leadership was too conservative and too indecisive. They viewed him as a weak wartime leader, who was the prisoner of the IDF top brass. The leadership of the IDF were well known to be reluctant to commit Israeli ground troops into Gaza for a prolonged period for fear of the number of casualties they would incur during such an extended operation. They also felt that the political case for reoccupation was not strong enough, and that Israel did not have a solid 'day-after plan' that would allow for an exit from Gaza in the short term.

During the course of the military operation, Netanyahu's policy options were governed by the IDF along with the ministry of defence, and the reaction of the international community to Israel's actions. It was a difficult tightrope for him to walk, and he largely ignored the calls from the right to broaden the objectives of the campaign.

The end of the war statement published by Netanyahu on 27 August 2014, after the ceasefire had come into effect, concentrated on what he argued were the positive military and diplomatic achievements from the campaign. He also wanted to remind those on the right in Israel that the military and diplomatic aims were inter-related. If he had broadened out the military aims this would have led to the loss of many of the diplomatic achievements that he heralded in the statement.

The tone of the statement was defensive. Netanyahu, more than anybody, understood that there would be political repercussions for agreeing to what many Israelis thought was a premature ceasefire. In his statement, he listed what he saw as the key military and diplomatic gains for Israel, and losses for Hamas. Before taking questions from the press he carefully read out the statement.

Upon the establishment of the ceasefire, I can say that there is a major military achievement here, as well as a major diplomatic achievement for the State of Israel. Hamas was hit hard and it did not receive even a single one of the conditions that it set for a cease-fire, not even one.

. . . From the first moment we set a clear goal: The goal was to strike hard at Hamas and the terrorist organizations and in so doing bring prolonged quiet to all Israeli citizens. I can say that Hamas was indeed hit very hard. First of all, we destroyed the network of attack tunnels that it built over the years. I would like to make it clear that we introduced the ground force for this goal.

When the mission was completed, when the IDF reported to us that this mission had been completed, we pulled the force back in order to deny Hamas the possibility of killing our soldiers or abducting them, goals that it very much aspired to.

We continued to attack from the air. Approximately 1,000 terrorists were killed, including senior terrorists, very senior terrorists from among its top command. We destroyed thousands of rockets, rocket launchers, rocket production facilities and other weapons, arsenals, command and control positions, hundreds of command positions, hundreds. We also foiled, of course, attempts by Hamas to attack us by land, sea and air.

Above all, thanks to Iron Dome, we foiled hundreds of attempts by Hamas to kill very many Israeli civilians. This was achieved, inter alia, thanks to a decision I made as Prime Minister, in my previous term, to equip the State of Israel with thousands of interceptors which, of course, blocked the murderous aerial assault by Hamas and the other terrorist organizations.

The blow that Hamas has now taken is unprecedented since it was founded, a very hard blow. I must say that it also took a diplomatic hit. See, Hamas set conditions at the outset for a ceasefire. We accepted the Egyptian initiative for a ceasefire, already in the first days, unconditionally and without time constraints whereas Hamas set conditions.

It demanded a seaport – it did not get one. It demanded an airport; it did not get one. It demanded the release of the Shalit prisoners, those who were released in the Shalit deal whom we returned to prison following the murder of the three youths, it did not get this. It demanded Qatari mediation; it did not get it. It demanded Turkish mediation; it did not get it. It did not receive any condition. It demanded further conditions. It demanded the rehabilitation of the institutions that we dissolved in Judea and Samaria; it did not get this. It demanded salaries and money from us; it didn't get them. It did not receive any of the conditions that it set.

. . . Moreover, I think that Hamas is also isolated diplomatically. We received international legitimacy from the global community. First of all, we received 50 days for very strong action against the terrorist organizations.

This was substantial. I think that we also instilled in the international community the fact that Hamas, ISIS and Al Qaida and other extremist Islamic terrorist organizations are members of the same family. We also instilled the understanding that the long-term goal is the demilitarization of Hamas and the terrorist organizations, the demilitarization of the Gaza Strip.

All of these are important achievements alongside the realignment of regional forces in the Middle East. The regional change of moderate forces in the Middle East is creating a possible diplomatic horizon for the State of Israel. I think that it contains within it new possibilities for our country. We will certainly try to advance these possibilities in a responsible and prudent manner as we have done up until now.[6]

Netanyahu's fears of domestic political consequences resulting from the ceasefire proved to be well founded. A poll taken by the Israeli daily newspaper *Maariv*, published on 29 August 2014, found that 58 per cent of Israeli Jews felt that it was a mistake for the government to agree to what amounted to an open-ended ceasefire with Hamas. An equally worrying statistic from the same poll for Netanyahu was that 61 per cent didn't think that the Prime Minister had achieved his main goal of achieving a state of prolonged truce with Hamas.[7]

At times of insecurity, the Israeli electorate usually shifts to the right. What was different after the war in Gaza was that parts of the electorate were shifting away from a right-wing Prime Minister, to parties further to the right that called for stronger action to be taken against the Palestinians.

The opposition to Netanyahu's decision to call time on the war was also present in the Likud. Arguably, the most vocal opponent of Netanyahu was the Likud MK Danny Danon, who had been fired as deputy Minister of Defence at the start of the war by Netanyahu. Speaking to the international press after the war ended, an angry Danon articulated the feeling of many Israelis:

> I think that there is a general atmosphere of disappointment after fifty days of war, seventy-two [Israeli] victims, billions of shekels lost, we are back at square one. You cannot ignore the fact that it's problematic.[8]

The reaction of Avigdor Lieberman was politically more important to the Prime Minister. Serving as Minister of Foreign Affairs, Lieberman, whose English was not considered fluent enough, was largely benched during the war. Netanyahu preferred to handle the foreign media directly from the Prime Minister's office. Naturally, this didn't please Lieberman, who was keen to try to get across his hawkish agenda to the media.

Lieberman was not alone in thinking that Israel needed to reoccupy Gaza and rid it of the Hamas threat. He was, however, the highest ranking minister to dissent from Netanyahu over the management of the war. As the war ended, and Netanyahu read the official Israeli statement, Lieberman took to social media to protest that the ceasefire was a mistake and that Netanyahu had erred by not allowing the IDF ground offensive to take and hold all of Gaza.

On his Facebook page Lieberman urged Israel: 'To free the Middle East and the Palestinians from the threat of Hamas', emphasizing that Israel must fight the terror organization 'without compromises'. 'So long as Hamas controls Gaza, we cannot guarantee safety for the citizens of Israel and we cannot reach a political arrangement,' he said:

> Hamas is not a partner for any sort of deal, neither a diplomatic [agreement] nor a security [agreement]. We cannot trust contempt-ible murderers. Therefore, we oppose the ceasefire, under which

Hamas will be able to continue to become stronger and wage another campaign against Israel at its convenience.[9]

Prior to the ceasefire, Lieberman had made his feelings clear to Netanyahu that Hamas had to be defeated. As he put it in an interview with Israel's Channel 2:

> Our strategic goal as a state must be either to defeat or force the surrender of Hamas. Surrender means that Hamas raises the white flag and begs for a ceasefire without any preconditions and requirements. Defeat means that Hamas has no ability to fire missiles, produce rockets or restore tunnels.[10]

Towards the end of the war both Lieberman and the Habayit Hayehudi leader, Naftali Bennett, had publicly pressured Netanyahu to adopt a tough stance against Hamas. Partly as a result of this pressure, and also down to other ministers opposing a truce, Netanyahu did not bring the ceasefire proposal to a vote in the Security Cabinet. This decision added to the sense of unease and displeasure felt by political leaders to the right of the Prime Minister in Israel that the war had been ended prematurely.

At the end of the war, while Netanyahu was heavily criticized from abroad for being too hard on Gaza, at home many Israelis saw him as being too soft.[11] This was made all the worse by the triumphalism of the Hamas leadership that claimed victory in the war and celebrated accordingly with their supporters in Gaza. All of the celebrations were screened back in Israel to an increasingly concerned public, who wondered what the costly operation in lives had achieved for the country.

Not for the first time, Netanyahu faced a potential rebellion from the right in Israel. At the same time, several wealthy liberal American Jewish businessmen were starting up and financing a new group to attack Netanyahu from the left. Netanyahu's tenure as Prime Minister, as a result, looked at its least secure in the final quarter of 2014 than at any time since he returned to the premiership in 2009.

When the German newspaper *Die Welt* had asked Netanyahu after the previous Gaza operation: 'What do you do for your personal peace? What do you do before you go to bed, just to lower your blood pressure after all this?', Netanyahu had replied, 'I watch the History Channel. If

it's good, I don't fall asleep quickly – and if it's bad, I fall asleep immediately. And I read a great deal.'[12]

After the war in Gaza in 2015, for a while Netanyahu looked like
a tired old leader who would soon hand over to a new generation of
presumably right-wing leaders.

Whether this was the case or not, both Lieberman and Bennett
saw the opportunity, in the weeks and months that followed the end
of the war, to try to assert their credentials to be the true leader
of the right and the heir to Netanyahu. All this left Netanyahu in
something of a bind. The good news for him was that support for the
right-wing block in Israel had been solidified by the war, and even
increased by it. The bad news was that the support had ebbed away
from him personally and the Likud, towards the more extreme end
of the block.

During the 2015 election campaign, Netanyahu found himself being
squeezed by both sides: on the right by Lieberman and Bennett and on
the centre-left by Herzog and Livni. Despite his best efforts to run the
campaign on his own terms and agenda, he soon discovered that this
was not possible. The centre-left were causing him to bleed support
on socio-economic issues, and the extreme right were damaging his
credentials on security.

Right up until the eve of the election, Netanyahu tried to dodge
the bullet by being pushed to the right. At countless campaign events,
when he got the question about the two-state solution he did not reply
in the negative. On 16 March 2015, with his political world falling
apart and facing the imminent prospect of a humiliating defeat, he took
the pledge and said no to a Palestinian state.

It was a huge political gamble, but, at the same time, from his
perspective the right thing to do. His argument that those who voted
for Bennett and Habayit Hayehudi in the election would lead to Herzog
becoming Prime Minister was not without merit. If he won the election, he genuinely believed that he would be able to walk the rejection
of a Palestinian state back before too much damage was done. On this
part of the play, he was plainly wrong.

Netanyahu went to bed on the night of 16 March believing that he
had done everything he could to win the election. There was no time
for any polling sample to test his shift to the right on the number of
seats that the Likud would win in the next day's election. Under Israeli

electoral law, the last day of publishing the results of opinion polls was five days prior to the election.

When the last polls had been published on 13 March, both Channel 2 and Channel 10 in Israel (in separate polls) had the Likud winning only a total of 20 seats compared to a mean of 25 seats for the Zionist Union, headed by Herzog and Livni.[13]

As Netanyahu went to sleep, it looked likely that the Zionist Union would prevail in the election and that Herzog would succeed him as Prime Minister. In addition to the Israeli press, there was a large contingent of foreign press crews covering the election. This number grew as it looked as if they might be witnessing the last chapter of Benjamin Netanyahu's controversial premiership.

Israelis, Palestinians, President Obama and interested onlookers all waited to see if this really would be the end of Benjamin Netanyahu, and if he would exit the political stage as quickly as he had done the last time he lost in 1999. Internationally, there was an air of cautious optimism that, if Herzog won, and formed a government, Israel would be more accommodating to the Palestinians and that prospects for peace would be on the up.

'Anybody but Netanyahu' was a rallying call for many people during the campaign, and the expectation was that the Israeli electorate was about to send him home.

29

Hail

As Israelis went to the polls on 17 March 2015, the headlines across the world were dominated by Netanyahu's apparent rejection of a Palestinian state. There was almost universal condemnation of his position, accompanied by opinion pieces and editorials in newspapers that he had unmasked himself as a hardline ideologue. His comments at Har Homa also attracted much international criticism with the belief that he was strongly committed to the settlement programme, and allied with the Settlers movement.

As Netanyahu surveyed the press and television channels, he wondered if his little dance for the right in Israel on the previous day had been enough to move the necessary votes to the Likud. His main fear, however, was voter apathy among the Likud supporters which had been so damaging to the party's performance in the 2013 Knesset elections. In what was expected to be a close race in 2015, voter turnout was considered a key factor in determining the eventual outcome.

By lunchtime, Netanyahu was deeply concerned and starting to panic that reports of lower than average turnout in Likud strongholds would cost him the election. As direct campaigning on the day of the election was not allowed Netanyahu took to social media after lunch and posted a hugely controversial video, which many people argued crossed the line into being racist.

The video was shot in an office with a map of the Middle East behind him. A stern-looking Netanyahu said, 'Arabs are going to the ballot boxes in droves, they are being bussed in by left-wing NGO's.'[1] The comments caused an immediate political storm in Israel as Netanyahu allegedly exercised racism towards Israeli citizens who were going to the polling stations to exercise their democratic right to vote.

The Obama administration were horrified by Netanyahu's statement both in terms of its content and by the fact that it came so soon after his flip-flop on his policy towards a Palestinian state from the previous day. Speaking to the *Huffington Post* about Netanyahu's rhetoric on the day of the election, Obama said it was:

> . . . contrary to what is the best of Israel's traditions. That although Israel was founded based on the historic Jewish homeland, and the need to have a Jewish homeland, Israeli democracy has been premised on everybody in the country being treated equally and fairly. To lose those values would give ammunition to folks who don't believe in a Jewish state, but it also I think starts to erode the meaning of democracy in the country.[2]

The full transcript of the video posted indicated that Netanyahu wanted his supporters to understand the extent of the campaign by the V15. At one point in the video Netanyahu said, 'Friends, we don't have a V15.' Here Netanyahu was clearly alluding to the foreign funding that he argued financed the V15 so-called non-partisan project. The fact that it was non-partisan meant that it could accept such funding, and this was what he meant when he talked of the Arab voters being transported by left-wing NGOs.[3]

Netanyahu's comments were truly horrible, but from an electoral point of view they achieved their intended purpose. Following the posting of the video, polling stations reported a late surge in the number of voters casting their ballots in the final hours of polling. The surge was particularly strong in areas where the Likud and right-wing parties were considered to be strongest. The outcome of the election that always looked to be close became even harder for the pundits to call.

One of the knock-on effects of the late surge in voters was its potential to distort the exit polls conducted by Israeli television. These exit polls largely finished gathering their data approximately two hours before the polls officially closed. Any changes in voting patterns after this time would come too late to be picked up in the polls. On top of this, there remained the Israeli national pastime of lying to the pollsters, which had distorted several exit polls from previous elections.

When the polling stations closed and the three exit polls from three Israeli television channels were flashed up on screen, there were cheers from the Likud party election headquarters, and a more muted reaction from the Zionist Union faithful. Two of the exit polls (from Channel 1 and Channel 10) had the Likud and the Zionist Union tied on 27 seats, while the other poll (from Channel 2) had the Likud ahead by one seat at 28 to 27 for the Zionist Union. Taking into account the margins of error of the polls, all three channels called the election a virtual dead heat between the Likud and the Zionist Union.[4]

As the votes were counted, it soon became clear that the exit polls were indeed wrong, and that Netanyahu and the Likud had won a clear victory in the election by securing 30 seats to the Zionist Union's 24. Netanyahu, with Sara beside him, was soon able to address the Likud faithful at their election headquarters. As the crowd chanted, 'Hail, Hail, Bibi', he said:

> Against all odds, we have scored a major victory for the Likud. We have scored a major victory for the nationalist camp headed by Likud. I'm proud of the Israeli people because at the moment of truth they knew to differentiate between challenge and nonsense and they took up the challenge
>   . . . Now we must form a strong, stable government that will know how to uphold security and socioeconomic wellbeing. We are faced with major challenges on the security and socioeconomic front. We promised to take care of cost of living and rise of housing costs, and we will do it.
>   I spoke to all of the nationalist party leaders, and I called on them to join me in forming a government without delay, because reality doesn't take a timeout. Citizens expect us to form a responsible leadership that will work for it, and that's what we will do.[5]

He then leaned across and kissed Sara, who feigned surprise, and put her hand on her neck as if to say 'Amazing'. The kiss annoyed many Israelis, just as much as when he kissed his wife after he had won the contest to become leader of the Likud in 1993. Over 20 years later the contempt of the Israeli media for Sara Netanyahu had not changed one bit, nor for the Netanyahu double act in general.

For Netanyahu it was a stunning victory, arguably the greatest of his career. He won the election by not going to the political centre, as had been the case in previous elections, but, rather, going to the right. In the sober light of day, when all the votes had finally been counted, it was clear that the results did not reflect any major political realignment in Israeli politics. Indeed, the percentage of votes that the right-wing camp received did not greatly increase from its performance in 2013.

As suspected, voter turnout was higher than in 2013 with 72.36 per cent of the electorate casting their ballots in 2015. Netanyahu's fear-mongering that the Israeli Arabs were going to polling stations in masses appeared to have done the trick for him. It would be wrong simply to say that this was the sole reason for his victory. In reality, the opposition lost the election as much as Netanyahu won it.

At the start of the campaign, the Zionist Union appeared to have everything going for them. The country was suffering from Netanyahu fatigue. Even the man himself looked tired and made noises about his increasing disillusionment about public life and its toll on his family. The campaign to oust Netanyahu was highly flawed. It made the same mistakes that had characterized the failed centre-left campaigns of Shimon Peres: too much preaching to the converted and not enough hard graft on the ground.

The campaign also missed the point that just because opinion polls found that the majority of Israelis wanted to get rid of Netanyahu, it didn't mean that they would actually vote at the polls to kick him out. There was also an unexplainable under-estimation as to the extent that Netanyahu would play dirty and push the boundaries of acceptable behaviour to their limits.

As Jonathan Freedland of the *Guardian* wrote about the centre-left opposition during the campaign, 'Right now his opponents look like a team facing an open goal and poised to miss.'[6] And miss they did. For all Netanyahu's bluster in his victory speech, for much of the campaign he had looked like a man who understood that he wouldn't win big time. His performance prior to 16 March had been one of the worst of his campaign career.

In essence, both Herzog and Livni failed to convince the voters that they would be any better at running Israel than Netanyahu. While the outside world ran to their tune of hope versus the fear factor of

Netanyahu, the election result was a timely reminder that many Israelis don't think about their country in the same way as foreigners.

On a deeper level, the rise of Netanyahu to power, and his ability to maintain a stranglehold over power, can be partly attributed to the failure of the centre-left to find a successor to the late Yitzhak Rabin who could appeal to voters beyond the traditional centre-left ones. For a while, Ehud Barak promised much, but his star soon faded and since then nobody has emerged, least of all Herzog or Livni.

It was no coincidence that for much of his political career at the apex of Israeli politics the major forces of opposition to him came from within the centre-right and the right-wing. In 2015, the election result reminded people that the centre-left's search for the new Rabin-style figure was not over. In the meantime, Netanyahu and the politics of fear continued to rule Israel.

Thomas Friedman, the *New York Times* columnist, argued that the real winner in the 2015 Israeli election was Iran. As he wrote the day after the Israeli election in his column, bubbling over with frustration:

> Oh, my goodness. They must have been doing high-fives and 'Allahu akbars' all night in the ruling circles of Tehran when they saw how low Bibi sank to win. What better way to isolate Israel globally and deflect attention from Iran's behavior?
>
> ... From Iran's point of view, it makes fantastic TV on Al Jazeera, and all the European networks; it undermines Israel's legitimacy with the young generation on college campuses around the globe; and it keeps the whole world much more focused on Israeli civil rights abuses against Palestinians rather than the massive civil rights abuses perpetrated by the Iranian regime against its own people.
>
> It is stunning how much Bibi's actions serve Tehran's strategic interests.[7]

Friedman's masterly argument was spot on. The re-election of Netanyahu suited the Iranians' needs perfectly. The continuation of the Netanyahu–Obama stand-off, and the increased international scrutiny of Israel under Netanyahu, suited Iran's aims perfectly.

A centre-left victory in Israel would have posed more difficult challenges for it. With a rekindling of warmer ties between Jerusalem and

Washington there would have been a greater squeeze on Iran's positions. International scrutiny of Israel might well have been less as it offered far-reaching concessions to the Palestinians.

The feeling among the centre-left in Israel was that it had missed a golden opportunity to get rid of Netanyahu, perhaps the last chance before Netanyahu became a truly important figure in Israel's relatively short history. After March 2015, Netanyahu could point to an electoral record of three wins and one loss. Viewed as an outsider and a lightweight by many Israelis, it looked perfectly possible that he would end up becoming the country's longest serving Prime Minister, replacing David Ben-Gurion.

While Netanyahu was untroubled by the feelings of the centre-left and the Israeli media, he was left with a bigger problem close to his political home. There was a feeling among several right-wing politicians that Netanyahu's victory had been achieved largely at their expense. In some ways, the 2015 election had produced the opposite outcome to the 1996 elections, when Netanyahu won the direct election for Prime Minister, but the Likud lost ground to other smaller parties.

In 2015, Bennett and Lieberman believed that Netanyahu's victory was secured at the expense of their respective parties. Bennett, in particular, felt that Netanyahu had stabbed him in the back as he shifted to the right in the final hours of the campaign. The additional seats that the Likud secured were taken from the Jewish Home rather than the centre-left.

In truth, as both Bennett and Lieberman viewed themselves as heirs apparent to Netanyahu as the darling of the Israeli right, the post-election manoeuvrings and coalition building took on even greater importance than was useful. The importance of both men to Netanyahu was further heightened when Yair Lapid made it clear that he would be taking his party, Yesh Atid, into opposition.

The political centrist Lapid also regarded himself as the next Prime Minister of Israel. Having served as Minister of Finance in the previous Netanyahu government – not usually a good route to the premiership – Lapid and Yesh Atid preferred to sit on the opposition benches and shout from the outside. In firing Yair Lapid (as well as Livni) in December 2014, Netanyahu had among other things potentially reduced his post-election coalition options.

Bennett and Lieberman both saw different opportunities created by the election. In some ways, Lieberman's choice was easiest. Yisrael Beiteinu won only six seats in the election and the preference was to go into opposition to rebuild the party and try to reconnect it with the voters. Bennett, on the other hand, wanted to go into government to maximize the number and the importance of the cabinet portfolios that the Jewish Home would be offered.

Immediately following the election, the headlines were dominated by the prospect of a government of national unity being established between the Likud and the Zionist Union. Although President Reuven Rivlin made it clear that this was his preference for the government, it was never a realistic prospect. Herzog and Livni preferred to take the Zionist Union into opposition from where they believed they would be able to develop an alternative to a Netanyahu government.

Netanyahu, as a result, was left in a strange position, having won a clear victory at the polls, but faced with problems in putting together a winning coalition. What followed was a game of poker with an old *Likudnik*, Moshe Kahlon, whose Kalanu party (All of Us) had won ten seats at the polls, holding most of the cards.

Kahlon, who had campaigned on socio-economic issues, particularly affecting the middle class, was regarded by several important commentators in Israel, such as Ari Shavit, as a potential heir to the old Likud school of Menachem Begin. During the campaign, Kahlon had been careful not to endorse either Netanyahu or Herzog for Prime Minister, and it was possible that he could sit in government with either block in power. His main demand was to be given the ministry of finance.

Given the complexity of forming a coalition, and with several of the party leaders involved having an eye on positioning themselves for the post-Netanyahu era, it was not surprising that the first deadline for forming a coalition was missed. On 20 April, President Rivlin granted Netanyahu a two-week extension until 6 May to form a government.

Negotiations went right up to the wire before, with only hours to spare, Netanyahu informed the President that he had put together a government coalition comprising 61 seats. In addition to the Likud the coalition comprised the Jewish Home, United Torah Judaism, Kulanu and Shas. Eyebrows were raised at Lieberman deciding not to join, and by the fact that Netanyahu announced he would not appoint a Minister of Foreign Affairs. It was widely presumed in Israel that he was keeping the post open to help entice Isaac Herzog to join the coalition with his Zionist Union colleagues at a later date.

The government was sworn in by the narrowest of margins (61 to 59) in the Knesset on 14 May 2015. During the fiery exchanges, Herzog once again stated that the Zionist Union would not be joining the coalition. It was a curious occasion in what was meant to be the start of the next chapter of Netanyahu's rule; all the headlines were grabbed by the opposition forces. The Prime Minister looked like a leader who understood that the chances of his coalition surviving its full term were limited.

The election had returned Netanyahu and the Likud to power, but the opposition to his rule from across the political spectrum did not bode well for his chances of doing much with the legislative power the election had given him. Israelis essentially voted for the status quo, and the known over the unknown.

The status quo, however, was about to end when the American-led efforts to secure a comprehensive nuclear deal with Iran bore fruit and robbed Netanyahu of the single issue that his politics of fear had centred upon. Israelis, and the rest of the world, looked on to see how Netanyahu would react to losing the debate on Iran, and whether, in the post-deal era, he could still remain relevant to Israeli and international politics.

30

D-Day

The nuclear deal, known as the Joint Comprehensive Plan of Action (JCPOA), between Iran and the five permanent members of the United Nations Security Council plus the European Union, was agreed in Vienna on 14 July 2015. The deal represented the total rejection by the international community of the central pillar of Benjamin Netanyahu's foreign policy since his return to power in 2009.

American, European and Iranian leaders rushed to herald the deal as the product of painstaking diplomacy that had averted a potential military clash between Iran and the rest of the world. In Israel the agreement was viewed with suspicion and fear. There was also a sense across the political spectrum that Netanyahu's confrontational tactics towards the Americans and the rest of the world over the Iranian nuclear programme had backfired spectacularly.

For Netanyahu 14 July 2015 was his D-Day, during which much of the world and Israel turned its attention to criticising his approach to the nuclear issue. It removed the prospect of any Israeli unilateral military action against the Iranian programme. Netanyahu had long prepared for this D-Day, believing that the Obama administration would lead the world into seeking an agreement of sorts with Iran. He was ready, as a result, to vent his frustration and opposition to the deal for the world to hear.

The headlines across the globe on 14 July were not dominated by the agreement, the contents of which most laymen failed to understand, but, rather, by the fierce reaction of Netanyahu to it, and his fears for the future of Israel and the Middle East. The king of fear-mongering went to task on the JCPOA, trying to rally support to prevent it from becoming law.

With much of Israel and the outside world watching, Netanyahu's statement was dramatic and full of rhetoric that made for good headlines:

> The world is a much more dangerous place today than it was yesterday.
>
> The leading international powers have bet our collective future on a deal with the foremost sponsor of international terrorism. They've gambled that in ten years' time, Iran's terrorist regime will change while removing any incentive for it to do so. In fact, the deal gives Iran every incentive not to change.
>
> In the coming decade, the deal will reward Iran, the terrorist regime in Tehran, with hundreds of billions of dollars. This cash bonanza will fuel Iran's terrorism worldwide, its aggression in the region and its efforts to destroy Israel, which are on-going.
>
> Amazingly, this bad deal does not require Iran to cease its aggressive behaviour in any way. And just last Friday, that aggression was on display for all to see.
>
> While the negotiators were closing the deal in Vienna, Iran's supposedly moderate President chose to go to a rally in Tehran and at this rally, a frenzied mob burned American and Israeli flags and chanted 'Death to America, Death to Israel!' Now, this didn't happen four years ago. It happened four days ago.
>
> Iran's Supreme Leader, the Ayatollah Khamenei, said on March 21 that the deal does not limit Iran's aggression in any way. He said: 'Negotiations with the United States are on the nuclear issue and on nothing else.' And three days ago he made that clear again. 'The United States', he said, 'embodies global arrogance, and the battle against it will continue unabated even after the nuclear agreement is concluded.'
>
> Here's what Hassan Nasrallah, the head of Iran's terrorist proxy Hezbollah, said about sanctions relief, which is a key component of the deal. He said: 'A rich and strong Iran will be able to stand by its allies and friends in the region more than at any time in the past.'
>
> Translation: Iran's support for terrorism and subversion will actually increase after the deal. In addition to filling Iran's terror war chest, this deal repeats the mistakes made with North Korea.

There too we were assured that inspections and verifications would prevent a rogue regime from developing nuclear weapons. And we all know how that ended.

The bottom line of this very bad deal is exactly what Iran's President Rouhani said today: 'The international community is removing the sanctions and Iran is keeping its nuclear program.' By not dismantling Iran's nuclear program, in a decade this deal will give an unreformed, unrepentant and far richer terrorist regime the capacity to produce many nuclear bombs, in fact an entire nuclear arsenal with the means to deliver it.

What a stunning historic mistake!

Israel is not bound by this deal with Iran because Iran continues to seek our destruction. We will always defend ourselves.[1]

It was a defiant statement that attempted to transmit the message that, as far as he was concerned, the battle over the Iranian nuclear programme was far from over. Central to his argument was that Iran must be prevented from obtaining nuclear weapons as the result of its programme.

In Israel, centre-left opposition politicians agreed with Netanyahu that the deal was bad for Israel, but blamed him for creating the conditions that encouraged the United States to sign the deal with Iran. A less confrontational stance would have produced better results for Israel and not damaged relations with Washington as much as Netanyahu's approach had done.

On the right, Avigdor Lieberman was predictably vocal in his opposition to the agreement, comparing it to Chamberlain's Munich Agreement with the Nazis. He said, 'It is an agreement of total capitulation to unrestrained terrorism and violence in the international arena.'[2]

President Obama telephoned Netanyahu on 14 July to try to reassure the Prime Minister that the agreement served American and Israeli interests, and that it would prevent Iran from acquiring nuclear weapons. Obama reminded him of America's commitment to Israel's security. As the White House phone read-out recorded:

The President also underscored his Administration's stalwart commitment to Israel's security and noted that the JCPOA will remove the spectre of a nuclear-armed Iran, an outcome in the national security interest of the United States and Israel. The President told the Prime Minister that today's agreement on the nuclear issue will not diminish our concerns regarding Iran's support for terrorism and threats toward Israel.

The President noted that Secretary of Defense Ash Carter's visit next week to Israel is a reflection of the unprecedented level of security cooperation between the United States and Israel, and that the visit offers a further opportunity to continue our close consultation on security issues with Israeli counterparts as we remain vigilant in countering the Iranian regime's destabilizing activities in the region.[3]

Obama's conversation illustrated his well-placed caution in dealing with Netanyahu. He understood that the Prime Minister would attempt to rally support in Congress to try to prevent the agreement becoming law. Netanyahu did exactly that, but his strategy failed as Congress was not able to prevent the implementation of the agreement.

For those Israelis who bothered to read the details of the JCPOA, the major problem that arose from it was over the question of verification. Inspectors would have limited access and the site visits were to be at registered plants. Inspectors would not be able to show up and conduct searches at previously unknown facilities.[4]

All of this sounded rather familiar to many nuclear experts in Israel. Its own nuclear weapons programme, devised in the late 1950s, had followed a similar path. First, the establishment of a nuclear programme for alleged peaceful purposes, which was then transformed into one that produced nuclear weapons by the start of the 1960s. Verification of Israel's nuclear facilities by American and British inspectors had been very poor, which allowed the Israelis to proceed towards the development of nuclear weapons with relative ease.

The most annoying aspect of the JCPOA for Netanyahu personally was that he understood perfectly well that he had not lost the argument on the merits (or not) of the agreement with Iran. He was correct in assuming that the world was not embracing a newly reformed despot regime, but, rather, had cut a deal with a dangerous regionally expansionist regime that wished to wipe Israel off the map.

Being right was one thing, but getting the agreement changed – or better still dropped altogether – appeared impossible. The world was not looking for a fight with Iran, and moved on to new, more pressing issues such as the rise of the Islamic State.

Netanyahu understood that he was beaten, and his pragmatic nature led him towards a reconciliation of sorts with President Obama. Part of his thinking was governed by his hope of extracting additional help from the administration towards protecting Israel in its, post-JCPOA, more dangerous neighbourhood.

On 9 November 2015, the two leaders met at the White House for the first time since the deal on Iran. For Netanyahu the meeting was about being seen to be mending fences with the Obama administration and securing a commitment from the President to bolster Israel's security. On Iran, the agenda shifted towards the implementation of the deal, and specifically making sure that the Iranians complied with its terms and conditions.

After the two and a half hour meeting, both Netanyahu and Obama were keen to emphasize that it was a return to business as usual. Obama argued that the time had come to set aside their differences over Iran, and to look towards negotiating a new ten-year package of military aid to Israel and to find ways to try to manage and calm the ongoing wave of violence between Israelis and Palestinians.[5]

Netanyahu described it as one of his best meetings with Obama, and during the course of his statement to the press offered the Americans a reminder of his apparently rediscovered acceptance of the two-state solution. As he put it:

> Equally, I want to make it clear that we have not given up our hope for peace. We'll never give up the hope for peace. And I remain committed to a vision of peace of two states for two peoples, a demilitarized Palestinian state that recognizes the Jewish state.[6]

Obama officials were quick to point out that despite Netanyahu's comments, they did not think it possible that there would be any Israeli–Palestinian agreement during the remaining time of the Obama administration. They also considered it pointless to try to start what they considered would be meaningless negotiations between the two sides. This was music to Netanyahu's ears.[7]

The meeting was important for both men, who understood the need to calm US–Israeli relations before any lasting damage was done to the relationship. Agreeing to differ over Iran was the best means to putting the row behind them, but, as Netanyahu quipped to the press, he remained convinced that he would be proved right. He said:

> It'll be left to history to see if Iran will modernize and reform under this clique. I have my doubts. I hope I'm wrong; I suspect I'll be proved right.[8]

The basic difference between him and Obama was that Netanyahu argued the deal would empower Iran, while the President thought it the best way to contain it. Netanyahu had never been a big fan of containment as a means to controlling troublesome regimes.

Not wanting to labour the point (again) Netanyahu was keen to move on from the subject area of his biggest political defeat and to focus on other aspects of Israeli security.

Reports from Israel indicated that Israel had been serious about attacking the Iranian nuclear programme in the past. Ehud Barak was said to have favoured a military strike along with the Prime Minister. In the period between 2010 and 2012, Israel came close to launching such a strike on three occasions.[9]

Alleged opposition from some other cabinet members and key figures in the IDF acted as a restraint on the Netanyahu–Barak axis and prevented any strike taking place. Once negotiations started between the Obama administration and Iran the potential for such a strike receded.[10]

Many leaders would have been crushed if the cornerstone of their foreign policy had failed, but not Netanyahu. He simply tried to move the political agenda on to something that he also felt passionate about, Israel's large resources of natural gas, that in his eyes needed to be tapped. A controversial issue with lots of opposition, it was perfect for Netanyahu to get his claws into.

In December 2015, and only after months of wrangling, he signed the deal that would lead to the start of the extraction of the gas from off the Israeli coast. Netanyahu labelled the discovery of the huge gas field as 'a gift from God'. It was one that had the potential to transform the energy map of the Middle East and bring great benefits to Israel.

This plan is important to our economy because it gives us a much cheaper source of energy . . . It makes us, if not an energy super-power, then definitely an important international force.

. . . There is no way to open up these additional gas fields without this plan. This is the only option . . . Unfortunately, this issue has become a political and populist discussion. This plan is vital to our security, because we don't want to be left with one power plant that's under fire; we need multiple gas fields.

This is essential for our foreign relations. Many countries have expressed interest [in buying the natural gas]. Not just Greece and Cyprus, whose leaders I am meeting in a few weeks. Jordan, and of course the Palestinian Authority as well, have shown interest. Turkey and Egypt are also interested, and we are in discussion with them.[11]

The development of Israel as an energy superpower was hugely attractive to Netanyahu and his vision of the future success of the Israeli economy. He continued to view the economy as both Israel's greatest strength, but also its major weakness. The strength lay in its high-tech boom and in other parts of the private sector. The weakness was prevalent in the public sector and its ties to the Zionist Labour movement.

Iran, by the end of 2015, while not forgotten, was no longer the hot topic of debate in the Netanyahu-led government. This revealing point indicates the notion of self-reinvention that Netanyahu had pulled off time and again in Israeli politics. Just when he looked cornered, with no exit possible, he discovered a way out and was able to enjoy a new lease of life.

The outside world, and much of Israel, continued to wait for the moment when the rise of Benjamin Netanyahu would come to an end and the start of his decline begin. As the British politician Enoch Powell had once said, 'All political lives, unless they are cut off in midstream at a happy juncture, end in failure, because that is the nature of politics and of human affairs.'[12] To date, despite his many setbacks and defeats, Netanyahu's own career has not yet ended in failure.

At the start of 2016, despite a formal investigation of his wife by the Attorney General in Israel, and a growing belief that his coalition would not last beyond the halfway point of the current Knesset, Netanyahu remained at the helm. Talk was of his chances of surpassing David Ben-Gurion as Israel's longest serving leader.[13]

Arguably, the most intriguing part of Netanyahu's rise was his ability to bridge (and at times divide) Israel with the United States. He viewed the dispute over the Iranian nuclear programme with President Obama as a one-off, and not as part of a weakening of ties between Jerusalem and Washington. That said, he would very much like still to be in power when the United States inaugurates President Obama's successor in January 2017.

PART TEN

Postscript

A Stranger in a Strange Land

The French moralist and philosopher Joseph de Maistre wrote in 1811: 'Every nation gets the government it deserves.' Maistre's point is important to note, as many people do not comprehend how Benjamin Netanyahu was able to win four elections and lead Israel for an extended period of time. To a large extent Netanyahu's political successes have been achieved as a direct result of the shortcomings of Israeli society and its political leadership.

Israel remains deeply divided and unsure of its place in the world. The notion of Netanyahu as the goalkeeper of Israel, protecting the country from physical and political attack, resonated with many Israelis, who remain deeply suspicious of the Palestinians, the Arabs and the rest of the world. This allowed Netanyahu's politics of fear to gain traction as he mirrored these suspicions in his appearance on the diplomatic stage.

Another factor in Netanyahu's longevity has been the lack of viable alternative candidates from the centre-left following the assassination of Yitzhak Rabin in 1995. For a time, it looked as if Ehud Barak would emerge as such a leader, but he failed to connect with the Israeli electorate, took risks on the peace front that many Israelis felt uncomfortable with and led the country into a war with the Palestinians. In the end, Barak turned out to be an invaluable number two and an effective Minister of Defence, but not a good Prime Minister.

Most of Netanyahu's opposition came from within the right-wing in Israel and specifically the Likud. Ariel Sharon was a formidable opponent who shared Netanyahu's deep distrust of the Palestinian leadership. The conclusions he eventually drew from this distrust, however, were different than those of Netanyahu.

Sharon argued the need to take unilateral action to divorce Israel from the Palestinians in the Gaza Strip, and, if he hadn't suffered a stroke, in all probability from the West Bank as well. Netanyahu settled for the status quo of no war–no peace with the Palestinians. He argued that it was a less painful and safer option than Sharon's unilateral disengagement plans. To give the Palestinians something for nothing was in his eyes wrong. Any territorial withdrawal needed to be the result of negotiations.

The stroke suffered by Sharon brought a premature end to his public service, which meant that the outcome in the hearts and minds of Israelis between Sharon's disengagement and Netanyahu's status quo would never be determined. With Rabin and Sharon gone, Netanyahu was left to compete with Sharon's successor, Ehud Olmert.

Allegations of corruption handicapped much of the Olmert era, and his departure from office came at a time when it appeared that he might be able to reach a comprehensive peace deal with the Palestinian Authority in the West Bank. Netanyahu spent the Olmert era as leader of the opposition, rebuilding the Likud following the exodus of a large number of its members to the Kadima party.

While Netanyahu regarded Olmert as a worthy adversary, he also understood that once the corruption investigation led to criminal charges and convictions, Olmert was politically finished. With Olmert gone he was left to face Tzipi Livni – who blew her chance in 2009 – and then more extremist and divisive figures in Lieberman and Bennett. In truth, neither Lieberman nor Bennett resembled national leaders, instead pandering to specific constituencies in Israeli society.

The last-man-standing argument appears to superficially fit the bill in explaining Netanyahu's extended period in office. Certainly, if Rabin had not been murdered and had Sharon not suffered a massive stroke, the resistance to the rise of Benjamin Netanyahu would have been stronger.

This argument is by itself simplistic. It is worth remembering that even if Rabin had lived, opinion polls taken shortly before his death indicated that there was a good chance that Netanyahu would have defeated him in the direct election for Prime Minister in 1996.

Presuming that Sharon had been able to carry out his plan of unilateral withdrawals from the West Bank, he would have encountered heavy opposition from many Israelis. As leader of the opposition in the

Knesset, Netanyahu would have been able to use this dissent to mount a credible and potentially successful challenge to Sharon's premiership.

For a deeper understanding of Netanyahu's resilience, it is important to look at his pragmatic skills of reinvention. Much of the outside world mistakes his apparent hawkish perspective towards the Palestinians, the Arab world and Iran as evidence of his strong ideologically motivated brand of politics. Added to this was the presence of a tough controlling father, who was steeped in the ideological history of Revisionist Zionist politics.

The debate over the influence of his father on Benjamin Netanyahu during his first term as Prime Minister was used to try to evaluate the ideological motivations for his actions during his premiership. In truth, while Benjamin Netanyahu sympathized with his father's brand of politics, in the real world his actions as Prime Minister were more pragmatically motivated.

Time and time again, Netanyahu performed flip-flops of key policies. In March 2015, his rejection of a Palestinian state in one television interview was quickly replaced by a back-track and a reassertion to President Obama of his commitment to the two-state solution.

The trouble that the world had in dealing with Netanyahu was not that he was an ideologue, but, rather, that he was too pragmatic, and prone to change his mind in order to curry favour with key voting groups in Israel. It should be remembered that Netanyahu won elections in Israel on different occasions by going to the centre (in 1996) and then going from the right (in 2015).

In this respect, Netanyahu more than casually resembled an American presidential candidate, trying to balance several divergent coalitions of supporters that were pulling him in different directions. Throughout his career Netanyahu has looked somehow out of sync with other Israeli politicians. A stranger in a strange land best characterized his dilemma as he struggled with his emotional commitment to the United States and Israel. David Remnick's profile of Netanyahu, 'The Outsider', published in the *New Yorker* in 1998, revealed him as a man who was in effect ill at ease with much of the country he led, and in particular its political, economic and media elites.

In the subsequent 18 years since Remnick's article, little has changed. Even today, Israel's second longest serving Prime Minister remains an outsider in the country he leads. His attempt to revolutionize Israeli politics (and economics) into a more modern American style remained far from complete.

In terms of political culture, Netanyahu continued to draw more from America than from Israel. Many Israelis squirmed with unease when he publicly lectured President Obama in the Oval Office over the Iranian nuclear programme. Israeli leaders simply didn't do such things. Whatever Netanyahu's motivations for giving the lecture, it didn't play well back in Israel.

Nearly all previous Israeli Prime Ministers liked to include aspects of history in their speeches, with a well-placed drop-in reference to a moment, or an event, in Jewish history. Netanyahu was also expert in doing this, but there was a subtle difference. Not only did he use Jewish history to illustrate a point or argument, he drew from the wider world history.

Well-known for his use of Winston Churchill quotes, he liked to use references to appeasement when talking about Israel's negotiating with the PLO and use the same imagery again when talking about the Iranian nuclear programme. Essentially, Netanyahu sounded like a more worldly man than his predecessors as Prime Minister.

With the American influence came the personal materialism, which many of his critics highlighted against him. Netanyahu's two predecessors as leader of the Likud, Menachem Begin and Yitzhak Shamir, lived in a modest manner. Netanyahu aspired to a rich lifestyle more in keeping with the chief executive of a major corporation, or a leading American Republican politician.

From time to time, this luxury lifestyle had got him into trouble, particularly when the Israeli taxpayer was picking up the bill. Investigations over the remodelling of his house, to his cigar tab, made the headlines with worrying frequency. Central to many of the investigations has been Sara Netanyahu, whose conduct has come under critical scrutiny in recent years.

To date, Netanyahu has stuck to his story that attacks against his family, and his way of life, are politically motivated with the intention of removing him from office. He sees little problem in his enjoying the good life, which he argues he largely paid for from his work in the private sector after he lost the 1999 election. His lifestyle, while nothing out of the ordinary in the United States, does not sit well so easily in Israel.

Netanyahu's more pragmatic American-orientated brand of politics helps explain why he was never taken down politically by a loss on a single issue. His political opponents who had hoped that the deal over the Iranian nuclear programme would mean the end of Netanyahu were sorely disappointed. He pragmatically admitted defeat on the deal, vowed to keep a careful eye on Iranian violation of it and moved on to the next issue.

In looking back over Netanyahu's political career, it can be seen that one reason for his prolonged success has been his ability to deal successfully with the decisive moments that have come his way. A tennis coach was once fond of saying that the difference between champion players and journeymen is that the former play the crucial points better than the others. This has been the case with Netanyahu.

Nine decisive moments have been highlighted in the course of this book, along with the reaction of Netanyahu. In each case, he understood the moment and used it to his advantage. Even his humiliating electoral defeat in 1999 created positives for him: an ability to earn a lot of money in the private sector, and, by leaving the stage straight away, holding the potential for a political comeback.

It is still not clear just how good a politician Netanyahu is, or how much of his success is down to the mediocrity of the rest of the political leadership in Israel. The present-day Israeli political elite contains few potential alternative leaders to Netanyahu.

Public service is no longer an attractive career option for Israel's best and brightest, who choose instead to go into Israel's vastly successful business sector or emigrate to the United States or Europe. The standard of the Knesset members has declined in recent years (from an already low position). The long-term impact of this on the state remains to be seen. In the short-term, Netanyahu, now considered one of the elders of the tribe, must look around him and wonder where the next leader will come from.

For all his many failings Netanyahu remains the man who a large part of the Israeli electorate feels most comfortable leading the country. His successes have been mainly at the polls and his failures mainly in governing the country. Two related key questions have still to be answered: will he eventually agree a deal with the Palestinians that involves major withdrawals from the West Bank, and will he beat Ben-Gurion's record to become Israel's longest serving Prime Minister? The answers to both questions will be of historic importance.

The final, cautionary words are left to Netanyahu's late brother, Yonatan, who, writing from Israel to Benjamin in the United States on 11 May 1975, summed up the political problems at the time in Israel. They remain just as relevant to the difficulties the country faces today.

No big news on the political scene. Everything as usual – i.e., pretty miserable and crying out for improvement. You hear the news as I do, or maybe more – and it'd therefore be a waste of time to write two lines about it. Sad! I'm beginning to feel like a little Vietnamese. What's needed is wisdom to fight the process of isolation that's closing in on us; but there are no wise men in Israel.[1]

Acknowledgements

This book has taken a long time to research and write and I owe an enormous debt of gratitude to a number of people who have helped over the years.

In Israel, I would like to thank everyone who gave up the time to be interviewed over the past 20 years. Many of these interviews were conducted off the record and helped me enormously with background information on Israeli politics and the Arab–Israeli conflict.

I am very grateful to the Palestinian leaders in the West Bank and the Gaza Strip who took the time to meet with me and to be interviewed over the last two decades. Their openness and candid discussions were extremely helpful for me to get the Palestinian perspectives on Netanyahu.

As always, the members of staff at the National Archives and Records Administration in the United States were hugely beneficial in helping me navigate around background documents that covered the early period of Netanyahu's career. Likewise, the British National Archives staff helped me do the same for a British perspective on the same period.

In Israel, I would also like to extend my grateful thanks to the staff at the Government Press Office for their prompt assistance with requests and queries, and for helping me source some superb images of Netanyahu from their extensive National Photo Collection.

At Bloomsbury, it continues to be an enormous pleasure working with my editor, Robin Baird-Smith. This is my third book with Robin, and it is a most enjoyable and rewarding experience to work with him again. Thanks also to assistant editor Jamie Birkett, and all the team at

Bloomsbury in London. At Bloomsbury in the US, I would like to give a particular note of thanks to George Gibson and his team in New York. It has been a pleasure to work with such a professional publishing house.

Thanks also to Matt Freeman who continues to do a fantastic job of helping to develop and evolve my website and social media.

At University College London, I would like to thank my colleagues. I am fortunate to work in a department that covers a variety of different disciplines, and one that has ancient and modern historians. There is a great deal that we learn from one another, and University College London continues to allow us to follow our research interests.

I remain most grateful to David Lewis for continuing to support my position at the College.

I would also like to thank the students of my Arab–Israeli Conflict class. I have found their questions and comments extremely stimulating and useful. Over the 15 years that the class has run there have been many changes to the course, but the study of Benjamin Netanyahu has remained a central feature of it.

On a personal note, I would like to thank my friends and family for their kindness and support, and most especially for their understanding for my long absences from home when I travel overseas for my research and during the various writing stages of the book – when I lock myself away in my study. Most of all, I am grateful for the love and support of my family: my mother, and my parents-in-law Patrick and Gillian Castle-Stewart.

A big debt of gratitude must go to my wife, Emma, and our two children, Benjamin and Hélèna. Emma, as well as keeping our home in one piece while I work, research and write, is also my agent – she helps me with the photographic research for my books, curates my exhibitions, reads my manuscripts, manages my website, organizes my talks, and much more. This book would not have been possible without her. My children are growing up fast and I am incredibly proud of them – they are both fantastic in knowing when to let their daddy get on with his writing tasks.

Neill Lochery

London
June 2016

Note on Sources

Writing about the life of Benjamin Netanyahu means producing a recent history of Israel, the Arab–Israeli conflict and US–Israeli relations. I have been following the development of his career for over 20 years, and in that time have collected a huge range of academic, and not-so-academic, sources about the subject matter.

The Arab–Israeli conflict continues to produce a huge number of books each year that are dedicated to various aspects of the conflict. For a country of only eight and a half million, Israel attracts an enormous amount of interest with studies from across the academic sphere ranging from political to economic and from legal to geographic.

In writing the book, I have made use of what is a large library of sources from the past quarter of a century. We now live in a much more instant world when even the 30-year rule for documents to be released is not as steadfast as it used to be. In light of this, I have been able to secure the release of some documents related to the period of Netanyahu's rule under the British Freedom of Information Act.

The documents proved useful in providing background detail and the occasional revelation that surprised even such a veteran Netanyahu watcher as myself. Like all selective releases of documents, it is important to issue a cautionary note in that their value and relevance will not be fully validated until we start to get a more comprehensive release of documents starting in 2023. This release will cover the year of 1993 when Netanyahu first became the leader of the Likud.

Over the past 22 years, I have conducted many interviews with Israeli leaders and other senior politicians, ex-military and intelligence leaders, business leaders, academics, journalists and writers. Almost all had an opinion on Netanyahu and many had worked with him or against him (and in some cases admitted to doing both at different times).

I have also been fortunate in interviewing Palestinian leaders (both the old guard and the younger generation) about Netanyahu and the peace process in general. I have been particularly intrigued by the attitude of the Palestinian economic elite on the subject matter of this book. Likewise, it has been a great pleasure discussing Netanyahu with Arab leaders, senior politicians and journalists over the past quarter of a century.

Foreign diplomats who have been based in Israel and the Arab world during the Netanyahu era have also been a rich source of information. In personal interviews, and in closed seminars and conferences, they have been very forthcoming about the career of Netanyahu, and specifically his impact on the peace process.

Many officials in both London and Washington who staff the Near East desk have been extremely helpful in helping me fill in some of the missing areas. Their expertise and information gathering provide many officials with almost encyclopaedic knowledge of Israel and its foreign relations.

Most of my personal interviews were conducted on the basis of being off the record. I chose to conduct the interviews in this way, as my main purpose was to gather background information and to cross-check information. That said, a number of the interviewees were more than happy to be recorded and some of these are sourced in the notes that appear at the end of this book.

The use of interviews as the main primary source material can be problematic. Bias, political colouring, memory loss and personal narrative-building are all common problems associated with this type of research. No amount of cross-checking of interviews can remove entirely these potential shortcomings.

Recently produced television and film documentaries on Netanyahu that used 'talking heads' to build their narrative and arguments provided a clear reminder of the problems of using the personal witness and active participant approach to present evidence. At the time of researching and writing this book, Netanyahu remains an active politician who is relevant not only in the past tense, but also to the present day and conceivably to the future as well.

A number of important participants in the narrative of Netanyahu's political career clearly still have an agenda to cause him as much damage as possible. Simple personal revenge against him, or a belief that he has damaged the peace process, are only some of the apparent motives for attacking him. Likewise, there remain a number of people who try to cover his many political and personal failings in order to try to protect him and his ongoing career.

So interviews can be useful, but also misleading (either deliberately or through mistakes). On their own they do not present a complete portrait of him.

Academic books and journal articles have been an invaluable help over the years. For such a small country, Israel has a large number of outstanding scholars in the fields of political science and history. The sources on Israel's elections were particularly helpful for the book, as were the more general accounts of Israeli politics and the peace process.

For parts of the book, I have drawn from personal memoirs to add colour to particular summits or decision-making processes. I am aware that memoirs contain many of the same pitfalls as using personal interviews. In some ways they can be even more distorted as the authors have had time to carefully plan their perspective on events and personalities. Wherever possible I have tried to double sources when using this genre of writing as supporting evidence, although in some cases this was not always possible.

Articles from the print media have been enormously useful in jogging my memory about certain events, and adding new perspectives to old stories. There remains a sizeable group of veteran journalists who have spent much of their careers as Israel watchers. Their insights into Netanyahu provided a lot of important clues to his thinking, regardless of their own, and their newspapers', politics.

The book is laced with direct quotes from Netanyahu and those figures central to the narrative. Some of these quotes are extended ones, particularly from key speeches and press statements that are of an extended nature. They are included to illustrate and underpin key moments and points in the narrative. Netanyahu's dialogue with President Obama represents one such moment where they were vital to the narrative of the book.

Finally, listed below are sources in a select bibliography. I chose not to present an exhaustive full bibliography of secondary sources on

Benjamin Netanyahu, and subjects relating to his career, in order to save space and paper. With the advent of electronic academic journal and search engines additional sources on the subject are easier to locate in 2016 than they were in 1993, when I first started working on this project.

Select Bibliography

PRIMARY SOURCES

Archival Material
British Public Records Office (National Archives), Kew
Central Bureau of Statistics, Jerusalem
Central Zionist Archives, Jerusalem
European Union Archives, Brussels
Knesset Archives, Jerusalem
Library of Congress, Washington, DC
Margaret Thatcher Foundation Archive
Ministry of Foreign Affairs, Jerusalem
Ministry of Defence, Tel Aviv
President Bush Presidential Library Archive
President Carter Presidential Library Archive
President Clinton Presidential Library Archive
President Reagan Presidential Library Archive
State Department Library, Washington, DC
UN General Assembly – Official Records, New York
UN Secretary General – Official Records, New York
UN Security Council – Official Records, New York
UN Security Council, Supplementary Records, New York

Freedom of Information Act Releases, Foreign Office, London
Annual Review for Israel for 1988
Annual Review for Israel for 1989
Annual Review for Israel for 1990
Annual Review for Israel for 1991
Annual Review for Israel for 1992

Annual Review for Israel for 1993
Annual Review for Israel for 1994
Annual Review for Israel for 1996

SECONDARY SOURCES

NEWSPAPERS, NEWS AGENCIES AND MAGAZINES

American Spectator
The Atlantic
Baltimore Sun
Daily Telegraph
The Economist
Financial Times
Forbes
Globe and Mail (Canada)
Globes
Guardian
Haaretz
Huffington Post
Independent
Jerusalem Post
Maariv
Moscow Times
National Post (Canada)
National Review
New Republic
New Statesman
New York Times
New Yorker
Newsweek
Prospect
Reuters
Spectator
Time magazine
The Times
Times of Israel
Vanity Fair
Wall Street Journal
Washington Post
The World Today
Yedioth Ahronoth

JOURNAL ARTICLES AND BOOKS

Abbas, Mahmoud, *Through Secret Channels: The Road to Oslo*, Garnet Publishing, Reading, 1995.

Albright, Madeleine, *Madame Secretary: A Memoir*, Macmillan, London, 2003.

Allen, Roger and Chibli Mallat (eds), *Water in the Middle East*, British Academy Press, London, 1995.

Arens, Moshe, *Broken Covenant: American Foreign Policy and the Crisis between the U.S. and Israel*, Simon & Schuster, New York, 1995.

Arian, Asher, *The Second Republic: Politics in Israel*, Chatham House, Chatham, 1998.

Arian, Asher and Michal Shamir (eds), *The Elections in Israel 1992*, SUNY, Albany, 1995.

— (eds), *The Elections in Israel 1996*, SUNY, Albany, 1999.

— (eds), *The Elections in Israel 1999*, SUNY, 2002.

Ayubi, Nazih, *Over-stating the Arab State: Politics and Society in the Middle East*, I. B. Tauris, London, 1995.

Bar-Joseph, Uri (ed.), *Israel's National Security Towards the 21st Century*, Frank Cass, London and Portland, 2000.

Bavly, Dan and Eliahu Salpeter, *Fire in Beirut: Israel's War in Lebanon with the PLO*, Stein and Day, New York, 1984.

Begin, Menachem, *The Revolt: The Story of the Irgun*, Steimatzky, Tel Aviv, 1952.

Beilin, Yossi, *Israel: A Concise Political History*, Weidenfeld & Nicolson, London, 1992.

—, *Touching Peace: From the Oslo Accord to a Final Agreement*, Weidenfeld & Nicolson, London, 1999.

Ben-Ami, Shlomo, *Scars of War, Wounds of Peace: The Israeli-Arab Tragedy*, Oxford University Press, New York, 2006.

Bentsur, Eytan, *Making Peace: A First Hand Account of the Arab-Israeli Peace Process*, Praeger, London, 2001.

Blair, Tony, *A Journey*, Hutchinson, London, 2010.

Bulloch, John and Adel Darwish, *Water Wars: Coming Conflicts in the Middle East*, Gollancz, London, 1993.

Caspit, Ben and Ilan Kfir, *Netanyahu: The Road to Power*, Vision Paperbacks, London, 1998.

Clinton, Bill, *My Life*, Hutchinson, London, 2004.

Cohen, Amnon, *Political Parties in the West Bank under the Jordanian Regime 1949–1967*, Cornell University Press, Ithaca, 1982.

Cohen, Mitchell, *Zion and State: Nation, Class and the Shaping of Modern Israel*, Basil Blackwell, Oxford and New York, 1987.

Corbin, Jane, *Gaza First: The Secret Norway Channel to Peace between Israel and the PLO*, Bloomsbury, London, 1994.

Cordesman, Anthony, *Perilous Prospects: The Peace Process and the Arab-Israeli Military Balance*, Westview Press, Boulder, 1996.

Darboub, Leila, 'Palestinian Public Opinion and the Peace Process', *Palestine-Israel Journal*, Vol. 3, No. 3–4, 1996, pp. 109–17.

Drezon-Tepler, Marcia, 'Contested Water and the Prospects for Arab-Israeli Peace', *Middle Eastern Studies*, Vol. 30, No. 2, 1994.

Elazar David J. and M. Ben Mollov (eds), *Israel at the Polls 1999*, Frank Cass, London and Portland, 2001.

Elazar, David J. and Shmuel Sandler (eds), *Israel at the Polls 1996*, Frank Cass, London and Portland, 1998.

Elmusa, Sarif, 'The Jordan-Israel Water Agreement: A Model or an Exception', *Journal of Palestine Studies*, Vol. 24, No. 3, Spring 1994, pp. 63–73.

Feldman, Shai and Abdullah Toukan, *Bridging the Gap: A Future Security Architecture for the Middle East*, Rowman and Littlefield, Oxford, 1997.

Feldman, Shai and Ariel Levite (eds), *Arms Control and the New Middle East Security Environment*, JCSS Study No. 23, Westview Press, Boulder, 1994.

Filc, Dani, *The Political Right in Israel: Different Faces of Jewish Populism*, Routledge, London and New York, 2009.

Flamhaft, Ziva, *Israel on the Road to Peace: Accepting the Unacceptable*, Westview Press, Boulder, 1996.

Freedman, Lawrence and Efraim Karsh, *The Gulf Conflict 1990–1991*, Faber & Faber, London and Boston, 1993.

Freedman, Robert, *The Middle East and the Peace Process: The Impact of the Oslo Accords*, University Press of Florida, Gainesville, 1998.

Freedman, Robert O. (ed.), *The Middle East after Iraq's Invasion of Kuwait*, University of Florida Press, Gainesville, 1993.

Gilbert, Martin, *Israel: A History*, Doubleday, London, 1998.

Gilmour, David, *Lebanon: The Fractured Country*, Sphere Books, London, 1987.

Golan, Galia, 'A Palestinian State from an Israeli Point of View', *Middle East Policy*, Vol. 3, No.1, 1994, pp. 56–69.

Goldberg, David, *To the Promised Land: A History of Zionist Thought*, Penguin Books, London, 1996.

Greene, Toby, *Blair, Israel and Palestine: Conflicting Views on Middle East Peace After 9/11*, Bloomsbury, London and New York, 2013.

Gresh, Alain, 'Turkish-Israeli-Syrian Relations and their Impact on the Middle East', *Middle East Journal*, Vol. 52, No. 2, Spring 1998, pp. 188–203.

Gruen, George, 'Dynamic Progress in Turkish-Israeli Relations', *Israel Affairs*, Vol. 1, No. 4, Summer 1995, pp. 40–70.

Hale, William, *Turkish Foreign Policy, 1774–2000*, Frank Cass, London and Portland, 2000.

Halevy, Efraim, *Man in the Shadows: Inside the Middle East Crisis with a Man who Led Mossad*, Weidenfeld & Nicolson, London, 2006.

Hallaj, Muhammad, 'Taking Sides: Palestinians and the Gulf Crisis', *Journal of Palestinian Studies*, Vol. 20, No. 3, Spring 1991, pp. 41–7.

Hart, Alan, *Arafat*, Sidgwick and Jackson, London, 1994.

Herzog, Chaim, *The Arab-Israeli Wars*, Vintage Books, New York, 1984.

Hinnebusch, Raymond, 'Syria and the Transition to Peace', in Robert Freedman (ed.), *The Middle East and the Peace Process: The Impact of the Oslo Accords*, pp. 134–53.

Hroub, Khaled, *Hamas: Political Thought and Practice*, Institute for Palestine Studies, Washington, DC, 2000.

Inbar, Efraim and Shmuel Sandler (eds), *Middle East Security: Prospects for an Arms Control Regime*, Frank Cass, London and Portland, 1995.

Karsh, Efraim (ed.), *From Rabin to Netanyahu: Israel's Troubled Agenda*, Frank Cass, London and Portland, 1997.

— (ed.), *Israel the First Hundred Years*: Volume One, *Israel's Transition from Community to State*, Frank Cass, London and Portland, 2000.

Katz, Shmuel, *Lone Wolf: A Biography of Vladimir (Ze'ev) Jabotinsky*, Barricade Books, New York, 1996.

Kedourie, Elie, *Politics in the Middle East*, Oxford University Press, Oxford, 1992.

Kellerman, Aharon, *Society and Settlement: Jewish Land in the Twentieth Century*, State University of New York Press, Albany, 1993.

Khadduri, Majid and Edmund Ghareeb, *War in the Gulf 1990–1991: The Iraq-Kuwait Conflict and its Implications*, Oxford University Press, Oxford, 1997.

Kimmerling, Baruch and Joel Migdal, *The Palestinians: The Making of a People*, Harvard University Press, Cambridge, Massachusetts, 1994.

Laqueur, Walter, *A History of Zionism*, Schocken Books, New York, 1989.

Levran, Aharon, *Israeli Strategy after Desert Storm: Lessons of the Second Gulf War*, Frank Cass, London and Portland, 1997.

Lewis, Bernard, *The Middle East: 2000 Years of History from the Rise of Christianity to the Present Day*, Phoenix, London, 1995.

Lochery, Neill, *The Israeli Labour Party in the Shadow of the Likud*, Ithaca Press, Reading, 1997.

—, 'Israel and Turkey: Deepening Ties and Strategic Implications 1995–98', *Israel Affairs*, Vol. 5, No. 1, Autumn 1998, pp. 45–62.

—, *The Difficult Road to Peace: Netanyahu, Israel and the Peace Process*, Ithaca Press, Reading, 1999.

—, *The View from the Fence: The Arab-Israeli Conflict from the Present to Its Roots*, Continuum, London and New York, 2005.

—, *Why Blame Israel?* Icon Books, Oxford, 2005.

—, *Loaded Dice: The Foreign Office and Israel*, Continuum, London, 2007.

Mahler, Gregory, *Israel: Government and Politics in a Maturing State*, Harcourt Brace Jovanovich, San Diego and New York, 1999.

Makovsky, David, *Making Peace with the PLO*, Westview Press, Boulder, 1996.

Malki, Riad, 'The Palestinian Opposition and Final-Status Negotiations', *Palestine-Israel Journal*, Vol. 3, No. 3–4, 1996, pp. 95–9.

Mansfield, Peter, *A History of the Middle East*, Viking, London and New York, 1991.

Massalha, Omar, *Towards the Long Promised Peace*, Saqi Books, London, 1992.

Mazzawi, Musa, *Palestine and the Law: Guidelines for the Resolution of the Arab-Israeli Conflict*, Ithaca Press, Reading, 1997.

Mitchell, Thomas G., *Likud Leaders: The Lives and Careers of Menachem Begin, Yitzhak Shamir, Benjamin Netanyahu and Ariel Sharon*, McFarland, Jefferson, 2015.

Milton-Edwards, Beverley, *Islamic Politics in Palestine*, Tauris Academic Press, London, 1996.

—, *Contemporary Politics in the Middle East*, Polity Press, Cambridge, 2000.

Morris, Benny, *Righteous Victims, A History of the Zionist-Arab Conflict, 1981–1999*, John Murray, London, 2000.

Netanyahu, Benjamin, *A Place Among Nations: Israel and the World*, Bantam Press, London and New York, 1993.

—, *Fighting Terrorism: How Democracies Can Defeat Domestic and International Terrorism*, Farrar, Straus and Giroux, New York, 1995.

Netanyahu, Jonathan, *Self-Portrait of a Hero: From the Letters of Jonathan Netanyahu, 1963–1976*, Warner Books, New York, 1980.

Nusseibeh, Sari, *Once Upon a Country: A Palestinian Life*, Farrar Straus and Giroux, New York, 2007.

O'Brien, Conor Cruise, *The Siege: The Story of Israel and Zionism*, Paladin, London, 1986.

Owen, Roger, *State Power and Politics in the Making of the Modern Middle East*, Routledge, London, 1992.

Peretz, Don and Gideon Doron, *The Government and Politics of Israel*, Westview Press, Boulder, 1997.

Peri, Yoram (ed.), *The Assassination of Yitzhak Rabin*, Stanford University Press, Stanford, 2000.

—, *Telepopulism: Media and Politics in Israel*, Stanford University Press, Redwood City, 2004.

Quandt, William, *Peace Process: American Diplomacy and the Arab-Israeli Conflict since 1967*, University of California Press, Berkeley, 2001.

Rabinovich, Itamar, *Waging Peace: Israel and the Arabs, 1948–2003*, Princeton University Press, Princeton, 2004.

Rahman, H., *The Making of the Gulf War: Origins of Kuwait's Long Standing Territorial Dispute with Iraq*, Ithaca Press, Reading, 1997.

Randall, Jonathan, *The Tragedy of Lebanon*, Hogarth Press, London, 1990.

Ranstorp, Magnus, *Hizb'Allah in Lebanon*, Macmillan, London, 1997.

Reich, Bernard and Gershon Kieval, *Israel: Land of Tradition and Conflict*, Westview Press, Boulder, 1993.

Reinharz, Jehuda and Anita Shapira (eds), *Essential Papers on Zionism*, Cassell (New York University Press), London, 1996.

Richards, Alan and John Waterbury, *A Political Economy of the Middle East: State, Class and Economic Development*, Westview Press, Boulder and Oxford, 1990.

Ross, Dennis, *The Missing Peace: The Inside Story of the Fight for Middle East Peace*, Farrar, Straus and Giroux, New York, 2004.

Rouyer, Alwyn, 'The Water Issue in the Palestinian-Israeli Peace Process,' *Survival*, Vol. 39, No. 2, Summer 1997, pp. 57–81.

—, *Turning Water into Politics: The Water Issue and the Palestinian-Israeli Conflict*, Macmillan Press, London, 2000.

Rubin Barry, *Revolution until Victory: The Politics and History of the PLO*, Harvard University Press, Cambridge, Massachusetts, 1994.

— (ed.), *The Middle East: A Guide to Politics, Economics, Society and Culture*, Routledge, London and New York, 2012.

Rubin, Barry, Joseph Ginat and Moshe Ma'oz (eds), *From War to Peace: Arab-Israeli Relations 1973–1993*, New York University Press, New York, 1994.

Sachar, Howard, *A History of Israel*, Volume 2: *From the Aftermath of the Yom Kippur War*, Oxford University Press, New York and Oxford, 1987. (NB: students need to read both volumes.)

—, *A History of Israel: From the Rise of Zionism to Our Time*, Knopf, New York, 1979.

Schiff Ze'ev and Ehud Ya'ari, *Israel's Lebanon War*, George Allen & Unwin, London, 1984.

—, *Intifada: The Palestinian Uprising, Israel's Third Front*, Simon & Schuster, New York, 1989.

Shafir, Gershon, *Land, Labour and the Origins of the Israeli-Palestinian Conflict, 1882–1914*, University of California Press, Berkeley, 1996.

Shamir, Yitzhak, *Summing Up: An Autobiography*, Weidenfeld & Nicolson, London, 1994.

Shapira, Anita, *Land and Power: The Zionist Resort to Force, 1881–1948*, Stanford University Press, Stanford, 1999.

Shapiro, Yonathan, *The Road to Power: Herut Party in Israel*, SUNY, Albany, 1991.

Sherman, Martin, *The Politics of Water in the Middle East: An Israeli Perspective on the Hydro-Political Aspects of the Conflict*, Macmillan Press, London, 1999.

Shimoni, Gideon, *The Zionist Ideology*, Brandeis University Press, Hanover and London, 1995.

Shindler, Colin, *Israel, Likud and the Zionist Dream*, I. B. Tauris, London, 1995.

Shlaim, Avi, *The Iron Wall: Israel and the Arab World*, Norton, New York and London, 2000.

—, *Lion of Jordan: The Life of King Hussein in War and Peace*, Penguin Books, London, 2008.

Shuval, Hillel, 'Approaches to Resolving the Water Conflicts Between Israel and her Neighbours', *Water International*, Vol. 17, 1992, pp. 133–43.

Sofer, Sasson, *Zionism and the Foundations of Israeli Diplomacy*, Cambridge University Press, Cambridge and New York, 1998.

Swisher, Clayton E., *The Truth About Camp David: The Untold Story About the Collapse of the Middle East Peace Process*, Nation Books, New York, 2004.

Tal, Israel, *National Security: The Israeli Experience*, Praeger, London, 2000.

Tessler, Mark, *A History of the Israeli-Palestinian Conflict*, Indiana University Press, Bloomington, 1994.

Watson, Bruce (ed.), *Military Lessons of the Gulf War*, Greenhill Books, London, 1993.

Woodward, Bob, *The Commanders*, Simon & Schuster, New York, 1991.

Yapp, Malcolm, *The Near East since the First World War: A History to 1995*, Longman, London and New York, 1996.

Notes

PREFACE

1 Jonathan Netanyahu, *Self-Portrait of a Hero: From the Letters of Jonathan Netanyahu, 1963–1976*, Warner Books, New York, 1980, p. 243.

1 INTERVIEW

1 Author's interview with Yitzhak Shamir, Tel Aviv.
2 Marvin Feuerwerger, 'Israel: the Gulf War and its Aftermath', in Robert O. Freedman (ed.), *The Middle East after Iraq's Invasion of Kuwait*, University of Florida Press, Gainesville, p. 144.
3 Moshe Zak, 'Israel and Jordan: Strategically Bound', *Israel Affairs*, Vol. 3, No. 1, Autumn 1996, p. 39.
4 Ibid.
5 Ibid., p. 55.

2 MADRID

1 FCO/FIA/Annual Review for Israel for 1991, p. 2.
2 Ibid.
3 Ibid.
4 Author's interview with Yitzhak Shamir, Tel Aviv.
5 FCO/FIA/Annual Review for Israel for 1991, p. 2.
6 *Washington Post*, 12 January 1999.
7 Ibid.
8 FCO/FIA/Annual Review for Israel for 1991, p. 5.
9 Ibid.

10 Author's interview with Yitzhak Shamir, Tel Aviv.
11 FCO/FIA/Annual Review for Israel for 1991, p. 3.
12 Ibid.
13 Author's interview with Moshe Arens, Tel Aviv.
14 FCO/FIA/Annual Review for Israel for 1992, p. 1.
15 FCO/FIA/Calendar of Events in Israel for 1992, p. 2.
16 Leon T. Hadar, 'David Levy: Can He Win the Likud's Succession War?', *Washington Report on Middle East Affairs*, March 1992, pp. 9–10, 48.
17 Author's interview with Yitzhak Shamir, Tel Aviv.
18 Ibid.
19 Author's interview with Moshe Arens, Tel Aviv.

3 EARTHQUAKE

1 FCO/FIA/ Annual Review for Israel for 1992, p. 2.
2 Ibid.
3 Author's interview with Benni Begin, Jerusalem.
4 Author's interview with Moshe Arens, Tel Aviv.
5 Quoted from FCO/FIA/Annual Review for Israel for 1992, p. 2.
6 Moshe Arens, *Broken Covenant: American Foreign Policy and the Crisis between the U.S. and Israel*, Simon & Schuster, New York, 1995, pp. 298–9.
7 FCO/FIA/Calendar of Events in Israel for 1992, p. 4.
8 Yitzhak Shamir, *Summing Up: An Autobiography*, Weidenfeld & Nicolson, London, 1994, pp. 182–3.
9 David Margolick, 'Star of Zion', *Vanity Fair*, June 1996.
10 Sam Lehman-Wilzig, 'The Media Campaign: The Negative Effects of Positive Campaigning', in David J. Elazar and Shmuel Sandler (eds), *Israel at the Polls 1996*, Frank Cass, London and Portland, 1998, p. 172.
11 *Haaretz*, 2 February 2015.
12 Author's interview with David Bar-Illan, Jerusalem.
13 Sam Lehman-Wilzig, p. 172.
14 Author's interview with David Bar-Illan, Jerusalem.
15 Ibid.
16 Ibid.
17 David Margolick, 'Star of Zion', *Vanity Fair*, June 1996.
18 Quoted from *Baltimore Sun*, 26 March 1993.
19 Ibid.
20 Ibid.

21 *Los Angeles Times*, 26 March 1993.
22 David Margolick, 'Star of Zion', *Vanity Fair*, June 1996.
23 Ibid.
24 Author's interview with Dan Meridor, Jerusalem.
25 Ibid.

4 REBUILDING

 1 Efraim Inbar, 'Netanyahu Takes Over', in David J. Elazar and Shmuel Sandler (eds), *Israel at the Polls 1996*, p. 34.
 2 Author's interview with David Bar-Illan.
 3 Efraim Inbar, 'Netanyahu Takes Over', in David J. Elazar and Shmuel Sandler (eds), *Israel at the Polls 1996*, p. 34.
 4 FCO/FIA/Annual Review for Israel for 1993, p. 1.
 5 Ibid.
 6 Ibid.
 7 Ibid.
 8 Ibid.
 9 Ibid.
10 Ben Caspit and Ilan Kfir, *Netanyahu: The Road to Power*, Vision Paperbacks, London, 1999, p. 139.
11 *New York Times*, 5 September 1993.
12 FCO/FIA/Calendar of Events for 1993, p. 5.

5 DANGEROUS GAMES

 1 Author's interview with Dan Meridor, Jerusalem.
 2 FCO/FIA/Annual Review for Israel for 1994, p. 4.
 3 Ibid.
 4 FCO/FIA/Annual Review for Israel for 1994, summary page.
 5 Ibid., pp. 3–4.
 6 Ibid., p. 2.
 7 Ibid., pp. 1–2.
 8 Ibid., p. 1.
 9 Ibid., p. 2.
10 Ibid.
11 Ibid.
12 Ibid., p. 3.
13 Ibid.
14 Ibid., p. 2.

6 DARK NIGHTS

1 Benjamin Netanyahu, *A Place Among Nations: Israel and the World*, Bantam Press, London and New York, 1993, pp. 329–57.
2 Benjamin Netanyahu, *Fighting Terrorism: How Democracies Can Defeat Domestic and International Terrorism*, Farrar, Straus and Giroux, New York, 1995, pp. 111–12.
3 Author's interview with Yitzhak Shamir, Tel Aviv.
4 FCO/FIA/Annual Review for Israel for 1995, p. 4.
5 Ibid.
6 FCO/FIA/Calendar of Events in Israel for 1995, p. 3.
7 FCO/FIA/Annual Review for Israel for 1995, p. 2.
8 Hendrik Hertzberg, 'Words and Deeds', *New Yorker*, 24 January 2011.
9 Mazal Mualem, 'Former Minister Warns of Settler Violence: Interview with Ben-Eliezer', *Al-Monitor*, 9 May 2014.
10 *Al-Monitor*, 9 May 2014.
11 Ibid.
12 Ibid.
13 Benjamin Netanyahu, *Fighting Terrorism*, p. 111.
14 FCO/FIA/Annual Review for Israel for 1995, p. 2.
15 Ibid.
16 Ibid., p. 6.

7 ELECTION NIGHT

1 'Israeli Election Too Close To Call', CNN, 29 May 1996.
2 'Israel Exit Polls Show Narrow Peres Lead', *Moscow Times*, 30 May 1996.
3 Ibid.
4 Ibid.
5 'Election for Prime Minister Is a Dead Heat', *New York Times*, 30 May 1996.
6 Ibid.
7 Ministry of Foreign Affairs, Jerusalem (MFA), Results of 1996 Elections.
8 Speech by Prime Minister Elect, Benjamin Netanyahu, International Convention Centre, Jerusalem, 2 June 1996.
9 Ibid.
10 Ben Caspit and Ilan Kfir, *Netanyahu: The Road to Power*, Vision Paperbacks, London, 1998, p. 166.
11 Ibid., pp. 168–9.
12 Neill Lochery, *The Israeli Labour Party: In the Shadow of the Likud*, Ithaca Press, Reading, 1997, p. 254.

8 CAMPAIGN

1 Barry Rubin, 'External Influences on Israeli Elections', in David J. Elazar and Shmuel Sandler (eds), *Israel at the Polls 1996*, Frank Cass, London and Portland, 1998, p.153.

2 'Likud Leader Fights for Voters' Confidence', *Financial Times*, 24 May 1996.

3 Yoram Peri, *Telepopulism: Media and Politics in Israel*, Stanford University Press, Redwood City, 2004, p. 178.

4 Ibid.

5 Serge Schmemann, 'Peres And His Foe Do Verbal Battle In Sole TV Debate', *New York Times*, 27 May 1996.

6 Ibid.

7 Ibid.

8 Efraim Inbar, 'Netanyahu Takes Over', p. 43.

9 Ibid.

10 Anton La Guardia, 'Netanyahu Will Seek to Rekindle Search for Peace', *Daily Telegraph*, 28 May 1996.

11 'Israel's Historic Choice', *Daily Telegraph*, 28 May 1996.

12 Ibid.

9 CHEQUES

1 Quoted from Efraim Inbar, 'Netanyahu Takes Over', p. 43.

10 ARAFAT'S HAND

1 Israeli Ministry of Foreign Affairs (IMFA), Israel's Foreign Relations (IFR), Vol. 16, No. 12, Press Conference with President Clinton and Prime Minister Netanyahu, Washington, 9 July 1996.

2 Ben Caspit and Ilan Kfir, *Netanyahu: The Road to Power*, p. 54.

3 On decline of the Labour Party see, Neill Lochery, *The Israeli Labour Party: In the Shadow of the Likud*, pp. 39–61.

4 Ben Caspit and Ilan Kfir, *Netanyahu: The Road to Power*, p. 65.

11 HEBRON

1 IMFA/IFR/16/38/ Interview with Prime Minister Netanyahu, *Haaretz*, 22 November 1996.

2 Ibid.

3 Neill Lochery, 'The Netanyahu Era: From Crisis to Crisis', *Israel Affairs*, Vol. 6, Nos 3 and 4, 2000, p. 229.

4 IMFA/IFR/16/69/ Press Conference with Netanyahu on the Hebron Accord, 13 January 1997.
5 Ibid.
6 Neill Lochery, 'The Netanyahu Era: From Crisis to Crisis', p. 231.
7 Ibid., p. 230.
8 IMFA/IFR/16/138/ Address by Prime Minister Netanyahu at the National Defence College, 14 August 1997.
9 Ibid.

12 WYE

1 Madeleine Albright, *Madame Secretary: A Memoir*, Macmillan, London, 2003, p 300.
2 Ibid, p. 303.
3 Ibid.
4 Associated Press, 4 January 1998.
5 Neill Lochery, 'The Netanyahu Era: From Crisis to Crisis', p. 233.
6 'Sharon Quits After Massacre Enquiry', BBC News, 8 February 1983.
7 Ibid.
8 Madeleine Albright, *Madame Secretary*, p. 310.
9 Ibid., p. 303.
10 Dennis Ross, *The Missing Peace: The Inside Story of the Fight for Middle East Peace*, Farrar, Straus and Giroux, New York, 2004, p. 419.
11 Ibid.
12 Bill Clinton, *My Life*, Hutchinson, London, 2004, p. 817.
13 Madeleine Albright, *Madame Secretary*, p. 310.
14 Bill Clinton, *My Life*, p. 816.
15 Madeleine Albright, *Madame Secretary*, p. 310.
16 Bill Clinton, *My Life*, p. 817.
17 Ibid.

13 DEAL BREAKER

1 Dennis Ross, *The Missing Peace*, p. 438.
2 Ibid.
3 Ibid., p. 439.
4 Ibid., p. 448.
5 Bill Clinton, *My Life*, p. 818.
6 Dennis Ross, *The Missing Peace*, p. 451.
7 Ibid., p. 452.
8 Bill Clinton, *My Life*, p. 819.

9 Dennis Ross, *The Missing Peace*, p. 455.

10 Ibid., p. 443.

11 Bill Clinton, *My Life*, p. 818.

12 Dennis Ross, *The Missing Peace*, p. 455.

13 Ibid., p. 457.

14 Ibid., p. 458.

15 Ibid., p. 459.

16 Bill Clinton, *My Life*, p. 819.

17 IMFA/IFR/17/75/ The Signing of the Wye River Memorandum-Statements, 23 October 1998.

14 HOME

1 IMFA/IFR/17/78/ Statement by Prime Minister Netanyahu, 25 October 1998.

2 Ibid.

3 Dennis Ross, *The Missing Peace*, p. 461.

4 Ibid., p. 467.

5 Ibid., p. 468.

15 END

1 Neill Lochery, 'The Netanyahu Era: From Crisis to Crisis', p. 234.

2 Ibid.

3 Ibid.

4 Nana Gilbert, 'Ramon: Netanyahu Agreed to 4th June 1967 Lines', *Jerusalem Post*, 13 January 2000.

5 Neill Lochery, 'The Netanyahu Era: From Crisis to Crisis', p. 234.

6 Author's interview with Yossi Beilin, Jerusalem.

7 Neill Lochery, 'The Netanyahu Era: From Crisis to Crisis', p. 235.

8 Ibid.

9 David J. Elazar and M. Ben Mollov, 'The Interplay Between Character, Political Culture and Centrism', in David J. Elazar and M. Ben Mollov (eds), *Israel at the Polls 1999*, Frank Cass, London and Portland, 2001, p. 6.

10 IMFA/IFR/17/131/ Interview with Prime Minister Netanyahu, *Time* magazine, 11 January 1999.

11 Ibid.

12 Neill Lochery, 'The Netanyahu Era: From Crisis to Crisis', p. 235.

13 IMFA/IFR/17/131/ Interview with Prime Minister Netanyahu, *Time*, 11 January 1999.

14 Ibid.

15 David J. Elazar and M. Ben Mollov, 'The Interplay Between Character, Political Culture and Centrism', p. 4.

16 Ari Shavit, 'Netanyahu's Secret', *Haaretz*, 4 March 1999.

16 LOSS

1 Deborah Sontag, 'The Israeli Vote: The Overview; Israelis Choose A New Leader And Remake Their Parliament', *New York Times*, 18 May 1999.

2 Ibid.

3 Joel Greenberg, 'Resigning From Parliament, Netanyahu Hints at Return', *New York Times*, 28 May 1999.

4 Ibid.

5 Deborah Sontag, 'The Israeli Vote'.

6 IMFA/IFR/17/131/ Interview with Prime Minister Netanyahu, *Time* magazine, 11 January 1999.

7 Karl Vick, 'Received Wisdom? How the Ideology of Netanyahu's Late Father Influenced the Son', *Time* magazine, 2 May 2012.

8 David Remnick, 'The Outsider', *New Yorker*, p. 80.

9 Ibid., p. 83.

17 FATHER

1 Benzion Netanyahu Obituary, *Guardian*, 1 May 2012.

2 Ibid.

3 David Remnick, 'The Outsider', p. 85.

4 Benzion Netanyahu Obituary, *Guardian*, 1 May 2012.

5 Karl Vick, 'Received Wisdom?'

6 David Remnick, 'The Outsider', p. 85.

7 Ibid., p. 84.

8 Ibid., p. 85.

9 Author's interview with Yossi Beilin, Jerusalem.

18 INVISIBLE

1 Lilach Weissman, 'Netanyahu Held Tax Haven Bank Account', *Globes*, 15 January 2014.

2 Ibid.

3 Ibid.

4 Marissa Newman, 'Netanyahu Kept Bank Account In Tax Haven', *Times of Israel*, 15 January 2014.

5 Ibid.

6 'Netanyahu Dubs BATM/Telco Systems the Grand Slam of the Desert;
   Former Israeli Prime Minister Reflects on Dynamic Technology Transfer Between U.S. and Israel', *Atlantic Business Wire*, 27 September 2000.
7 See for example, Clayton E. Swisher, *The Truth About Camp David: The
   Untold Story About the Collapse of the Middle East Peace Process*, Nation
   Books, New York, 2004.
8 Suzanne Goldenberg, 'Netanyahu Set for a Comeback', *Guardian*, 28
   September 2000.
9 Ibid.

19 FALSE START

1 http://www.mfa.gov.il/mfa/aboutisrael/history/pages/elections.
2 'Barak Concedes Israeli Prime Minister Election', CNN, 6 February
   2001.
3 Ibid.

20 INVITATION

1 MFA/President Shimon Peres Tasks MK Benjamin Netanyahu with
   Forming Government, 20 February 2009.
2 Ethan Bronner, 'Netanyahu, Once Hawkish, Now Touts Pragmatism',
   New York Times, 20 February 2009.
3 Ibid.
4 MFA/Incoming Prime Minister Benjamin Netanyahu Presents his
   Government to the Knesset, 31 March 2009.
5 Ibid.
6 Ibid.
7 Ibid.
8 Ibid.

21 NOVEMBER

1 Barak Ravid, 'Iraq 2002, Iran 2012: Compare And Contrast
   Netanyahu's Speeches: The Arguments Are The Same, The Intonation Is
   The Same, Even The Advisors Are The Same', *Haaretz*, 4 October 2012.
2 Adapted from Address by Benjamin Netanyahu, House Committee on
   Government Reform, 12 September 2002.
3 Chris McGreal, 'Israel Faces Swing to Right as Coalition Falls',
   Guardian, 31 October 2002.
4 Caroline Glick, 'Interview with Benjamin Netanyahu', *Jerusalem Post*, 7
   November 2002.

5 Ibid.
6 'Middle East Timeline', *Guardian*, 2003.
7 Ian Fisher, 'Six Israelis Die at Polling Station; Sharon Wins', *New York Times*, 29 November 2002.
8 MFA/FM Netanyahu Addresses to EU Ambassadors Conference, 17 December 2002.

22 FINANCE

1 Joshua Brilliant, 'Israel's Sharon Presents New Government', *UPI*, 27 February 2003.
2 Chris McGreal, 'Sharon Sacks Netanyahu to Smooth US Ties', *Guardian*, 27 February 2003.
3 MFA/Address to the Knesset by Prime Minister Ariel Sharon on the Presentation of the New Government, Jerusalem, 27 February 2003.
4 Nehemia Shtrasler, 'Netanyahu: Economic Reforms are Vital', *Haaretz*, 1 October 2004.
5 'Netanyahu's Economic Reforms and the Laffer Curve', *Forbes*, 13 November 2015.
6 On the reforms see, Dani Filc, *The Political Right in Israel: Different Faces of Jewish Populism*, Routledge, London and New York, 2009.
7 'Netanyahu's Economic Reforms and the Laffer Curve', *Forbes*, 13 November 2015.
8 Nehemia Shtrasler, 'Netanyahu: Economic Reforms are Vital', *Haaretz*, 1 October 2004.
9 Ibid.
10 Patrick Clawson, 'Middle East Economics', in Barry Rubin (ed.), *The Middle East: A Guide to Politics, Economics, Society and Culture*, Routledge, London and New York, 2012, p. 208.

23 SEPARATION

1 Nehemia Shtrasler, 'Netanyahu: Economic Reforms are Vital', *Haaretz*, 1 October 2004.
2 Scott Wilson, 'Netanyahu Resigns In Protest of Pullout', *Washington Post*, 8 August 2005.
3 Ibid.
4 Ibid.
5 David Makovsky, 'Sharon, Netanyahu, Disengagement, and Likud Leadership', *Policy Watch 501*, The Washington Institute, 17 August 2005.
6 Ibid.

7 Conal Urquhart, 'Netanyahu Quits over Withdrawal from Gaza', *Guardian*, 8 August 2005.

8 'Netanyahu to Challenge Sharon Leadership', CNN, 30 August 2005.

9 Ibid.

10 Caroline Glick, 'Netanyahu's Great Gamble', *Jerusalem Post*, 8 August 2005.

11 Jonathan Spyer, 'Likud and the 2006 Election', in Shmeul Sandler, Manfred Gerstenfeld and Jonathan Rynhold (eds), *Israel at the Polls 2006*, Routledge, London and New York, 2008, p. 66.

12 Reported on CNN, 29 March 2006.

13 Chris McGreal, 'Kadima Wins Israel's General Election As Likud Humiliated', *Guardian*, 29 March 2006.

14 Jonathan Spyer, 'Likud and the 2006 Election', p. 71.

24 THE SPEECH

1 Israel Army Radio = Likud 22 and Zionist Union 24. Joint Poll for Television = Likud 21 and Zionist Union 24, Polls published on 3 March 2015.

2 Benjamin Netanyahu Address to Congress on 3 March 2015, Prime Minister's Office, Jerusalem.

3 Ibid.

4 Ibid.

5 Ibid.

6 Ibid.

7 Ibid.

8 Ibid.

9 President Obama's Remarks After Netanyahu's Speech, 3 March 2015.

10 Separate polls for Channels 1 and 10 in Israel taken on 4 March 2015 put the Likud at 23 seats. A poll taken published in *Maariv* on 6 March 2015 put the Likud on 22 seats.

25 CHALLENGE

1 Jeff Zeleny and Alan Cowell, 'Addressing Muslims, Obama Pushes, Middle East Peace', *New York Times*, 4 June 2009.

2 'President Obama's Remarks to the Muslim World', Cairo, White House, 4 June 2009.

3 Ibid.

4 Ibid.

5 Ibid.

6 Ibid.

7 Address by Benjamin Netanyahu, Bar-Ilan University, 14 June 2009.
8 Ibid.
9 Ibid.
10 Isabel Kershner, 'Netanyahu Backs Palestinian State, With Caveats', *New York Times*, 14 June 2009.
11 Ibid.
12 Ibid.
13 *Haaretz*, 25 November 2009.
14 Ethan Bronner and Mark Landler, 'Israel Offers a Pause in Building New Settlements', *New York Times*, 25 November 2009.

26 RELATIONSHIPS

1 Barak Ravid, 'Netanyahu: Arab Spring Pushing Mideast Backward, Not Forward', *Haaretz*, 24 November 2011.
2 MFA/Prime Minister Netanyahu Addresses Opening of Knesset Winter Session, 31 October 2011.
3 Mark Landler and Steven Lee Myers, 'Obama Sees 67 Borders as Starting Point for Peace Deal', *New York Times*, 19 May 2011.
4 Remarks of President Barack Obama: A Moment of Opportunity, the State Department, Washington, DC, 19 May 2011.
5 Ibid.
6 *New York Times*, 19 May 2011.
7 MFA/Statement by Prime Minister Netanyahu on Address by US President Obama, 19 May 2011.
8 Jeremy Bowen, BBC News, 20 May 2011.
9 Remarks by President Obama and Prime Minister Netanyahu of Israel after Bilateral Meeting, White House, 20 May 2011.
10 Ibid.
11 Ibid.
12 Ibid.
13 'Israeli Rebuke of Obama Exposes Divide on Mideast', Reuters, 22 May 2011.
14 'Sarkozy Tells Obama Netanyahu is a Liar', Reuters, 8 November 2011.
15 'Sarkozy, Obama Bemoan Netanyahu over Open Microphone', CNN, 8 November 2011.

27 PROTESTS

1 Address by Prime Minister Netanyahu at the Graduation Ceremony of Course 38 of the National Security College, 25 July 2011.
2 'Biggest Rally in Israel's History Presses PM', Reuters, 4 September 2011.

3 MFA/Prime Minister Netanyahu Addresses Opening of Knesset Winter Session, 31 October 2011.
4 Channel 10 News, 2 August 2011.
5 'Israel's Netanyahu, Lieberman Merge Parties for Ballot', Reuters, 25 October 2012.
6 BBC News, 26 October 2012.
7 Poll published by Channel Two, 25 October 2012.
8 Reuters, 25 October 2012.
9 David Remnick, 'Netanyahu's Dark Choice', *New Yorker*, 28 October 2012.

28 INDEED

1 Polls from Channel 10 and Channel 2, 13 March 2015.
2 'Netanyahu: No Palestinian State on My Watch', *Times of Israel*, 16 March 2015.
3 Barak Ravid, 'Netanyahu: If I'm Elected, There Will Be No Palestinian State', *Haaretz*, 16 March 2015.
4 PMO/Netanyahu at the Opening of the Knesset Winter Session, 27 October 2014.
5 Ibid.
6 MFA/PM Netanyahu sums up Operation Protective Edge, 27 August 2014.
7 Joshua Mitnick, 'Israelis Frustrated With Outcome of Gaza Conflict', *Wall Street Journal*, 29 August 2014.
8 Ibid.
9 'Lieberman Pans Ceasefire with Contemptible Murderers', *Times of Israel*, 27 August 2014.
10 Ibid.
11 'Long May It Hold', *The Economist*, 30 August 2014.
12 Interview with Netanyahu, *Die Welt*, 5 December 2012.
13 Channel 2 and Channel 10 Television Opinion Polls, 13 March 2015.

29 HAIL

1 'Netanyahu's Election Day Talk of Arabs Voting in Droves Was Not Racist', *Times of Israel*, 26 November 2015.
2 Interview with President Obama, *Huffington Post*, 21 March 2015.
3 Gil Troy, 'In Defense of Netanyahu: Appalling, Yes. Racist, No', *Policy Magazine*, May–June 2015.
4 'Israel's Election Results', *Independent*, 17 March 2015.

5 'Israel Election: Netanyahu Claims Victory as Main Rival Concedes',
   CNN, 19 March 2015.
6 Jonathan Freedland, 'Israelis Have a Chance to Dump Netanyahu.
   I Fear They Won't Seize It', *Guardian*, 6 February 2015.
7 Thomas L. Friedman, 'Netanyahu Will Make History', *New York Times*,
   18 March 2015.

30 D-DAY

1 MFA/Statement by PM Netanyahu on Iran, 14 July 2015.
2 Isabel Kershner, 'Iran Deal Denounced by Netanyahu as 'Historic
   Mistake', *New York Times*, 14 July 2015.
3 Readout of the President's Call with Prime Minister Benjamin
   Netanyahu of Israel, White House, 14 July 2015.
4 *New York Times*, 14 July 2015.
5 Ibid., 9 November 2015.
6 PMO/Remarks by PM Netanyahu, White House, 9 November 2015.
7 *New York Times*, 9 November 2015.
8 Ibid.
9 'Israel's leaders Furious over Barak Tapes Describing Aborted Plans to
   Hit Iran', *Times of Israel*, 22 August 2015.
10 Ibid.
11 Quoted from *Times of Israel*, 17 December 2015.
12 Enoch Powell, *Joseph Chamberlain*, Thames & Hudson, London, 1977,
   p. 151.
13 Gil Hoffman, 'With Full Term Possible, Netanyahu May Outlast
   Ben-Gurion (and Obama)', *Jerusalem Post*, 24 March 2015.

POSTSCRIPT

1 Jonathan Netanyahu, *Self-Portrait of a Hero: From the Letters of Jonathan
   Netanyahu, 1963–1976*, Warner Books, New York, 1980, p. 265.

Index

W

Wachsman, Nachshon 65, 66

Washington Post 24, 141

welfare state, Israeli 237, 238, 241

West Bank 12, 15, 28, 29, 36, 38, 49, 57–8, 63, 68, 70, 74, 80–1, 94–5, 98–9, 120, 121, 134, 135, 136, 141, 147, 198, 200, 203, 229, 249, 251, 275, 276, 277, 280, 281–3, 287

Hebron 65, 121, 129, 131–5, 141, 155

see also Palestine and territories

White, John 85

Wiesel, Elie 265

World Trade Centre attacks (2001) 225–7

Wye Summit and Memorandum 140, 142–3, 145, 146–50, 153–9, 161–3, 164, 165–9, 172–3, 198

Y

Yachimovich, Shelly 196–7

Yedioth Ahronoth newspaper 247

Yesh Atid 303, 304, 324

Yisrael Ba'aliyah 74, 201

Yisrael Beiteinu 252, 253, 300–1, 303–4, 325

Yom Kippur War 123, 124–5, 126

Z

Zabludowicz, Poju 196

Zaghal, Tarek 232

Zarif, Mohammad Javad 264

Zionist Union 259, 318, 321, 322, 325, 326

About the Author

Neill Lochery is a world-renowned source on the politics and modern history of Europe and the Mediterranean Middle East, and is the Catherine Lewis Professor of Mediterranean and Middle Eastern Studies at University College London.

He has authored a series of critically acclaimed books, including *The View from the Fence: The Arab-Israeli Conflict from the Present to its Roots*, the international bestseller *Lisbon: War in the Shadows of the City of Light* and most recently *Brazil: The Fortunes of War, World War II and the Making of Modern Brazil*. His next book *Out of the Shadows: Portugal from Revolution to the Present Day* will be published in 2017.

Neill has served as an advisor to political and economic leaders from both sides of the Arab–Israeli conflict.

He frequently appears on TV and radio around the world, and is a contributor to leading newspapers, including the *Wall Street Journal*.

www.neill-lochery.com

Note on the Type

The text of this book is set in Adobe Garamond. It is one of several versions of Garamond based on the designs of Claude Garamond. It is thought that Garamond based his font on Bembo, cut in 1495 by Francesco Griffo in collaboration with the Italian printer Aldus Manutius. Garamond types were first used in books printed in Paris around 1532. Many of the present-day versions of this type are based on the *Typi Academiae* of Jean Jannon cut in Sedan in 1615.

Claude Garamond was born in Paris in 1480. He learned how to cut type from his father and by the age of fifteen he was able to fashion steel punches the size of a pica with great precision. At the age of sixty he was commissioned by King Francis I to design a Greek alphabet, and for this he was given the honourable title of royal type founder. He died in 1561.